To Bill

wildside

CEK

D1132283

LUCIANO AND THE MAFIA

Despite all the white-washings and breast-beatings of recent years, it is a fact that the Mafia did and does exist.

"Lucky" Luciano himself describes it, "There's always been a Mafia but it's not like those sons-a-bitches tell it in the newspapers . . . the Mafia's like any other organization, except we don't go in for advertising. We're big business, is all."

Here, then, is Luciano and his Mafia as they both grew into enormous power in the United States.

This is not a rehash of his legend, an advertisement for gangsterism, or a slick fabrication from disputed sources . . . this is *the* story of Charles "Lucky" Luciano.

WRITE FOR OUR FREE CATALOG

If there is a Pinnacle Book you want but can't find locally, it is available from us—simply send the title and price plus 25¢ to cover mailing and handling costs to:

PINNACLE BOOKS
275 Madison Avenue
New York, New York 10016

__Check here if you want to receive our catalog regularly.

__Check here if you wish to know when the next_____will be published.

Luciano:
the man who modernized the American Mafia.

by Tony Sciacca

PINNACLE BOOKS • NEW YORK CITY

LUCIANO: THE MAN WHO MODERNIZED THE
AMERICAN MAFIA

Copyright © 1975 by Tony Sciacca

All rights reserved, including the right to reproduce this book
or portions thereof in any form.

An original Pinnacle Books edition, published for the first
time anywhere.

ISBN: 0-523-00679-9

First printing, July 1975

Printed in Canada

PINNACLE BOOKS, INC.
275 Madison Avenue
New York, N. Y. 10016

For Ernie, The Hawk, Rupolo,
whose luck ran out at the bottom
of Gravesend Bay.

FOREWORD

I never met Lucky Luciano. I never interviewed him. I don't have tapes of his reminiscences.

But I think I know Luciano well. As a journalist and investigative reporter in the New York City area for more than twenty years, most of my adult life has been devoted to an investigation and exploration of the Honored Society, the Mafia.

Through those twenty years I've been fortunate enough to develop sources within the Mafia who have talked with me about their past, and particularly about Luciano. Some of those Mafia members were the fathers and uncles of my childhood friends in Brooklyn. I was born and raised in an Italian-American section of Brooklyn. My father is Sicilian and my mother's parents came from southern Italy.

From the time I was a child growing up among people of Sicilian and Italian ancestry, I have known about the Mafia. The men of the Mafia discuss their business among themselves; they frequently gossip to their wives, and their wives gossip to demonstrate to their neighbors that they are people of substance. Mafia.

During my two decades as a journalist I've read most of the books and the newspaper and magazine articles on the Mafia and its members. Much of what I've read has been myth, some of it created by writers more interested in sensationalizing their sketchy information than in digging for the facts. To be fair, most writers get their information from the police, who often exaggerate to demonstrate their own knowledge.

But many books on the Mafia demonstrate more imagination than truth. The worst offender of all is the now discredited "personal memoir" of Luciano, *The Last Testament of Lucky Luciano,* which was publicized as being based on tapes of Luciano's recollections until it was admitted that no such tapes have ever existed. A detailed analysis of this book will be provided in the Appendix.

I first became aware of journalistic myth-making while still in my teens. It was sometime in 1949, and the newspapers had discovered that Frank Costello had sponsored a fund-raising benefit for the Salvation Army, in the Copacabana nightclub. The press immediately selected Costello as "boss" of the American Mafia and ran long articles about him and his power.

Over in Brooklyn, I was attending high school. On my way home each day I'd drop into a candy store on Thirteenth Avenue in the Bay Ridge section for a soda or malted and a little play on the illegal pinball machine. The machine was immune from police interference because the store was operated by Ernie "The Hawk" Rupolo (and owned by the family of the pastor of our local church).

Ernie, who was called Hawk because of his beak nose and the patch he wore over the eye he had lost in a knife fight years before, was a very talkative man for one who had been in the Mafia all his life and knew the ground rules. Perhaps he believed he could get away with his careless chatter, perhaps he believed newspaper stories about his "charmed life"—he had once named Luciano's chief assistant, Vito Genovese, as the instigator of a murder, and he was permitted to live despite this gross violation of the Mafia ethic.

Years later Ernie was finally murdered because he had never understood that his habit of talking about his Mafia superiors was more dangerous to his health than the cigarette that always dangled from his lips, Bogart style.

In any case, I stopped in at Ernie's store as usual that day in 1949 when Costello's name was making headlines as the Mafia boss. I ordered my chocolate malted, and began reading the newspaper that Ernie had left on the counter, folded at the Costello story; Ernie was never very subtle about things like that. I'd barely read through the first paragraphs when Ernie asked:

"What do you think of that garbage?"

"Makes good reading," I replied, not having much opinion about the sanitary value of the newspaper.

"That's all it makes," Ernie said. "It's garbage. Costello ain't nothin' but a messenger boy for Charlie Lucky."

"Really?" I asked. (Years later that word, "really," said with a large measure of awe and a trace of doubt, opened up more mouths than the culinary abilities of the Neapolitan chef at Patsy's.)

"Damn right," Ernie said. "Charlie Lucky is still *numero uno* even from Italy. He was *numero uno* even when they locked him up for being a whoremaster. A frameup, you know . . ." And Ernie went on and on.

Thus ended my faith in newspaper stories about the Mafia. And a couple of years later, when I became a newspaper reporter, I resolved to keep Ernie in mind whenever I wrote a story about the Mafia. Ernie was the very critical audience-of-one for whom I wrote.

It's unfortunate that some of the writers who have turned out biographies of Mafia members didn't have their own Ernies to calm down their excesses. One thing has often annoyed me about those biographies: The writer always feels compelled to make *his* subject the most cunning, feared, brilliant and powerful man that the American underworld has ever produced.

Dozens of men have been selected for the title "King of Organized Crime" or some variation thereof, including Luciano and Meyer Lansky, Costello, Genovese, Capone, and many more.

I've always tried to avoid that trap. In all my writing about the Mafia that has been published in newspapers and magazines I've attempted to let the story speak for itself, vowing never to oversell any particular individual.

And yet . . . and yet.

The fact remains that, of all the men whose deeds of violence are scattered through the files of investigative agencies in America and abroad, whose mystique has been recounted by Joe Valachi, Ernie the Hawk, and other informers from inside the Mafia, of all the figures in the modern American crime syndicate only two deserve the overused title, King of . . .

One of them is Johnny Torrio, the man who created and controlled Al Capone. While Capone was the best-known gangster during the insanity called Prohibition, Torrio was undoubtedly the smartest. He was probably the most efficient organizer of large-scale criminal enterprises that the U.S. has ever produced; he comes closest to being the mythical "criminal mastermind" than anyone else. He died in his sleep in the late 1950's, still a man of mystery.

The only other man who deserves the accolade is Lucky Luciano. With Torrio as his teacher, with Torrio guiding him and supporting his radical ideas, Luciano brought together dozens of disparate criminal groups and forged them into the cartel that is the modern American Mafia. Charlie Lucky ruled it even after being sent to prison for compulsory prostitution, a crime that he never committed; he continued to maintain at least some control over the Americanized Mafia even after being deported to Italy.

A note about the use of the word "Mafia." Joe Valachi has said that the men of the Mafia stopped using that term in the 1930's, that it became Cosa Nostra after the old-fashioned Sicilian immigrants in the Mafia were disposed of and Luciano had forged his confederation. But I shall continue to call it Mafia, for several reasons.

Today's crime cartel, which rules so much of organized crime in America, is a direct descendant of Mafia and many of its now elderly rulers were members of Mafia.

4

What Valachi referred to as Cosa Nostra is the Italian-American syndicate in the New York area, which is only one criminal group among many in the U.S.

Most of all, Valachi notwithstanding, the word Mafia is still used by police officials, journalists, the public—including descendants of Sicilian and Italian immigrants who were most exploited by Mafia—and it is still used by younger members of the national crime syndicate. Even Luciano himself, a couple of years before he died, said to an undercover agent of the Federal Narcotics Bureau:

"I'll tell you something, kid. There's always been a Mafia but it's not like those sons-a-bitches tell it in the newspapers . . . The Mafia's like any other organization, except we don't go in for advertising. We're big business, is all."

So, Mafia it will be.

Many men and women have helped me build this portrait of Charlie Lucky. Some, like Ernie the Hawk and Polly Adler, who talked about Luciano during interviews, are now dead. Others are "retired." Several are still actively engaged in Mafia business and will be surrounded throughout this book with pseudonymity.

I wish to thank, especially: "Frankie Bath Beach"; "Sal Martello"; "Harry Rizzo"; "Moe Cohen"; the men from the Federal Narcotics Bureau, who kept close watch on Charlie in exile and who gave me much help in my work as a writer in the 1950's and 1960's—Charles Siragusa, George Gaffney, and several others who have always asked to remain anonymous; those men in the FBI who, with the permission of their superiors, gave me material from their Mafia files, the late Robert F. Kennedy, who served on several Senate committees investigating organized crime and who never hesitated to answer my questions or supply copies of documents. I owe a large debt to Leonard Katz for making available to me the material, much of it fresh and from the inside, which he amassed during research on his excellent biography of Frank Costello, *Uncle Frank*. And to Vincent Barbi.

And to those I may have overlooked, and those confidential sources I dare not grace with a *nom de gang*: Much thanks.

1

At a few minutes before eleven o'clock on the night of Sunday, November 4, 1928, Patrick Kelly was sitting inside the service elevator he operated at the Park Central Hotel in Manhattan, when he heard someone shuffling down the stairs nearby.

"I go to look," he later told police, "and this guy is walking down slow. I say, 'Are you sick?' and he says, 'Get me a taxi. I've been shot.' This ain't none of my business, so I go looking for the house detective."

Joseph Fallon, the hotel's security director, went to investigate. "I see this man," he said in his statement to police. "He is hanging on to the banister with one hand and he is holding his belly with the other. He says, 'Call me a taxi. I've been shot.'

"I send Kelly to look for a cop. I take a good look at this fellow . . . Sure, I recognize him. Everyone knows Arnold Rothstein."

Nearly everybody in America did know of Arnold Rothstein. He was believed to be the man who fixed the 1919 World Series between the Chicago White Sox and the Cincinnati Reds. He was the "King of Gamblers" to some newspapers, "The Brain" to Damon Runyon, he was the character Wolfsheim in *The Great Gatsby*.

A.R., as he liked to be known, was the bankroll, loan shark, and business organizer of the New York underworld, financing narcotics, bootlegging, gambling, anything that would make him a dollar. And he amassed great political power with his money.

The shooting of Arnold Rothstein was the sensation of the era. Police, and the newspaper reporters—among whom were many, such as Damon Runyon, who considered A.R. a friend—soon learned why he had been shot. Rothstein, they said, had refused to pay more than three hundred thousand dollars which he had lost in a poker game more than two months earlier. He hadn't welshed, exactly, but he was forcing his creditors to sweat it out, knowing they would eventually be happy to settle for half the debt. And one of them shot him in a drunken rage.

As Rothstein lay dying in a hospital bed, from a bullet that had ripped through a couple of vital organs and, traveling downward, had severed an artery in his leg, police did not push their investigation too strenuously. To do so would have meant jeopardizing every corrupt policeman (and there were many) and every corrupt politician (there were also many) in the city of New York. Leaders of both political parties had been bought by Rothstein. Every police official with any power was owned by Rothstein. Many judges, many prosecutors—and the Mayor himself, dapper and debonair Jimmy Walker—had been corrupted by Rothstein's wealth.

They had all protected him and the men who worked for him, and they had grown rich by selling such protection. Mayor Walker, it was disclosed several years later, had almost a million dollars credited to him in a secret account at a brokerage house. Other more important politicians banked even larger sums.

And the politicians knew that the evidence that could destroy them all was in Rothstein's "insurance company" office in a midtown building.

Thirty-six hours after he had been shot, A.R. died of his wounds. Less than a half-hour after the official pronouncement of death, three men unlocked the door to Rothstein's office and began going through his files. Several policemen, sent to safeguard the office, arrested the men. They were identified for the newspapers as Rothstein's bodyguard, Fats Walsh; Rothstein's business associate, George Uffner; and "a waiter," Charles Lucania. Fame had not yet arrived for Lucky Luciano; he preferred it that way.

Police released the "waiter" and the other two men after receiving word "from City Hall" that they should not be held unless a murder charge could be placed against them. The police did not know—they did not care to know—that the three had gone to Rothstein's office to confiscate several sheets of paper with cryptic notes upon them.

The papers told them the names of dozens of the most powerful political figures in the city—names which they already knew—and the amounts of money that Rothstein had been paying each of them. Money that would continue to be paid by A.R.'s successor. Equally important, the papers told them the location of the different caches of narcotics in this country, the shipments on the way from foreign countries or awaiting Rothstein's command to dispatch them, and orders from buyers which must be filled immediately from Rothstein's storehouses.

Years later, while an exile in Naples, Luciano reminisced about A.R. with an old friend. And Charlie laughed when he recalled his arrest in Rothstein's office:

"The dumb cops frisked me for a gun, but they never looked at any of the papers in my pocket. I got everything from that office I went lookin' for."

Charlie Lucky didn't say it, but in the few minutes he spent in Rothstein's office on that day in 1928 he became one of the biggest men in the narcotics trade, and the most powerful in New York's political-criminal structure.

Luciano felt warmly about Rothstein, as well he should have. "Arnold taught me a lot," he told his visitor in Naples. "Not only me, but Frank (Costello), Vito (Genovese), and just about anybody who worked with me. We all learned by A.R."

In the spring of 1933 Charlie Lucky Luciano, supported by the elder statesman of organized crime, Johnny Torrio, called a meeting of gang leaders from all across the country. Present at the week-long conferences in a Park Avenue hotel were not only the leaders of Mafia groups, composed solely of Italian-Americans, but every bootlegger, narcotics importer, and union racketeer of consequence, regardless of national origin.

Among them were Meyer Lansky, Louis Lepke, Moe Dalitz of the Cleveland organization, three representatives of Chicago's mob, Longy Zwillman from New Jersey, and at least a dozen others of equal prominence in all the rackets across the nation. So far as I have been able to learn, no one attending that conference has ever discussed it in detail with authorities; none of them ever became an informer.

But Joe Valachi later heard about it and told officials the little he knew. So did Nicola Gentile, who had been a Mafia leader in Pittsburgh, Cleveland, and Kansas City through most of Prohibition, had fled to Sicily to avoid prosecution on narcotics charges in the mid-1930's, and who wrote his memoirs twenty years later. Although never published, parts of his memoirs were quoted in the Italian press, and Gentile elaborated on them during interviews. The information that reached Valachi, Gentile, and others in the Mafia was eventually passed on to authorities, and all the accounts strongly support one another.

That information has it that Johnny Torrio opened the meeting by recounting the dreadful toll in death and in unwelcome publicity that had resulted from the inability of Chicago gangs to agree to divide the city in a business-like manner so that all could share in the wealth and none would suffer.

Torrio spoke from firsthand knowledge of Chicago; it had been "his" city, from the Mayor to the cops on the beat, for more than a decade. He had gone to Chicago in 1909, after being a New York gang leader for a dozen years, and through much of Prohibition he had controlled Chicago's rackets from the shadows while his protege, Al Capone, made the headlines. It had been Torrio's dream to form an area-wide syndicate of all the gangs in Chicago, to cut down on competition and violence. But his plan had failed because of hotheads like Capone, and the Irish and Polish gang leaders who hated Capone's strength and his ego.

They all listened quite attentively as Torrio spoke at this conference that he'd organized with the hope that it would finally bring order to the chaos of gang rivalries. "Johnny was like a god," Valachi has said. "He built up Chicago for the boys so everybody got rich, and he got out with his skin and his money. By this time he's a secret partner in everybody's racket, and all the cops believe he's retired."

Torrio then proceeded to describe the way in which all the bootleg gangs on the East Coast had, four years earlier, formed a monopoly in which each cooperated with the other. Working from an office in a West Forty-Eighth Street hotel, the combination had set quotas on the liquor to be imported each month, set the price to be charged the retailer, and even established the design of bottles and labels to be used after the liquor was landed and cut. In other words, the gang leadership had established a cooperative monopoly which governed the illegal importation of liquor, and they had ended the kind of competition that had caused thousands of violent deaths in the first decade of Prohibition. Much of the credit for the formation of the bootleg cooperative, Torrio reportedly said, belonged to Charlie Luciano.

When Torrio completed his low-key recitation of what had been achieved in the illegal liquor industry, he turned the floor over to Luciano. And, according to reports in the files of federal agencies and the story within the Mafia, Luciano began to outline a scheme that would place all major criminal gangs into one national syndicate. A cooperative similar to the East Coast rum-running combination.

What Luciano was proposing would have horrified the old "Mustache Petes"—the provincial, clannish Mafia immigrants who had controlled a part of the criminal rackets a decade earlier and who believed that all those who did not possess one hundred percent Sicilian or Italian blood were the enemy. Charlie's plan was a complete break with the clannishness and exclusivity of Mafia traditions.

Under that plan, the country would be divided into spheres of influence and the "outfit" then in control of each area in its city or state, as of the year 1933, would be confirmed as supreme in that particular area. Moe Dalitz and his Jewish syndicate in Cleveland, for example, would be recognized by every other local syndicate as supreme in the territory they had carved out during Prohibition.

It didn't matter that they were not Mafia, in the old sense. They had proved their ability to create a functioning, politically connected, money-making organization, and they deserved to be recognized by every other syndicate.

And on and on, down the line of the leaders in attendance, Luciano made it clear that the New Yorkers—heavily Italian and the wealthiest and most powerful racketeering group in the nation—would cooperate with every other syndicate then in control.

Cooperate. And that, Luciano said, was the primary reason for bringing them all together. Now that Prohibition was coming to an end it was essential to create a board of directors that would meet whenever necessary, to vote on issues brought before it—issues that in the past had led to gang wars.

For example, if a member of the New York syndicate encroached upon the business of the Cleveland syndicate —perhaps by hijacking a shipment of narcotics—the Cleveland men would no longer have the right to go gunning for the New Yorkers. A meeting would have to be called, and all the members of the board of directors would discuss the matter and then vote on a solution. The

12

penalty imposed upon the malefactors would be executed dispassionately, as in any business organization.

More important, however, were the overall syndicate operations. If one group wished to branch out beyond its assigned territorial limits, or if one group was about to conduct a piece of business that could affect any other group—for example, fixing a horse race, which was a common occurrence—then the other groups must be advised so that they wouldn't be caught short.

Further, there must be a sharing of certain resources. Political power, for one thing. Should a local syndicate "own" a senator, or even a president, and should another local syndicate require that politician's aid, then the first syndicate must accept and carry through on a contract for the political fix.

And, finally, certain areas of the country which did not fall under the control of any present local syndicate must always be considered "open" territory. There would be no exclusive franchises in those areas. The gangs from each section would pool resources and jointly "invest" in any open area which might prove in the future to be worth developing. Luciano couldn't have realized it at the time, but the flexibility provided in his blueprint would later bring about the very orderly development of gangster control of gambling casinos in Nevada, Cuba, the Bahamas, and even in London for a brief time.

The meetings which set up the present structure of organized crime in America lasted for several days, according to information that came out years later. When those conferences were ended and agreement reached, the modernized Mafia came into existence. The structure is basically the same today, more than forty years later—dozens of independent syndicates, each tied to the other through a cooperative national syndicate council, in which each "company" in the cartel has a single vote.

Because of the composition of the gangs in control back in 1933, that national syndicate is primarily Italian and Jewish.

13

During those meetings Luciano—strongly supported by the highly respected Torrio and by Lansky, whose Jewishness eased the suspicions of the Jewish gang leaders—insisted that there would never again be a "boss" in this national syndicate he was proposing. However, after agreement had been reached and handshakes formalized the verbal compact, Luciano was in actuality the boss.

He was simply one of about thirty-five Italian and Jewish gang leaders. Each of them had equal rank. But as Joe Valachi put it:

"Charlie was the first among equals. He was the boss. He just didn't act like a dictator because he was too smart."

The "boss" of a national commission of criminal businessmen was not the future that anyone would have predicted for Luciano in the early days, when he was just another wild street kid carrying a gun and anxious to use it at every possible opportunity. "I buried a hundred guys," Luciano had said to several people in the final years of his life, including undercover narcotics agent Sal Vizzini.

Charlie Lucky wasn't exaggerating. In his later years others pulled the trigger for him, at his command. But during his teens and his twenties, when he was hustling on New York streets, and after his formal induction into Mafia at the start of Prohibition, Luciano killed at least twenty men, by all believable accounts.

"I put a few of them (bullets) into other people," Luciano told Vizzini.

The first bullet from a Luciano gun that ever brought blood, so far as can now be determined, spilled Charlie's own blood. He was fourteen at the time, a street hoodlum on the Lower East Side. He was proudly displaying to a friend the shiny new revolver he had just bought. The friend asked to hold it, and Charlie handed it to him. As the friend was fondling the weapon it went off. The bullet

14

grazed Charlie's left leg. Until the day he died, he carried the scar of that accidental shooting—the only time in his life he'd ever been shot.

Luciano, as a child, must have been very much like a minority of the young men who still inhabit Italian-American neighborhoods in New York, and probably every urban area. Although born in the United States—often as third generation Americans—they are only slightly educated and seldom very bright. They spend their days running errands for the local don, and their nights practicing for their initiation into Mafia manhood, when they will get the call to murder someone. In the dank cellars of one of the dozens of "social clubs" that dot their neighborhoods, they practice for hours by shooting at targets nailed into the brick wall. They are most anxious to kill someone, for only by killing for the don will they be able to prove they are brave, fearless, and loyal—following a code that is a perversion of the Boy Scout ethic.

(Almost twenty years ago, when he was just such a young man, Vincent Gigante practiced his marksmanship in one of those cellars. He then proceeded, on orders from his don, to murder Frank Costello. But, after at least a week of intensive practice in the use of his gun, Gigante barely grazed Costello's scalp. No matter that he failed. He has achieved heroic stature; he is the man who shot Frank Costello, and all the young simpletons of the neighborhood idolize him. And hope to emulate him.)

"I was just a little kid when my old man took us to New York," Luciano recalled in a talk with friends a few years before he died. "My father was a laborer in Sicily, and he really believed all those fairy tales about the streets paved with gold in America. He never did admit it was bullshit.

"Christ, we were starving. I was hustlin' in the streets when I was twelve, stealing and runnin' penny ante crap games, and running errands for the cocksuckers who thought they were big shots because they ran a couple of cat houses, and got scared little shopkeepers to pay protection, and had gunmen to take care of their problems.

"But I looked up to those bastards, I gotta admit that. You're a kid in the slums, and you see your old man bustin' his hump for peanuts. At the same time you see the local sharpies—the bookies and the torpedoes—all makin' dough and drivin' limousines.

"So what's the kid do? He's gotta decide whether he's going to be a crumb, or make dough. Me, I made up my mind pretty young. I'd rather shoot myself than be a crumb.

"When I was fourteen, just before I got shot, my old man caught me with the gun. He always beat me a lot, when he heard about some of the things I'm doing. Runnin' with a gang and stealing. This time he didn't beat me. He just aimed the gun at me and said he oughtta pull the trigger, because I'd grow up to bring disgrace on the family. But he didn't have the guts to do it.

"So I stopped coming home, when he was around. I'd sleep in empty apartments in the neighborhood, or in pool halls. I'd only go home in the daytime, to get a hot meal from my mother. But I stayed away from my old man as much as I could."

Charlie had been born on November 24, 1897, in a drab, stinking, sulphur-mining town in the hills just southeast of Palermo. He was the son of Antonio and Rosalia Lucania. Baptized Salvatore—meaning "savior"—he began calling himself Charlie after arriving in New York with his family in the spring of 1907, when he was not yet ten; Salvatore was too Italian-sounding, and Charlie wanted to be an American.

The Lucania family settled into a slum tenement on Tenth Street and First Avenue, in a mixed neighborhood of Sicilians, mainland Italians (the Sicilians always made that distinction), Eastern European Jews, and a smattering of immigrants of other nationalities. Young Salvatore was sent off to the public school a few blocks from his home, and he detested it almost immediately.

"The teachers treated Italians like they were dirt, just

16

stupid people who would never learn," Charlie told a probation officer after his first arrest in 1916. "I hated the teachers, and hated school. So I dropped out and started to hustle."

In truth, he had begun to hustle long before he left school when he could legally quit, at fourteen. The Lower East Side was at that time one of the primary recruiting grounds for the raw muscle talent of New York's criminal gangs. Every slum neighborhood in the city had its gang, which usually controlled several square blocks. Within its boundaries the gang would run the gambling enterprises, the pool halls, bars, and whorehouses, and would sell narcotics.

Police ignored most gang activities, being handsomely paid to look the other way. Politicians were "patrons" of the gangs, providing bail and friendly judges in times of need (which were frequent) in return for the gangs' talents at stuffing ballot boxes and at persuading voters of the wrong political ideology to stay away from the polls.

Gang members were despised by the honest citizens sweating to make an honest dollar in a land paved not with gold, but with the same type of corrupt power structure from which the immigrants had fled. But to the young men in a hurry to become wealthy and influential, the young men who believed that normal opportunity was denied them because their names were Lucania, Lansky, or Costello, the gang leaders presented the quickest way out. The gang leaders were men of substance, they commanded respect, they were on a first-name basis with the powers of Tammany Hall, they had conquered the ghetto.

Charlie played truant through most of his school years, preferring to get his education on the streets. His probation report said that after he had been picked up by the local truant officer several times, "he threatened to kill said officer," who wisely refrained from annoying Charlie again.

To placate his father, to obtain his father's permission to leave school on his fourteenth birthday, Charlie took a

17

job as a shipping clerk in a hat factory. The pay was five dollars a week for a six-day, sixty-hour week. He quit after a couple of months. In later years he would always say he quit because he didn't want to be a "crumb."

One of the myths created by some writers, most notably by Sid Feder and Joachim Joesten in their book *The Luciano Story,* is that Charlie had always been a rather decent boy at heart, except that he loved to gamble a few pennies at a time. He had been working hard in the hat factory, the myth continues, bringing money home to his mother to help support his two brothers and two sisters. One night, on the way home from work with his five dollars salary in his pocket, he got into a crap game in an alley and won $244. Instant corruption! Salvatore, the good boy, became Charlie the hoodlum.

That myth, Charlie has told friends, "is a crock of shit." And, depending on his audience, he sometimes added, "Sure I won 244 bucks. With loaded dice."

When he quit the factory, more than ever determined to go the way of the "bookies and the torpedoes," Charlie no longer slept at home. He was afraid to face his father, especially after his father had pointed Charlie's own gun at him, and he began living in any apartment he could find available.

He was a darkly handsome young man, small and wiry and full of energy, and very street wise. Any number of young, street-hustling women offered to take him in. Although he liked women, as many and as frequently as possible, he preferred living much of the time in a rooming house on Fifteenth Street that was filled mostly with young men who also carried guns, and stole, and ran errands for the neighborhood mobsters.

The hoodlum who controlled Charlie's neighborhood was Monk Eastman. He was to be the last in a long line of gang leaders who, between the Civil War and Prohibition, controlled small pieces of urban territory and fought it out with leaders of other territories because none of

18

them had the intelligence to cooperate and place crime on a more businesslike basis.

Charlie seemed to understand early that there was little future for the Monk Eastman brand of criminality, and he soon began to frequent bars and pool rooms at the lower end of the East Side, in Little Italy. Here, in Mulberry Bend, just a score of blocks south of where Charlie lived, the Sicilian and Italian gangs had created a small but very secure organization.

Protected by Paul Kelly (real name Vaccarelli), a gangster who survived several murder charges in his battles with the Monk Eastman gang and then stepped up into criminal politics and had much influence in Tammany Hall, the leader of Little Italy's Mafia was Ignazio Saietta. Known as "Lupo," or "The Wolf," he was a vicious, sadistic Sicilian who was really Mafia. He had joined the Honored Society back in Sicily and had fled to New York in 1899, to avoid prosecution for murder.

The men of the Mafia had an advantage over the Monk Eastman type of gang leader. No matter what neighborhood he may have settled into, a Mafia member had blood ties—through a semireligious rite of induction into the group—with every other Mafia member in the world. A Mafia man in New York knew that his Mafia brothers in New Jersey or Louisiana would lend aid and assistance when called upon. A network of gangs interconnected through Mafia began to achieve criminal and political power in the first decade of the century.

Johnny Torrio had been a member of the Lupo-Kelly gang in Mulberry Bend, and young Charlie had early contact with the legend and the man.

Torrio was a small, slim, and very reserved sort who never appeared to become angry but who was known in certain elements of society in New York and Chicago as "Terrible Johnny." It was a nickname that fitted him perfectly.

Born in Naples in 1882, Torrio came to New York in his teens, settling with his family in that section of Brooklyn between the docks of Red Hook and the political power of Borough Hall. Before he was twenty he had opened a saloon that became a meeting place of gangsters and politicians, and by 1905 he formed the Johnny Torrio Association, a political club that formalized the criminal-political structure in Brooklyn.

Around the same time, in the first years of this century, Torrio opened a saloon in Manhattan, on James Street, near Paul Kelly's saloon and political center on Great Jones Street. Torrio became associated with Kelly and Lupo in their criminal and political fiefdom in Mulberry Bend.

Through those early years he made frequent trips to Chicago to aid his uncle, Jim Colosimo, who ran a small empire built on brothels, gambling, and political corruption. It was those visits to Chicago that earned Torrio his nickname.

Back then all sorts of dastardly criminals were attempting to extort money from Colosimo. Most of them signed their threatening letters *La Mano Nera,* the Black Hand, and embellished them with quaint symbols such as daggers and skulls. Colosimo had killed several Black Handers himself, but grew tired of such sport and summoned Torrio whenever another letter arrived.

Torrio made at least ten such trips between 1905 and 1909, and the bodies of thirty-two Black Handers bore witness to his no-nonsense approach. Eventually, Colosimo was left alone.

It would have been difficult for any outsider to believe Torrio was a killer. While others boasted about their marksmanship, or their skill at avoiding bullets during the frequent gang battles of the day, the nearest Torrio ever came to bragging about anything was when he spoke of his friendship with Enrico Caruso. Rather well-educated —he spoke five languages and actually read most of the books in his extensive library—Torrio was an opera lover and Caruso was his idol.

As an Italian of fame and wealth, Caruso became a

natural target for Black Hand extortionists. In New York, when he received a Black Hand letter, Caruso went to police. The Black Handers were caught and sent to prison for a few years. In Chicago, after receiving a similar letter, Caruso went to Torrio with his problem. The Black Handers were caught, and their mutilated bodies were found in the stockyards.

Torrio eventually moved to Chicago in 1909, to assist his uncle in the operation of his growing empire. Now he was commuting regularly to New York, to look after his political club and the power it brought him, and his gambling and bordello investments.

A year later, Torrio was summoned back to New York by Paul Kelly and other Mafia leaders, for a crisis had developed which needed Terrible Johnny's wisdom—and murderous reputation—to settle. It seems that Lupo, then generally conceded by all to be the leader of the Mafia in America, had been made foolish by greed and became involved in counterfeiting. It is a business that the government discourages more than any other. Lupo was sentenced to thirty years in the penitentiary. And a dispute had arisen over who would be caretaker of the New York Italian rackets in his absence.

Torrio, it is said, settled the matter rather intelligently. He advised that while Lupo was away, the Mafia's business should be conducted by Ciro Terranova, who was Lupo's brother-in-law and who controlled things in the Italian ghetto uptown, and by Joe Masseria, who had been Lupo's chief assistant in the Mulberry Bend section. Each man, Torrio said, should have control of his area, should consult with each other in matters of city-wide policy, and should seek the counsel of Lupo in prison as frequently as possible. Torrio's advice was accepted.

It was around this time, early 1911, that Luciano began to hang around Martinghetti's Pool Hall, which was one of those places referred to as "a den of thieves" in those days. Young Charlie, carrying a gun and obviously anxious to use it, came to the attention of Masseria's men in Martinghetti's and similar places in Little Italy.

There is little doubt, for Charlie has himself said it, that within a couple of years after arriving down around Mulberry Bend he had proved himself by killing several men who did not fit into the Lupo-Masseria gang's plans. There were many opportunities for an Italian-American gunman of Charlie's age, for the Monk Eastman gang members continued to behave in their primitive fashion, more anxious to war with other gangs than concentrate on money and power.

Slowly, the Eastmans and their ilk were disposed of. Luciano most certainly had a hand in several of the murders.

So also did a young man, two years Luciano's junior, named Alphonse Capone. Born in Brooklyn, Capone had followed Luciano's path—away from the crumbs—and had gone to work as a waiter in Torrio's Brooklyn club. When Capone was about fifteen, Torrio placed him in the Masseria gang.

"Al was just a great big lug, as a kid," Luciano was to recall in later years, sitting with friends in Celano's Gardens in Little Italy sometime around 1934, when Al Capone had been in Alcatraz a few years. "But he was strong and useful, and Johnny Torrio sure brought him up fast."

2

The first official recognition of Luciano came in April, 1916, a few months before his nineteenth birthday, when he sold a packet of opium to an undercover agent and was arrested. Charlie refused to tell police the name of his wholesaler, and claimed he just happened to find the narcotics in the gutter and decided to "make a few bucks."

According to a report by investigators, made a part of Luciano's probation report years later, police had developed information that Luciano was selling opium and heroin for one of Masseria's aides, whose name was given as Big Nose Charlie. Luciano denied ever hearing of Big Nose, and he was sentenced to a year in the penitentiary. He was paroled on December 30, 1916, after serving six months.

When he returned to Mulberry Bend on New Year's eve, he was acclaimed a "stand-up guy" who hadn't given police a bit of information. Charlie now had a "rep," as they still refer to it in those circles. Eventually he was given the supreme accolade of induction into Mafia.

The precise date of the grand honor heaped on Luciano is not known. Nor are the details of the initiation ceremony. Statements of informants, however, place the date as somewhere around the autumn of 1919. Most of the information compiled by the Federal Narcotics Bureau from informers indicates that in the few months after the 1919 summer there was a wholesale induction of young Italian-Americans into Mafia.

Among them, besides Luciano, were Vito Genovese

and Al Capone. Genovese, who would later play a major role in Luciano's rise to power, had been living on Mulberry Street since 1914 and had become a gunman and narcotics pusher for one of Masseria's lieutenants. Luciano and Genovese, upon discovering they had been born only three days apart, always held a joint birthday celebration for as long as they were together in New York. Capone, in the meantime, had been assigned to work for a Masseria associate in Coney Island, the Brooklyn resort area, where he had become chief suspect in at least two murders. Married in late 1918, Capone had become the father of a son within ten months. Albert Francis was born around the time of the Mafia induction of new members. Capone was a very important young man, for Johnny Torrio had come east to be the child's godfather and, probably, to be Capone's sponsor at the initiation rite into the Honored Society.

That society, founded in Sicily a couple of centuries before and traditionally limited to Sicilians, had already become slightly Americanized by 1919, after less than two decades in the melting pot. So many gangsters from the Italian mainland—such as Torrio, Genovese, and Capone, whose parents were from Naples—had become so indispensable to the American Mafia that the doors of the organization were opened to non-Sicilians.

But Luciano, as a Sicilian, could still be assured of special treatment by the leaders of the Mafia.

As difficult as it may be to believe, a man brought into Mafia was made to go through an intitiation that seems just a cut above the adolescent. Joe Valachi described his initiation when he testified before a U.S. Senate investigating committee. Although Valachi glibly named dozens of underworld killers and gave detailed accounts of the murders they had performed for Mafia, and though he didn't evidence any fear about revealing those secrets, he appeared almost terrified when he was asked about the rites of initiation. As he was questioned about the initiation, Valachi broke in:

24

"Can I say something? As to what I am telling you now, I need go no further to say nothing else but this here, what I am telling you, what I am exposing to you and to the press and everybody. This is my doom. This is the promise I am breaking. Even if I talked, I should never talk about this, and I am doing so."

The initiation he should never have talked about was described in this fashion by Valachi:

"They called us into this big room one at a time. When I came in, there was this long table running down the middle of the room with chairs all around. There was about thirty or thirty-five, maybe even forty guys sitting around this table. They all got up when I came in. I was led to the other end of the table past all the guys that I knew and one of the guys said, 'Joe, meet Don Salvatore Maranzano. He is the boss for all of us.' So I met the boss for the first time, and others I never met before.

"Then they sat me down at the table, we were all tight together in the chairs. Maranzano tells me to sit down on an empty chair at his right. There was a gun and a knife on the table in front of me. Maranzano motions us up again, and we all hold hands and he says some words in Italian or Sicilian that I didn't understand too well, but that meant, 'One for all and all for one.'

"Then we sit down and he turns to me, Maranzano talks to me about the gun and the knife. Still in Italian. I couldn't understand the words and Maranzano explains to me in English that they lived by the gun and the knife and they died by the gun and the knife. He said when you took that oath, you were expected to die by the gun and the knife. That was your oath.

"Then he gave me a piece of paper, and told me to make a cup out of my hands. The piece of paper is put in my hands and he lit the paper. The piece of paper is burning and Maranzano told me to say after him, in Italian, 'This is the way I will burn if I betray the secret of this thing of ours—this *cosa nostra*.' I repeated the words until the piece of paper is burned, meaning I would

25

be burned to ashes like the paper if I expose this organization.

"Maranzano said, 'To betray the secret of *cosa nostra* means death without trial.'

"After that, Maranzano said to draw numbers. Everybody at the table holds up a finger, one to five. You add them all up and then you start counting around the table till you reach the number added up. That man is what you call my godfather, he is responsible for me. The man it fell to was Joe Bonanno, known as Joe Bananas.

"Joe Bananas comes to me and says, 'Give me that finger you shoot with.' I give him my finger and he pricks it with a needle, and he makes a little blood come out. That's the blood relationship. Mr. Maranzano, when the blood comes out, says, 'This blood means that we are now one Family.' Then we all shake hands."

According to reports from within Mafia, after taking part in an initiation ceremony that must have been very similar to Valachi's, Luciano was assigned to work directly under Joe Masseria. If that is true, and it seems to be so, then Masseria may have perhaps drawn the number that made him Charlie's Mafia godfather. In any case, Charlie seems to have been placed at the right hand of the trustee of Lupo's domain and probably the second most powerful *mafioso* in America.

Masseria, who was about forty, was built like a fire hydrant, short, thick-necked, and very muscular. And he was also very shrewd. It had been his decision, made while Lupo was in prison, to expand the rolls of Mafia by recruiting younger Sicilians like Charlie, and "outsiders" like Genovese and Capone. These newer members owed their allegiance to Masseria, not to Lupo, and within a few years Masseria became the boss in name and in actuality.

Joe the Boss he was called, and he swaggered around the Mulberry Street area with the self-importance of a matinee idol.

He was the leader not only of the Mafia, but also of the Unione Siciliane, an organization that Lupo had seized some years before and turned into a Mafia subsidiary. Unione had been formed around 1900 as a mutual aid society for Sicilian immigrants. It was an organization of the honest immigrants who decided to band together to assist their countrymen in finding jobs, in explaining to them the intricacies of citizenship papers, life insurance, and burial plots, of all the enormous complexities of American society.

Some old-country Mafia members also joined, for the men of the Honored Society were as bewildered about American customs as were the honest immigrants. Eventually the Mafia, in the person of Lupo, gained control of Unione Siciliane; in the earliest years the Mafia's sole plunder was from fellow Sicilian immigrants, and having large numbers of immigrants together in one organization simplified the plunder.

When Masseria opened the doors of the American Mafia to non-Sicilians he put his own pure-blood Sicilian gangsters into Unione, achieving two ends: He had total control of an organization of Sicilian-Mafia elite, the Unione, and he maintained his grip on the greatly expanded Mafia, now swollen with Neapolitans, Barese, Calabrese, and others from the Italian mainland.

Joe the Boss was as cunning as he was power hungry. He knew that the imprisoned Lupo would not quietly stand by and permit him to confiscate the power structure that Lupo had begun to erect before his prison sentence. Lupo's relatives and Mafia blood brothers in East Harlem, his loyal aides in Mulberry Bend and in Unione Siciliane—who continually spoke of the day that Lupo would be released and return to the leadership that was rightfully his—all of them were a potential source of inter-Mafia strife should the psychotic Lupo object to Masseria's expansion of his personal power.

And so, after giving it much thought, Joe the Boss decided that the time had come to secure Lupo's release from prison. But he wasn't about to give up to Lupo everything that he, the Boss, had so carefully built. Instead, he

27

sent emissaries to Lupo in prison, messengers instructed to convince Lupo that, should he be paroled, the spectre of a return to prison for parole violation made it wise for Lupo to go into semiretirement. Joe the Boss would run the American Mafia, with Lupo as an unofficial advisor, immune from reimprisonment by remaining in the shadows. In this way, Joe would be the Boss with the blessings of Lupo, who would be forever grateful to Joe for freeing him from prison.

The legend in Little Italy has it that Lupo agreed to accept retirement. A movement to secure his parole was immediately begun.

As much as Masseria and most older Sicilian-Italian gangsters distrusted the "Jew boys," as they called them, only one man in New York, a Jew, could help Lupo get a parole. That man was Arnold Rothstein, the Brain.

By all accounts of criminal figures who were around in those days and who later reminisced to friends or let pieces of information slip to authorities, Masseria chose Charlie Luciano to seek Rothstein's help.

When he was approached by Charlie, the story within Mafia has it, Rothstein was only too glad to see what he could do for Masseria. At a price, of course. Everything Rothstein did had a price. How much the parole of Lupo cost, precisely who received the payment, and any other question that would occur to an inquisitive mind will never be answered, for there weren't too many investigators who were inquisitive enough to look into the actions of the President of the United States.

All that is known beyond dispute is that one of Warren G. Harding's first acts, upon assuming the Presidency in 1921, was to parole Lupo. Harding acted at the urging of his Attorney General, Harry Daugherty, who claimed that Lupo had been reformed and would never again become involved in criminal activities. To make his parole request even more palatable, Daugherty drew up a parole document giving the President the exclusive right to judge Lupo's future activities and to rule on whether or not he had ever broken parole.

In effect, the President was Lupo's parole officer.

(Daugherty was later prosecuted for his role in the Teapot Dome scandal, in which huge oilfields in Wyoming were raped by oilmen close to the President, but he was acquitted.)

When Lupo was released, he returned briefly to New York, kissed Joe the Boss on both cheeks to show his appreciation and to confirm Joe as Mafia leader, then sailed for Sicily. Though he returned in less than a year he lived up to his agreement—a rare event in Mafia, when a crown is at stake—and never again was an important figure in Mafia history and legend.

Luciano had been the most logical choice to bring to Rothstein the contract to free Lupo. Normally, such a contract is handled only at the highest levels, by the oldest and most seasoned gangsters. But Luciano had already established a relationship with Rothstein, through a number of business deals.

While growing up around Fourteenth Street in a neighborhood in which crime was controlled by Jewish gangsters, Charlie had run small crap games and other enterprises with several young Jews of his own age. Including Meyer Lansky, Bugsy Siegel, Louis Lepke, and George Uffner. One of the activities of all of these men, especially Uffner, was dealing in narcotics. Uffner's narcotics trade was financed by Rothstein, who extended Uffner loans to import narcotics from abroad, loans for which he charged twenty percent interest a month. Luciano by now was distributing the Uffner-Rothstein merchandise, and had met Rothstein and done several jobs for him. Primarily, it is said, as a gunman.

Rothstein had been primarily a gambler and a loanshark. He entered the narcotics market when he discovered he could compete with the licensed drug manufacturers by undercutting their prices.

At the turn of the century the drug manufacturers were

doing a sixty million dollar annual business in patent medicines, which were laced with opium, morphine, and cocaine. There was big money in peddling narcotics, and it was part of American big business; the drug lobby was the largest of any then in existence, and it fought off all attempts to control the sale of drugs.

Back then the use of narcotics of every type was probably as common in the urban ghettoes as the smoking of marijuana is in today's society. The official government blindness, a myopia purchased by the drug lobby, created hundreds of thousands of addicts. For those who desired more excitement than drinking their narcotic in a bottle of "cough syrup," there were any number of places to obtain drugs straight, in more potent form, and in more adventurous surroundings.

In the early years of this century the entire area around Mulberry Bend, the lower part of which was becoming Chinatown, was filled with stores and tenement flats that had been converted into opium dens. The term seems rather quaint now, sixty years later, but opium dens were the reality of tenement and gangster life. A certain percentage of the young men and women of the ghetto were destined to become hopheads, addicts who emerged from narcotic hazes only long enough to rob a pedestrian or burglarize a store, so that they could get the price of another few pipe loads of the narcotic in their favorite opium den.

Young Charlie used opium from the time he began hustling on the streets, at least until he was inducted into Mafia. He has admitted to friends, "I used to hit the pipe joints in Chinatown when I was a kid, we all did it." Those pipe joints abounded in Mott, Pell, Doyers, and Catherine Streets, the neighborhood in which Paul Kelly and Johnny Torrio still had their saloons when Charlie had begun hanging around the Italian gangsters.

Charlie once remembered with fondness the man who had given him his first pipe filled with opium. "He was a dentist we all called Doc," Charlie told a visitor during his

30

enforced exile in Naples, a few years before he died. "He was a hophead who never bothered getting a license, but he worked on everybody's teeth in the neighborhood and he was good. And cheap, too. Had a place over on Catherine Street, in Chinatown.

"I was about fourteen, and one of the boys needed some work on his teeth. He told me to come along, that the Doc was always good for some opium. I did, I'd try anything when I was a kid. And I liked it, the stuff did funny things to my head. But I'd never let it suck me under."

Charlie could never forget Doc, he said. "Because he got killed a couple of days after I had my first smoke with him. He took away the broad of some hophead, think his name was Brady. A cheap burglar and stickup man who was so crazy with opium all the time that he'd kill you if you got in his way. Brady got mad at losing his girl, so he went up to the Doc's place and put a few bullets in the poor guy. The whole neighborhood was talkin' about it, how they lost a good dentist."

Luciano used opium and other drugs in moderation. He had seen too many men, like Brady and Doc, destroyed by dope, and he was much too ambitious to seek that way out of the ghetto.

While the opium dens were frowned on by the police, and occasionally raided when newspapers complained about them, there was such a thin line between the legal narcotics of the drug companies and the illegal dope peddled on the streets that a young man never had to fear more than a few months in prison if he was caught selling the stuff and was unable to buy his way out of an arrest.

The legal drug trade was not without its detractors, however. The muckrakers, America's first investigative journalists, had been publishing exposés in the popular magazines from about 1900 on, depicting the horrors of drugs and the political corruption spawned by the drug lobby. As a result, Congress passed the Harrison Drug Control Act in 1916. Originally designed to fully halt the flow of drugs to an unsuspecting public, which was turning many of its infants into addicts, the Act had been so weakened by the drug lobby that it was no more than a tax on the legal drug trade.

Which is when Rothstein entered the market. He had found the gambler's "edge"—he could compete with drug manufacturers by producing narcotics and failing to pay the newly imposed taxes. Within a year, his bankroll was financing the manufacture and distribution of more drugs in the New York area than were sold through recognized drug houses.

Charlie Luciano was one of those selling Rothstein's drugs, buying the narcotics in pound lots from George Uffner and selling it at a large markup to the addicts on the street. But his association with Uffner was a freelance activity separate from the Mafia business of Joe the Boss.

Joe's mob family was buying narcotics in huge wholesale lots from the Rothstein-financed factories. Occasionally, between the time money and narcotics would change hands uptown and its scheduled delivery downtown in the wagon or truck of a Masseria associate, the dope would be hijacked by a gang of gunmen. Being ever so suspicious, Masseria was certain he was being robbed by Rothstein's own men, most notably the Diamond brothers.

Eddie Diamond and his younger brother Jack, known as Legs for his youthful ability to steal a package from a delivery truck and outrace all pursuers, were thieves, narcotics peddlers, and hijackers who operated chiefly on the West Side and in midtown, Rothstein's territory. Originally from Philadelphia, the Diamonds had come to New York in 1914 and immediately carved out a reputation for themselves. They came to the notice of Rothstein and within a couple of years they had become his bodyguards and he had become the financier of their various activities, especially narcotics.

Now, it was rather well known in certain sectors of underworld society that Rothstein was never above the

32

double cross if he was certain such unethical behavior would not be traced to him. Thus it was only natural that Joe the Boss should suspect the Diamonds of hijacking his narcotics shipments.

Masseria had two options. He could order the death of Rothstein and the Diamonds, which would disrupt the enormously profitable narcotics trade. Or he could have the Diamonds watched closely, so that they would not dare strongarm any *mafioso* again.

Joe the Boss chose the latter and much wiser option. He ordered Charlie Luciano to join the Diamonds' gang, to be "temporarily attached" to Legs Diamond and the other "Irishers" who were causing Masseria so much financial loss. Luciano did so, and he became the liason between the Rothstein-Diamond syndicate and the Italian gangsters.

That assignment, and the years of contact with Rothstein that it brought him—the years of education in crime, business, and politics—is perhaps the primary reason that Luciano would later become the moving force in the creation of the modern American Mafia. Rothstein's power must have greatly impressed a man like Luciano— and other ambitious young men such as Costello and Lansky. It couldn't have taken Charlie long to realize that Rothstein's power derived from one basic strength: He knew the price of every man—whether politician or killer —and he always had the money to pay for it.

"He was a genius, just a genius," Charlie would later say. "I mean, it's one thing to fix a traffic ticket or get a gambler let go with no fine, but to put a fix in at the White House . . ."

3

Despite the awe in which he held Rothstein, it is apparent that Charlie, before he was twenty-three, gave the underworld's financier a bit of advice that expanded Rothstein's power even further. According to journalist Leo Katcher, who detailed Rothstein's life in *The Big Bankroll*, one of the few literate books ever written about gangsters, it was Luciano who suggested to Rothstein the then innovative idea of importing opium and heroin directly from the Mideast and Europe.

The development of an international narcotics pipeline, at the young Luciano's urging, had its origin in the insanity called Prohibition. On January 17, 1920, the Volstead Act became effective. This federal law, which set up the apparatus by which the Eighteenth Amendment would be enforced, made it a crime to manufacture, transport, or sell beverages containing more than one half of one percent alcohol by volume.

According to his biographer, Rothstein did not immediately understand that the Volstead Act would open for every gambler and criminal the greatest "edge" they could ever ask. Rothstein believed the law would be obeyed and that only the very wealthy, who could use influence and bring in a few cases of Scotch or gin from Canada and Europe, would be drinking as they usually did.

It was probably the only time in his life he didn't see, in advance, the potential for profit. Masseria, Luciano, Lansky, and perhaps every Italian, Jewish, and Irish gangster saw what was coming with Prohibition. They had an advantage over Rothstein. He came from a moderately wealthy, respectable family. The Lucianos and Lanskys had been raised in the ghettoes, where immigrants from Europe had long been making small quantities of their own wine, liquor, and liqueurs.

In the six months between the ratification of the Eighteenth Amendment and the effective date of the Volstead Act, the ghetto gangsters were preparing for the great booze binge. They had spread the word among their fellow immigrants that they would pay well for homemade alcoholic beverages, and they encouraged immigrant families to increase production. They began setting up trucking companies to bring in liquor from Canada. They had begun making contacts with agents in England, who would buy and ship back to America huge loads of liquor. And they had accumulated millions of dollars worth of liquor, laying down stock for the future.

Although he became involved in bootlegging comparatively late, Rothstein apparently was the first to actually bring whiskey into the U.S. by the shipload. Several months after the Volstead act had become effective, Rothstein was approached with a proposition by "Waxey" Gordon—his nickname came from the days he was a pickpocket, and his victims' billfolds seemed to stick magically to his fingers —and by Max Greenberg of Detroit. Greenberg said he had been bringing in whiskey from Canada, which had been very profitable, and now he wanted to expand. He needed $175,000, at the usual rate of interest.

Rothstein said he would let them know the next day. Before that second meeting he made dozens of phone calls across the country and to England, exploring every facet of the whiskey trade. When he met with Greenberg and Gordon, he was ready with a counterproposal.

Instead of buying the whiskey in Canada, why not buy it in England and ship it over? Of course, such an importing business would cost much more than $175,000. But he, Rothstein, would be happy to finance the operation. He would make Greenberg a partner to the extent of $175,000, would lend him this money at the usual high interest rates if Greenberg gave him as collateral the real estate and trucks Greenberg owned in Detroit.

This proposition was not quite what Greenberg had in mind when he first approached Rothstein, but he accepted it. He now owed Rothstein $175,000, but he didn't get a penny of the money; that was simply his "piece" of the importing business, to be paid back with interest when the first shipload was disposed of.

Rothstein then contacted in London an agent with whom he had already made arrangements the day before, during his exploration of the liquor business. That agent was Harry Mather, a stock swindler who had fled to England to avoid prosecution. He commissioned Mather to buy twenty thousand cases of Scotch, and to find a ship and crew that could be bought or leased.

While Mather was making arrangements in England, Rothstein proceeded to set up an organization that could facilitate the landing and selling of the whiskey in America. On some of these activities he dispatched Charlie Luciano, Legs Diamond, and other members of the Diamond gang.

The Diamonds and their associates, using Rothstein money and Rothstein influence, bought in New Jersey a half-dozen large speedboats which would each carry eight hundred to a thousand cases of whiskey from the cargo ship anchored offshore. They bought off practically the entire staff of the Coast Guard station at Montauk Point, Long Island, which patrolled the waters in the area where Rothstein intended to land his cargo. They made arrangements with police, so that the trucks carrying the whiskey into the city could travel unmolested.

When the ship eventually did arrive with its cargo of Scotch some time early in 1921, Luciano and the Diamonds, with Costello, Lansky, and other young men who worked with Rothstein, were on hand to greet it. They were helped enormously, in transferring the whiskey from the ship to the smaller boats, by the Coast Guard crew; a

36

number of cases went into the Coast Guard cutters as a bonus. Once the whiskey was ashore, the bootleggers were also greatly assisted by police, who helped load the cargo into the trucks and then provided a motorcycle escort to Rothstein's warehouse in the city.

Included in that cargo was a watertight box containing about fifty pounds of narcotics, primarily opium and heroin.

The narcotics importation, as already noted, had been Luciano's idea. While much energy was being devoted to bootlegging, Luciano did not forget the profits he had made in narcotics.

At around the same time that it passed the Volstead Act, Congress had also strengthened the Harrison Drug Control Act. Amendments to that ineffectual law now required drug companies to maintain detailed records of every gram of narcotics that they maufactured and sold, and it barred physicians from writing unlimited prescriptions for drugs.

The legal market for narcotics was drying up, but the demand remained as great as ever. Thousands of men, women, and even children, made addicts by patent medicines more than by drug pushers, wanted something to alleviate their craving. Luciano had been supplying the needs of some of them, on a small scale. Now he saw a way by which he could expand into wholesale dealing.

According to Katcher, in his biography of Rothstein:

"Luciano . . . suggested to Rothstein that there was money, big money, in dope. It was as a result of this suggestion that Rothstein entered the traffic when he started to import whiskey."

By early 1921, Luciano had become one of the largest wholesalers in New York of Rothstein's imported narcotics. More important, he had become very closely associated with the man whose money, organizational talent, and political influence had been slowly turning anarchic criminal gangs into underworld business firms. There was much that an ambitious young man could learn from A.R.

Luciano, of course, did not drift away from Masseria and the Little Italy crowd of gangsters. Though he was establishing relationships with every important criminal in the city, Mafia was his primary responsibility. Rothstein might be his teacher, a few hours a day; Mafia was his family, his blood.

There was much work to do for Mafia.

The bootleggers had found that getting their hands on enough whiskey to satisfy the public's suddenly awakened thirst presented no real problem. Some of it rolled down the highways in trucks from Canada. Much of it was stolen at gunpoint from government warehouses, or removed without violence through forged or illegally purchased federal "medicinal withdrawal permits." Some liquor was distilled in tenement bathtubs, or in distilleries that were constructed overnight in vacant factories and warehouses, or any building that could hold a still.

The problem was getting all of this liquor into the hands of consumers. Masseria's gangsters, suddenly become businessmen, were the first to establish a commodities market for bootleg liquor.

The Curb Exchange, as it was wryly called in imitation of the Wall Street market for the movement of stocks not listed on the Big Board, came into being in the heart of Masseria's territory, just one block from police headquarters. At the intersection of Mulberry and Grand Streets, and for several blocks around, the liquor vendors met through the day and night to carry on their business.

The Curb Exchange was created so that a wholesaler could purchase the brand of whiskey that his retail outlets demanded. A man who had been able to get two hundred cases of whiskey out of a government warehouse with his real or forged permit might find that the only brands available were those his customers did not want. So the bootlegger went down to the curb exchange and traded his two hundred cases for a similar quantity of the brands in demand in those speakeasies he supplied.

Joe the Boss established his headquarters in a "social

club" at the corner of Kenmare and Mulberry Streets, which became the communications center of the curb exchange. Directly across the street, in a garage and loft building, Charlie Luciano set up his office. Though still rather young, he was important enough to have an office and staff of his own, for he was the link between the Italian mob and the outsiders.

It was here, at the curb exchange, that Luciano became even more closely associated with a number of younger racketeers with whom he was beginning to forge alliances and with whose assistance he would later propel himself, and those friends, to the control of the Americanized Mafia.

Meyer Lansky and Bugsy Siegel, both of whom Charlie had known from Fourteenth Street when they were hustling teenagers like himself, came around to buy and sell liquor. Vito Genovese had already been in the neighborhood since 1914, living on Mulberry Street and working for some of Masseria's men, and he and Charlie became close friends. And then there was, most vital of all to Charlie's later development, the arrival of Frank Costello.

Costello came down to the curb exchange from East Harlem accompanied by his brother, Eddie, to deal in whiskey. Frank had been born in Calabria, on the Italian mainland, in 1891. He was brought to New York by his family when he was four, and followed the standard pattern: truancy, quitting school at fourteen, gambling, robbing people at gunpoint.

He no longer carried a gun, however. In 1915, after joining the West Side gang of robbers headed by Owney Madden, a tough and wily kid from Liverpool, Costello was charged with carrying a concealed weapon. He was convicted and served eleven months in the City Penitentiary. He came out vowing he would never do another day of time, and he stopped carrying a gun.

Many years later, Costello told friends that in those early days of their relationship he considered Luciano to be "just a punk kid"—there was a violence in Charlie that sometimes exploded for no just cause, Costello said, "as if he had to prove something by beating people up, and by letting everybody know he carried a gun and used it."

As an example of Charlie's volatile nature, Costello liked to tell dinner companions about the night Luciano almost stabbed him. According to Costello's biographer, Leonard Katz, some time shortly after they met in 1920 Costello and Luciano quarreled in a speakeasy near the curb exchange. Luciano suddenly pulled out a knife. Costello didn't panic. He gently lectured Charlie that it was necessary for intelligent men to discuss their differences, that fighting led to the death of good men and brought unwanted police investigations, that "violence is ignorance."

Luciano put the knife away. "We got very close," Costello reminisced in the last years of his life. "I think he looked up to me, as a father figure." Luciano was twenty-three at the time, and Costello twenty-nine.

Luciano continued to carry a gun, and to use it, for by the end of 1920 he had become one of Joe Masseria's bodyguards. The position of bodyguard is quite an honor in Mafia. A bodyguard is more than just a gunman-sentinel. He is the confidant of the criminal executive, the buffer between the executive and the employees. By promoting Charlie to bodyguard, Masseria was signaling to all that he believed Charlie was destined for high rank in Mafia.

The job kept Luciano quite busy; it seemed for a time that everybody was trying to kill Joe Masseria. For more than a year the curb exchange itself became as much a battleground as a brokerage business. Some hoodlum was constantly shooting at another, in spite of the exchange's proximity to the police headquarters complex. "Fledgling detectives did not have far to walk to practice the investigation of murders," one writer has remarked about those days.

Much of the gunfire involved Masseria. It began in the summer of 1920. A pair of ambitious bootleggers, by name Sal Mauro and Umberto Valenti, could not reconcile themselves to the fact that Masseria was the Boss and his crowd controlled the whiskey trade among the Italians. They decided to correct the injustice that had forced inferior roles upon them.

One afternoon, in front of 222 Chrystie Street, just a few blocks from the curb exchange, Mauro ambushed Masseria. Mauro must have been a poor gunmen for, in spite of his advantage of surprise, Mauro was quite dead when the gun battle ended. Masseria was arrested on homicide charges. As so frequently happened when one paid close attention to political connections, the case was dismissed for "lack of evidence" and Masseria was not even inconvenienced by a single night in jail.

Finding it impossible to get near Masseria, surrounded as he was by Luciano and other bodyguards after that first abortive attempt on his life, Umberto Valenti adopted guerilla tactics. He, or his men, executed at least a half-dozen of Masseria's men over the next several months, some of them in the midst of the curb exchange.

Masseria apparently did not at first suspect that it was Valenti who was trying so desperately to kill him and his people, for Valenti lived in Mulberry Street and traded on the exchange yet was never harmed.

It wasn't until May 8, 1922, that Masseria finally realized Valenti was behind the slow decimation of his gang, and vowed that he would personally execute this mosquito that was trying to sting the Boss. On that morning several gunmen positively identified as in the employ of Valenti murdered Vincent Terranova, one of Lupo's relatives, in East Harlem; that afternoon the same gunmen shot down Terranova's bootlegging partner in Broome Street, right on the curb exchange.

It all became too much for Joe Masseria. The insult, to kill a Terranova in front of his house, and to kill another dear friend of Masseria on the exchange, must be avenged.

That evening Joe the Boss and two of his men—one of them Luciano, according to Mafia historians still living in the area—waited in a doorway at 194 Grand Street. This strategic position was less than two blocks from Police Headquarters, which troubled the Boss not at all, and only a block from Valenti's speakeasy in Mott Street.

They hadn't been waiting very long when Valenti and his bodyguard left the Mott Street speakeasy and turned into Grand, walking toward Masseria. When the targets were two doors away, Masseria gave orders to open fire. Valenti and his bodyguard returned the fire, forcing the Masseria group to duck for cover. When they peeked out, Valenti had run off and the bodyguard was on the pavement, bleeding from several wounds.

The man took two months to die. Joe the Boss had been seized by police as he fled the scene of the shooting, and was charged with murder when Valenti's bodyguard died. Luciano and the other gunman with him had been able to escape into the curb exchange crowds.

Valenti went into hiding for a while, hoping that the courts would complete the job of removing Masseria that he and his men had bungled. Perhaps they would send the Boss to the electric chair. But Masseria was promptly freed on bail, provided by Arnold Rothstein's bonding company, and his case was delayed again and again through political influence. Valenti grew impatient.

On August 9 he sent gunmen to murder the Boss in front of his home at 80 Second Avenue, near Fifth Street. The assassin failed. According to an eye witness, Masseria dashed into a millinery shop at No. 82 when the first shots alerted him to the danger of remaining on the streets, and the gunman followed him inside. The owner of the shop reported, in his statement to police:

"The man with the revolver came close to the other fellow and aimed. Just as he fired, the man jumped to one side. The bullet smashed the window of my store. Then the man fired again and the fellow he aimed at ducked his head forward. The man with the gun fired again, and again the other man ducked his head forward."

The gunman was out of bullets by now, and he fled to a waiting car. When the reports of Joe the Boss's dancing act spread through the area, and were confirmed by that afternoon's newspapers, his reputation became greatly enhanced among his superstitious countrymen, who began to whisper that the Boss was immortal.

Masseria knew better, of course. If Valenti was not stopped, Masseria might soon be dead. Giving it much thought, he sent to Valenti a neutral emissary, reported to be one of Luciano's non-Italian friends, either Meyer Lansky or Legs Diamond. The emissary bore good tidings: Joe the Boss wanted a peace conference.

Valenti, who must have been a rather stupid sort, agreed to a meeting. The conference spot selected was a spaghetti house on East Twelfth Street, near Second Avenue. It was Luciano's neighborhood. He knew every inch of ground, every alley, back yard, and doorway.

Valenti arrived with one retainer and Masseria with one, as had been previously agreed upon. Masseria's bodyguard, according to Mafia legend, was Luciano. They ate pasta for lunch, and talked quite seriously, and seemed to come to an amicable agreement. After lunch the quartet walked together along Twelfth Street toward Second Avenue. At the corner two other Masseria men came up and, at a nod from Masseria, they and the bodyguard who is said to have been Luciano opened fire on Valenti.

He was hit, but he ran diagonally across the intersection toward a taxi, firing over his shoulder. Masseria's men ran after him, and brought him down with a bullet through the head as he was opening the door of the taxicab.

Finally, Valenti the mosquito had been disposed of. He was the last threat, for some years, to Masseria's rule of Mafia.

In spite of the frequent murders and shootings through all the Prohibition years and later, assassinations and gun battles took up only a small part of the life of any gangster. If it sometimes appears that murder and mayhem was the only business of the mob, that's only because the killings made the newspapers while the important business was conducted in relative secrecy. That business, for the Mafia and the outsiders with whom it was associated, first and always was the making of money and the building of political power.

For Luciano, too young and inexperienced to have gained political influence, the major business activity outside the duty owed to Masseria and the Mafia in the whiskey trade, was narcotics. Luciano and others were grossing enormous sums from bootlegging, and yet the narcotics business was of special importance to Charlie. His first large income had been derived from narcotics, as a young boy who refused to be a crumb. His special relationship with the great Rothstein was through their mutual business interest in narcotics. His growing importance to Joe the Boss and his Mafia organization stemmed at least in part from the money he helped them make in narcotics.

4

By 1923, Charlie Luciano was quite a wealthy young man, one of the many thousands of beneficiaries of Prohibition and of the government-protected drug industry that created so many customers for men like Charlie.

The extent of Luciano's resources may be gauged by an incident which occurred in June of that year, and which has always been misunderstood by Mafia watchers.

Luciano at that time was a major distributor of narcotics. Entering into partnership with Rothstein, he would frequently own an investor's share in much of the dope that was flowing from Turkey through Europe and into Rothstein's New York storehouses. Once the narcotics were landed, Charlie would pick up his share and secrete it in an apartment in a tenement he owned—under the legal front, The Downtown Realty Corporation—at 163 Mulberry Street. His narcotics were quite safe there for he employed guards and no one would dare rob the Little Italy apartment of Masseria's chief executive.

Luciano apparently did not have a large organization to distribute his narcotics. He had few employees to sell the stuff several ounces at a time to the actual street pushers. He sold most of the dope to retailers himself.

On June 2, Charlie sold two ounces of morphine to a man named John Lyons, a pusher who had been a steady customer for several months. On June 4, he sold an ounce of heroin to Lyons. The next day, in a pool room on East Fourteenth Street, Charlie sold him another two ounces of morphine. And was arrested by federal narcot-

45

ics agents. John Lyons, it turned out, had become a federal informer.

Charlie was taken in for questioning. He was now twenty-six, no longer to be treated with leniency as a minor, as he was when first arrested for a narcotics violation in 1916. Now he could be sent to prison for ten years or more.

He offered to make a deal. If the federal agents would promise to release him, he would tell them where to find "a whole trunk full of narcotics." Charlie bargained for a while with Joseph van Bransky, agent in charge of the New York office. An agreement was shortly reached: Should Charlie be able to deliver the batch of narcotics, the agents would inform the judge that Charlie was working for them, as an undercover agent, and persuade the judge to dismiss the charges.

Luciano directed the agents to his apartment storehouse in Mulberry Street. There they found a trunk containing heroin, opium, and morphine, then valued at $150,000 wholesale. Charlie was taken before a judge that afternoon and, without having to say a word, heard the charges against him dismissed.

It wasn't until twelve years later that the story of Charlie's escape from a long prison sentence became public knowledge. By that time, in 1936, Luciano was on the witness stand testifying in his own defense. It is almost unheard of for a Mafia leader to voluntarily take the witness stand, but Luciano was vainly hoping to refute the long string of low-class prostitutes whom an ambitious District Attorney named Thomas Dewey had persuaded to swear that Charlie was the head of a citywide prostitution conspiracy.

During his cross-examination of the witness, Dewey recited the facts of Charlie's 1923 drug arrest and his information to agents about the several pounds of drugs in Mulberry Street. And then the examination went like this:

"What were you—a stool pigeon?"

"I only told him what I knew."

To the newspaper writers, and to those who later wrote books about Luciano and the Mafia, there could be little doubt: Charlie had been an informer. Some writers went so far as to claim that a number of men had been arrested as a result of Charlie's information. (Research in the files indicates there had been no arrests.) One or two writers flatly stated that Luciano built up his own "narcotics empire" by informing on the competition, using the federal government to help him create a monopoly.

The truth, as sworn to by the old-timers around Mulberry Street whom I've interviewed over the past twenty years, has a greater logic to it than the version promoted by Dewey and accepted by the newspapermen. That truth is, simply, that Charlie Luciano sacrificed his own cache of narcotics in barter for his freedom. To Charlie, in 1923, the loss of $150,000 in drugs was as nothing compared to the loss of the ten most productive years of his future.

As an old man known as Funzi, who had been a young Masseria man with Charlie in those days and still operated a few pieces of business in Little Italy in the 1950's, once explained it to me:

"Charlie Lucky didn't stool on nobody but himself. That was *his* dope he gave up. Smartest thing he ever did, 'cause it wasn't no more different than payin' that amount to judges and politicians to get let off."

It was around this time, shortly after Charlie's near-imprisonment, that Frank Costello had a long talk with him. Speaking very softly, as he always did, Costello advised Luciano to give up narcotics, to concentrate on bootlegging and gambling.

"Dope is for suckers," Costello said, according to friends with whom he reminisced years later. "Dope isn't like booze and gambling. The best people want to drink. The best people want to place a bet. They'll thank you for helping them drink and gamble. But they'll take a walk if they learn you're spreading dope around."

47

The "best people" had by now become one of Costello's main concerns. For Costello craved respectability above all else. With the riches that had become his in the very first year of Prohibition, Costello had begun to ease away from the Masseria types, gun-happy Sicilians whose egos needed the very flashy show of power.

Costello sought power as much as they, but on different terms. To be most effective, he realized, power must be totally secret. Passing ten thousand dollars to a Tammany politican and thereby manipulating the political process was, to Costello, much more rewarding than shooting down an enemy and being hailed by the *paisans* on Mulberry Street. Especially when that politician would be forever in your debt, and would come sucking up as a friend so that the money would continue to flow.

The politicians, many of them morally lower than the mobsters from whom they took a fortune, nonetheless had entree into "polite" society. For one thing, a few members of old and respected New York families would generally enter politics, either to fulfill their own special needs or sincerely to help the city and its enormous problems. For another, the city's bankers, brokers, and businessmen would be helpless in face of the city bureaucracy did they not cultivate, and bribe, political leaders in exactly the fashion of the bootleggers and gamblers.

Frank Costello had begun to walk among these men, at political receptions, charitable affairs, private dinner parties.

Costello had gained access to that society of "respectable" merchants who manipulated the political structure and skimmed the wealth of the city, through his association with Jimmy Hines, a Tammany Hall leader whose political influence was for sale to any and to all.

Hines was a muscular blacksmith from the Upper West Side who had become a Tammany district leader several years before Prohibition. Partially through his association with West Side gangs and with Arnold Rothstein, partially as a result of his behind-the-scenes support of Tammany Hall boss Charlie Murphy, Hines by 1920 had become one of the most vitally important men in the criminal-political system that has always dominated New York City.

Hines's role was a very special one. He was the bag man who received payoffs and bribes from Rothstein and most of the other gangsters, including the Masseria-Mafia complex; Hines passed the bribes to police officials, judges, to Charlie Murphy and others in Tammany Hall, after a certain percentage stuck to his fingers, of course. And he was the man who made the phone calls which ordered a police official to halt an investigation, which ordered a judge to dismiss a charge for "lack of evidence," which ordered the Mayor to award a contract to a certain firm, and which warned a gambling hall or bootleg warehouse of the rare raid that could not be halted.

Without Hines, or someone like him, the Rothsteins, Lucianos, and Costellos could never have functioned. With Hines, the only risk faced by a businessman-racketeer through the 1920's and 1930's was from the guns of overambitious competitors.

It has long been the established wisdom that Prohibition was responsible for the corruption of police and politicians. The truth is that police and political leaders had always been in the employ of criminal gangs in New York, taking bribes and performing extralegal services, since at least 1840 when the Five Points gang attained prominence in Mulberry Bend. Prohibition simply increased the flow of monies to the corrupt and helped create a more civilized, more highly organized channel for the movement of those funds. Jimmy Hines, for one, had always been corrupt; after Prohibition began, however, his income from the gangs changed from a fee-per-favor arrangement to a weekly retainer of thousands of dollars and, in several instances, an actual partnership in a bootleg or gambling enterprise.

Costello, operating his bootleg business from the West

Side, had purchased Hines's services quite early. While Joe Masseria was dodging bullets around the curb exchange in the first two years of Prohibition, Costello was developing his political contacts uptown. His role in Mafia had become, by 1922, that of the bridge between the so-called respectable world, and the Italian mobsters; most of the contracts for political favors required by the Mafia were assigned to Costello by Masseria.

As Leonard Katz, Costello's biographer, has written:

"The role of advisor and fixer suited Costello's aims perfectly. He had no ambition to become another Joe the Boss in the secret society. He was too busy carving out his own empire. His careful ties with the Mafia gave him the muscle he needed, and his place in the outside world gave him the respectability he craved."

Costello's image of himself was that of a businessman, supplying services—liquor and gambling—to a public that demanded them in spite of the bluenoses who had made them illegal. He invested in real estate, an ice cream factory, an automobile agency, and he cultivated the image of a prosperous businessman. He dressed conservatively, selecting his suits with great care. There was nothing flashy about Frank Costello, nothing that would bring him to the notice of the press, the income tax agents, or any of the forces beyond his control which could, if he were not careful, destroy his world.

He advised Luciano to do the same. To get out of narcotics. To change his showy style of dress and his openly expensive tastes—Luciano had become a Broadway "sport," gaudily dressed, escorting chorus girls and stars to flashy nightclubs in which gossip columnists found their titillation, making himself much too obvious in the better bordellos and gambling dens and at the race tracks.

Luciano, according to Costello, ignored the advice at first. In fact, Luciano at that time was still such a *cafoni* —a peasant—that he actually had himself tattooed. One of those tattoos, on his right forearm, was the nickname by which he would later become famous, "Lucky."

Another of those myths promoted by many writers, and most recently repeated in the questionable Luciano "memoirs," *The Last Testament,* is that Luciano earned his nickname in 1929, when he was kidnapped by a rival gang that had decided to kill him and somehow failed. The truth about the severe beating Luciano suffered that night will be discussed later. As for the myth about his nickname, the fact is that Luciano had begun calling himself "Lucky" in the early 1920's.

Frank Costello would tell friends years later that Charlie gave himself the nickname because "He felt that people are attracted to a guy when he's lucky; everyone wants to be with a winner." Luciano pushed the name on others, Costello said, until many began to accept it. Charlie even fabricated stories about his incredible winnings at dice, cards, and the horses because he wanted everyone to believe he was a lucky man.

So he became Lucky Luciano in certain circles around 1924. And he was all flash. Along with many other bootleggers and gamblers who partied along Broadway in that Runyonesque era, Luciano invested in Broadway musicals. Being angels gave the boys a certain status among the sporting set. It also gave them the pick of chorus girls, or at least those women of the chorus who were strangely attracted to men of sinister background. One chorus girl would move in with Charlie for six or eight months, to be replaced by another. And another.

But as Prohibition ground on, Lucky Luciano would begin to realize that Costello's advice was sound. By the second half of the 1920's he would adopt a low profile, would work as hard at keeping his name off the lips of Broadway and underworld gossips as he had earlier worked at spreading the word about his fabulous luck.

A part of the reason for Charlie's later caution was the very dreadful things that happened to men of his profession whose activities made newspaper headlines.

5

Prohibition has been called the dry and lawless years. It wasn't dry, but it was certainly lawless.

Police and politicians were owned by the likes of Rothstein and Costello in New York, by Johnny Torrio and Al Capone in Chicago. The few federal Prohibition agents who had not been purchased by the bootleggers could not begin to halt the flow of alcohol. The only law was the gangsters' own law; the only means of enforcement was by the gun.

And the guns, which often killed the innocent along with the underworld malefactor who had been sentenced to death—for bootleg gangsters were almost as dreadful at marksmanship as the legendary outlaws of the Wild West were—the guns brought unwelcome publicity that sometimes threatened to destroy the criminal-political structure.

Chicago was far worse than New York. Luciano, who maintained close business and personal contact with Torrio and Capone in Chicago, remarked to friends after one visit to that city: "A real goddamn crazy place! Nobody's safe in the streets."

Charlie Lucky was absolutely correct. From the first notable murder at the start of Prohibition, a murder which made Torrio and then Capone the rulers of the Midwest, until the incredibly arrogant Valentine's Day Massacre in 1929, at least five hundred people were slain in Chicago. Among them were a newspaper reporter and an assistant district attorney; the sort of victims that brought much protest from respectable society and much "heat" on the gangsters.

That first notable Prohibition murder in Chicago can be fixed with exactitude. It occurred on May 11, 1920, only four months after the Volstead Act had become law. The victim was Big Jim Colosimo, uncle to Johnny Torrio, the man who brought Torrio to Chicago.

In the ten years since he had gone to Chicago to help Uncle Jim operate his businesses, Torrio had developed what was by far the largest and wealthiest criminal enterprise in the nation. He and his uncle were the sole owners of a syndicate of bordellos (in those quaint days whorehouses could be found six to a block in business and entertainment districts, complete with red lights at the front doors). They operated taverns, horserooms, gambling dens designed after the salons at Monte Carlo, anything in which large sums of money could be made. Much of Torrio's success came from the money and ballot box stuffers he employed to guarantee the election of Big Bill Thompson as Mayor of Chicago in 1915.

When Torrio realized that the fanatics of the temperance movement were winning their fifty-year fight to dry up America, he astutely began to look ahead. He understood that millions of dollars could be made by supplying thirsty Americans who didn't care to stop drinking.

Torrio tried to interest his uncle in the coming bonanza of Prohibition, but Colosimo was hardly enthusiastic. He insisted that prostitution and gambling would forever be the large money-makers; that Prohibition was a passing fancy not worth investing in because it would quickly pass into history.

Torrio, of course, knew better. He began preparing for the new era by purchasing partnerships in breweries and distilleries before the Volstead Act became law. The proposition was simple: the legal owner would remain in the background as an anonymous partner, providing only professional advice to Torrio and his men, who would accept all responsibility should there be raids and arrests.

Few businessmen, faced with the prospect of losing their investment and their annual profits, resisted the offer. Those who did resist were bought outright. There was no violence.

Torrio also laid in a large supply of liquor—several million dollars' worth, it is said in Chicago. He knew that once the liquor supply was frozen by law, his investment would double or triple in value.

While Torrio was racing about, preparing for Prohibition locally, he did not ignore his roots in New York. He invested in several distilleries back East. And, most important, he set up alliances with his old associates, particularly Joe Masseria in Little Italy and Frankie Yale in Brooklyn. There were many conferences, and much talk of shipping whiskey from England; Torrio began establishing the supply line that would transport his share from the rumrunners off the Atlantic coast to his Midwest customers.

A word about Frankie Yale is necessary here, for he would be at least partially responsible for the inter-Mafia rivalry out of which Luciano would, in the 1930's, create the modern American Mafia. Born Uale, he grew up in Brooklyn and as a young man Americanized his name. He joined Torrio in several joint enterprises involving gambling and political corruption, establishing a power base along the Brooklyn docks and in Coney Island. It was Yale who owned the tavern in that seaside resort to which the young and inexperienced Al Capone had been sent, about 1917, to learn the business.

Yale was the most powerful *mafioso* in Brooklyn, and was recognized by all in the Honored Society as second only to Joe the Boss throughout the country. Yale had always had close ties with Masseria. When Masseria had decided to infiltrate Unione Siciliane and turn it into an elite arm of Mafia, still pure for only Sicilians could become members, Yale became president of the organization. Much of his power as a "man of respect" flowed from that office.

It was such alliances as these, men all across the country linked into what was known as "the Italian mob," that helped Mafia become the dominant criminal group in the country.

Part of Torrio's preparation for the illegal liquor business was to call Al Capone to Chicago, no doubt because he had heard good things from Brooklyn concerning his young protege's education under Frankie Yale. Capone's first assignment was as a bouncer in a tavern-bordello, but he had obviously been chosen for greater glory because Torrio suggested he adopt a legitimate facade. Al Capone just loved to hand out his business card: "Al Brown. Antique Dealer."

Uncle Jim Colosimo continued to deride Torrio's interest in alcohol, even after the Volstead Act became law and the money flowed in on a tidal wave of booze. Colosimo's problem was not so much stupidity as it was an ailment that has affected the judgment of so many middle-aged men: He had fallen in love and really didn't give much damn about business. He had divorced his wife, making her a fifty-thousand-dollar settlement, and married a young and quite beautiful singer. He must have been still rather virile for his age, because he spent more time with his bride than in his business.

And so Uncle Jim was murdered on a May afternoon, during one of his rare visits to his restaurant that was the most fashionable in Chicago. The police have always maintained that it was Frankie Yale who put several bullets into Colosimo's body in the foyer of his restaurant. From underworld sources, they said, they learned Torrio had discussed his problem with his old "goombah" during a trip back East, and Yale offered to personally handle the removal of Big Jim. He went West by train, the story goes, waited at the restaurant for Colosimo, who had been lured there by a phone call from Torrio requesting an urgent meeting, and killed him. Then Yale boarded the next train for New York, and was home in bed before police had gotten over their shock at the demise of the man who made half the force wealthy.

With Colosimo gone, Torrio began to spread his word among rival gangs: cooperation. In conference after conference with Irish, Polish, and Jewish groups, Torrio preached the benefits of cooperation. In essence, Torrio recommended the division of Chicago into districts roughly conforming to each gang's historic territory. There would be no encroachment by one gang upon the district of another. Within each district, the ruling gang would be the sole supplier of whiskey and beer to speakeasy and private customers, and would operate all illegal enterprises in its territory. Should there be encroachment, the matter must be settled at Torrio's conference table. If no solution was possible, then every gang would join the injured group to punish the encroacher.

Every gang would be free to operate its own breweries and distilleries. If some chose not to get into that line of work, Torrio would be happy to sell some of his enormous supplies to them.

Every Chicago gang of substance agreed to the proposal. Johnny Torrio was general supervisor over a dozen gangs, comprising more than a thousand combat-hardened musclemen.

Although the alliances he made were sometimes shaky, they generally held together for some time because Torrio was a master at conciliation, a diplomat who somehow settled disputes among men who'd rather shoot than talk. Most important, it was well recognized in Chicago's criminal circles that Torrio possessed an added persuader: He was making regular payments to everyone who counted, from Mayor Thompson to district police captains, to the patrolman on the beat. (In fact, every bootleg warehouse or distillery had a policeman or two acting as guards, every liquor-laden convoy had policemen riding shotgun. They usually worked in full uniform.)

The operations of the syndicate were so efficient and so lacking in scandal or bloodshed that politicians in the suburbs practically begged Torrio to bring similar enlightened criminality to their towns. Most notable was the suburb called Cicero, which quickly became as wide open as Las Vegas would be a quarter-century later, and which would eventually attain a worldwide notoriety under Al Capone. It was in 1923 that Torrio promoted Capone by giving him the complete responsibility for the operations in Cicero; by now Al had justified his mentor's faith in his abilities.

Torrio had demonstrated that crime could be civilized. As Paul Sann put it in his history of that era, *The Lawless Decade,* Torrio was "the Supreme Court, the Chairman of the Board. He made the rackets Big Business. He brought civilization to the gangland jungle. He kept the peace."

But, through no fault of his own, the peace was short-lived. In the spring of 1923 Edward O'Donnell and his three brothers, all throwbacks to an earlier era when gangs fought each other for the pleasure of the fight, decided that their gang was not receiving sufficient reward for their labors. Rather than bring their complaint to the syndicate conference table, the O'Donnells hijacked liquor trucks and attacked protected speakeasies.

Torrio sought a meeting with the O'Donnells. But Edward O'Donnell refused. "Tell that miserable wop to drop dead," he reportedly said. "I ain't holding no conference with a dago."

Over the next several months about a dozen men on both sides were killed. The headline-provoking guns continued to roar until the next winter, when every member of the O'Donnells was killed, except their leader, who was seriously wounded and who slipped out of town after recovering.

Peace returned to the syndicate for several months. Then Dion O'Banion, known to all as Deanie, became overly ambitious. Little Deanie, a major partner in the combination, was the boss of Chicago's North Side. He ruled his domain from the flower shop he operated as a hobby.

Deanie had been one of the first gang leaders to have seen the wisdom of Torrio's blueprint for criminal cooperation, and his membership in the "outfit" made him one of Chicago's most powerful hoodlums. But he had never liked the feeling he got that Torrio was actually in control of Chicago, and he was soon plotting to remove Torrio.

Trying to kill Torrio would be foolish, of course, although Deanie had killed at least twenty-five men by official reckoning. But the murder of Torrio would have led to dreadful consequences, for Al Capone was more crazy and vengeful than most. Another way must be found to dispose of Torrio, and Deanie found it.

One of the inducements by which Torrio had originally persuaded O'Banion to join the gangster cooperative had been the offer of a half interest in the large and very profitable Sieben Brewery, which Torrio had bought from the owners who wanted no part of illegal brewing. In the early spring of 1924, O'Banion had received information that federal agents were planning to raid the brewery. He rushed to confer with Torrio.

However, he did not sound a warning. He offered, instead, to sell his share in the brewery back to Torrio, claiming that he intended to retire and open a ranch in the West. Torrio agreed.

On May 19, a week after O'Banion had been paid a half-million dollars for his share, he and Torrio were making a final tour of inspection at the brewery. They had gone there at O'Banion's insistence. Federal agents raided the place while they were there, and arrested them both.

O'Banion, a first offender, got off with a small fine as he knew he would. Torrio, who had somehow been arrested once before, was given a nine-month jail sentence for his second violation. He remained at liberty pending appeal. Once more, according to Chicago crime authorities, he summoned his good friend, Frankie Yale.

One afternoon shortly after Torrio's arrest, three men entered O'Banion's florist shop to order a wreath for a well-beloved hoodlum who had died of a heart attack, an unusual avenue of exit, considering his trade. O'Banion knew two of the men as bootleggers but the third—Frankie Yale—was a stranger. They were introduced, and shook hands. Yale suddenly pulled Deanie toward him, throwing the florist off balance. At the same time all three men drew guns and, at handshaking range, carefully placed several bullets into little Deanie, who never even got a chance to draw.

The men of O'Banion's gang swore revenge, most naturally. On a chilly afternoon in January, 1925, Torrio and his wife stepped out of their car in front of their home. Mrs. Torrio was unlocking the front door while Johnny and his chauffeur fumbled with a mound of packages on the back seat, the fruits of a shopping excursion. Three men leaped out of a car parked across the street and ran toward Johnny. They fired with sawed-off shotguns and an automatic pistol but, apparently overwhelmed by their audacity in trying to kill the most important man in Chicago, they missed Torrio with their first round.

Crouching low, Johnny sprinted toward the front door of his home, which his wife had thoughtfully left open for him before running for cover. Torrio never made it. A blast from a shotgun caught him in the left arm, wheeling him around. A charge of buckshot hit him in the face, tearing away part of his jaw. Two .45 caliber bullets hit him, one in the chest and the other in the abdomen. The gunmen fled.

Torrio was near death in a hospital for several weeks, guarded by police and a dozen gunmen commanded by Al Capone. When he had recovered enough to think about his obviously shaky future, Torrio told Capone that Chicago was now his, that Torrio was going to take his wife to Naples for a vacation and then settle down in New York.

That's how Al Capone came to possess Chicago. As for Johnny Torrio, he didn't retire, of course. After a year in Italy he returned to New York and took a more active interest in his investments there. He remained behind the scenes for more than a decade.

In the meantime, with Al Capone now in charge in Chicago, the reputation of that fair city plunged from dreadful to ghastly. Capone did not possess the calmness and judiciousness of Torrio. Capone was, basically, an overweight pasta-consuming slob who could never advance beyond the muscle-man's mentality because he was limited in outlook and in intellectual capacity. He was a goon. He stood above all the rest because he had more goons at his command than any other gang leader in the Midwest.

From the moment he was elevated by Johnny Torrio's very wise abdication, Chicago's streets, stockyards, and streams became the recipients of more bodies than the legendary Boot Hill of Western Americana fame. The "pineapple"—the bomb thrown through a competitor's window—was made famous in Capone's Chicago. So was the "one-way ride." And so was the Thompson submachine gun, a marvelously efficient killer of men—and, on occasion, of children who happened to get in the way. And every time there was a shooting or a bombing, Capone's name was broadcast across the land.

Back in New York, Johnny Torrio warned all who would listen that such unfortunate publicity would eventually be the downfall of Big Al, and of anyone who received such public notoriety. Although the New Yorkers did not indulge in the brutalities and excesses of their colleagues out in Chicago, there were enough shootings and killings to keep the police reporters quite busy in the early years of Prohibition. Joe Masseria—and Luciano—contributed their share of the excitement, although Charlie never did get his name into the papers.

It took a little time, but the advice given him by Torrio and Costello began to have its effect. Luciano began to drift into the shadows, pulling as far away from publicity as he could get.

6

It must have become obvious to Luciano that the men who were progressing most brilliantly in assorted rackets and were accumulating the greatest wealth and influence without much police interference, were those who avoided the flash of the hoodlum speakeasy scene and who kept their names out of the newspapers.

Arnold Rothstein was an obvious example. As far back as September, 1921, Rothstein had announced that he was retiring from gambling "to devote most of my attention to my racing stables and my real estate business." The newspapers announced the "retirement" in bold headlines and, even as he was stepping into whiskey and dope smuggling, into the garment center unions, into a half-dozen illicit enterprises, Rothstein began getting the anonymity he craved.

Frank Costello was an even better example, and much closer to Luciano's own background. Costello had become the political fixer for the small group of gang leaders who were forming an organization around Luciano. He had married, was living quietly, had actually moved into a small surburban home in an attractive middle-class neighborhood in Bayside, Queens. He was known as a businessman.

The benefits of keeping the low profile became clear to Charlie in December, 1925, when the U.S. Justice Department announced that twenty persons had been arrested and a forty-million-dollar-a-year international liquor smuggling ring had been smashed. The stories, bannered in the newspapers, stated that the ring was headed by William Dwyer, known as Big Bill, a noted sportsman and owner of race tracks. Buried on the inside pages were the names of two others, identified as "pay-off men" who had bribed Coast Guard crews to ignore the landing of liquor—Frank and Eddie Costello.

Charlie, and everyone in the business, knew that that particular bootleg operation was owned and managed by Frank Costello, who ran it like a large corporation from a suite of offices at 405 Lexington Avenue; they knew that Dwyer worked for Costello and not the other way around. But Dwyer made the better newspaper copy. He owned racetracks in Montreal and Cincinnati, was the original owner of the football Brooklyn Dodgers, and was the man who imported ice hockey from Canada to New York. His name was constantly in the sports pages and gossip columns. And when the government induced several Coast Guardsmen to talk, and indicted most members of this particular importing business, Dwyer was named its head even though Costello was the actual leader.

Dwyer was convicted, and his trial made the front pages. Frank Costello, tried later as a minor member of the ring, was freed when the jury couldn't reach agreement as to his share of the guilt; his trial never earned more than a couple of paragraphs at the back of the newspapers.

That made a lasting impression on Luciano. In Naples, a few years before his death, Charlie told an old New York friend: "Big Bill getting stuck with the rap taught me a lot. You gotta stay out of the papers, you gotta pay people good to stick their necks out while you stay in the background. Arnold did that, Frank did it, Johnny Torrio did, all the smart ones stayed out of the papers. Christ, do you know that even Joe the Boss moved into a place on Central Park West and called himself an importer. And he was a greasy old *cafoni*."

In the early years Charlie had insisted upon being called "Lucky" and had even been tattooed with the nickname. Now, starting some time around 1925 or 1926, he demanded that everyone call him Charlie, never Lucky. He tried to have the tattoo erased from his arm.

"The tattoo guy couldn't get it all off, but he made it fuzzy enough so you couldn't read it," Charlie told a friend years later. "Then I had him put a heart around the name you can't read anymore, so anybody seeing it would think it was a dame."

He moved out of the ghetto into a large apartment on the East Side, near where the UN stands today. He imitated Rothstein and Costello in their conservative dress, in their impeccable manners and their facade of respectability. Costello introduced him into his growing circle of friends in the business, social, and political life of the city and state. Charlie was attaining some class; a very shrewd man, he emulated others but he was no doubt his own Pygmalion.

His newly developed desire for anonymity worked marvelously well for several years. There are only occasional glimpses of him in the public prints during this period. He went out on the town but he avoided the mobster joints, the speakeasies and clubs in which hoodlums loved to gather with their chorus girls of the moment. Luciano chose only the finest places, those patronized by the politicians and socialites and in which the hoodlum custom was quietly but firmly discouraged. He was welcome in the better places for he was no longer a hoodlum.

Charlie's sexual life also changed around this time. In the past he would live with one young woman for several months and, when the affair broke up, another woman would move into his apartment. But as he began to attain some wealth and power, and a great deal of polish for a Little Italy street punk, Charlie would no longer permit a woman to live with him. He believed there was a danger in having a woman around, almost as a wife; no matter how secretive he might be, she could not help but learn some things about his business.

There were frequent lapses between women. Charlie would be chaste for months at a time, grown impotent because he believed an old case of syphillis which had kept him out of the World War was now flaring up. Years later he would be embarrassed by prostitutes who testified that he "couldn't get it up."

For Charlie, however, business was always more important than any woman. And the business had become enormous by now, and much diversified.

If there was one thing well understood by Luciano, Costello, Lansky, and others who had established a close relationship from the start of bootlegging, it was that they could never surrvive in the jungle without an organization. A mob, a gang. Not like the gangs of Monk Eastman and the Five Pointers, battling it out for some small piece of territory and some *macho* glory. They needed a business organization that would demonstrate its strength, not publicly, but through the underworld gossip mills which would spread the word of the alliances which had created a gang to be feared.

Lansky especially preached the formation of a strong group. Born Maier Suchowjansky in Grodno, Russia, in 1902, Lansky was brought to the Lower East Side by his parents in 1911; within a few years he had Americanized his name and became a street brigand. Soon, he began to work with Legs Diamond and grew friendly with Luciano and other men in the Diamond gang. He was a killer, but he was also highly intelligent and the friends around him were soon calling him Brains, a flattering comparison to Rothstein.

A strong gang was needed, they all knew, because the one obvious fact of Prohibition life was that treachery abounded everywhere. Bootleg whiskey caravans were hijacked. Narcotics shipments stolen. One group encroached upon the other in every sphere of operation. Men were killed—but quietly, not like in Chicago. If a group were weak, the vultures would tear it apart. Even within Mafia, among the various men who belonged to the Honored Society, were factions preying upon other factions. Only the strong could survive, only in numbers could there be survival.

So it was, through the need for mutual protection, through the friendships they had formed in working for Rothstein and others, that a group began to slowly form around Luciano, Costello, and Lansky in the first half of the 1920s—and by mid-decade had become almost formalized into an underworld organization of great strength. Most important in this partnership were:

Lepke Buchalter. Born Louis Buchalter on Lincoln's birthday, 1897, he was the youngest child of a pious hardware merchant. His mother always called him Leb, his Jewish name, which he mispronounced "Lepke" as a child. Lepke it became among the gamblers and thieves he joined after his father's death in 1915. During the garment center strikes of 1919 and 1920, which Arnold Rothstein was called on to resolve, Lepke worked as a Rothstein-union goon for $7.50 a day, and met Luciano and the others working for A.R.

Benjamin Siegel. Darkly handsome, the glamour boy of the crime syndicate which would be formed in the 1930's, Siegel was so headstrong and possessed such a low boiling point that he earned the nickname, Bugsy, which he hated all his life. Born in Brooklyn in February, 1906, Bugsy was only fourteen when Prohibition overwhelmed the nation, fifteen when he attached himself to Meyer Lansky and began to work with him as a guard on Rothstein's liquor trucks, sixteen when he killed his first hijacker—according to his own boast years later—and seventeen when he became part of the Luciano organization. He was so volatile, so quick to shoot, that many men stronger and better armed than he would walk blocks out of their way to avoid a confrontation with Bugsy.

Vito Genovese. Inducted into Mafia with Luciano, Genovese was his closest friend from the Masseria group. Ruthless, constantly scheming, he was loved by Luciano and distrusted by many of the others in the organization.

Waxey Gordon. By 1926 this former pickpocket, after

becoming associated with Rothstein in the whiskey deal that brought the first shipload from England, had grown as rich as any man in bootlegging. He was the owner and operator of a fleet of seagoing ships that imported fine whiskey from Nova Scotia and the Bahamas. He owned several hotels in midtown Manhattan, including the popular Piccadilly; he owned breweries and distilleries in Philadephia; and he had as a rum row partner one Nucky Johnson, who was political and criminal leader of Atlantic City and who guaranteed complete protection for all rum-runners unloading along the small stretch of Jersey coast which he controlled.

Willie Moretti. Costello's younger cousin, he had gambling interests in Brooklyn and bootleg interests in New Jersey, and a small regiment of gunmen which proved quite useful to the Luciano organization.

Louis Shomberg. Known as Dutch Goldberg, he was born in New York around 1895, making him older than everyone else in the group with the exception of Costello. He spent a few years in prison after his conviction on murder charges in 1915, was paroled at the beginning of Prohibition, and gravitated toward Luciano. Goldberg was the liason between all the members of the group; more than a messenger by far, he was a counselor and adviser to the other partners. He also appointed himself Luciano's unofficial bodyguard. "Dutch was Charlie's arm, his muscle arm," a friend of Goldberg recalls of those days.

They were a formidable group, for each of them had their own followers and employees, gunmen and sluggers and head-breakers who constituted a small army. And there were many others in the partnership, most notably a contingent from Brooklyn's Italian gang, young men also drawn to Luciano because of his obvious ability to lead. Among these were Joe Adonis (real name Doto) and Anthony Carfano, known as L'il Augie Pisano, both of whom were closely aligned with Frankie Yale. Plus Albert Anastasia, a growing power in Brooklyn dock unions and the most feared killer in all Mafia.

From the beginning, Charlie Luciano was recognized as leader of the group. The role fell to him for several reasons. Most important was his position as the strong right hand of Joe the Boss; none of the other gangs would risk crossing Luciano for they knew—or believed, which amounted to the same thing—that a fight against Charlie was a fight against every *mafioso* in New York. Further, his alliance with Torrio and Capone gave him additional strength.

But Charlie also possessed certain vital qualities of leadership within himself. As an observer of the scene in those days wrote: "He was calm and firm in times of danger, never emotional or flighty as were so many of his Latin confreres. He spoke slowly and always thought before he spoke. Ruthless with his enemies, he was, like any good politician, one who would go down the line for his friends."

The corporation, and it was run almost along the lines of a major business enterprise, had by 1925 expanded beyond liquor and narcotics. Gambling was a major source of revenue for the group—bookmaking on the streets and in horserooms, slot machines that Frank Costello was beginning to place all over town by the hundreds and, as a fringe benefit, loansharking to provide gamblers with even greater sums to lose to the organization.

But it was, foremost of all, the group's entry into "labor-management relations" which would give criminals enormous control over many unions in the country and, as a result, add what in actuality was an underworld "tax" on most foodstuffs and manufactured products sold to the American public. That entry into the unions would eventually place a union official who was controlled by the Luciano group very close to the seat of Presidential power.

As in so many things, Arnold Rothstein had been the first to see the possibility of making money by "settling" union-management disputes.

New York had been the center of the nation's garment trades since the 1890's, when thousands of immigrant women and children formed a cheap pool of labor in the sweatshops. In 1897, Monk Eastman and his gang had been hired by several sweat shop owners for a few dollars, to break up a threatened strike for higher wages. Eastman did his job, collected his pay, and thought no more of this potential source of racket income.

In 1909, two years after Luciano came to New York, the first large scale garment strike hit the industry. Sweatshop workers were primarily Jewish and Italian, and all the gangsters and hoodlums in the ghettoes knew about the long hours and low pay in the garment factories. They knew, also, that their relatives and their friends were being manhandled by "guards" hired by the employers to break the strike.

The unions, weak and ineffectual, turned to the gangsters for help. In many cases, local hoodlums volunteered to assist the unions which their relatives had joined. Those gangsters beat down the employers and helped the unions seize a small foothold in the shops. When the strike ended with partial union recognition, some of the gangsters had a stake in the unions, hired on as "organizers." One of them, Benny Fein, was employed by twelve union locals, drawing a salary from each and using his gang members as organizers and bodyguards for union leaders. Besides their salaries, the unions also provided Fein and his gang with a guarantee of protection—lawyers, bail, and political influence.

To make good on that guarantee the union leaders hired the only man they knew who could protect them. Arnold Rothstein.

Rothstein had his own crew of gangsters. Over the next several years, Fein and many of his men went to prison and Rothstein placed his own men within the unions. The gangster in charge of it all, for Rothstein, was named Little Augie Orgen, who had been one of Benny Fein's lieutenants and whose loyalty had been purchased by Rothstein.

The garment factories were hit with a major strike in

1919 and 1920, and the employers once more brought in their "guards." Orgen, on Rothstein's orders, increased the number of his troops to beat back the employers' goons. Among those he recruited for the widespread battles in the garment center were Legs Diamond, who had been working for Rothstein in other ventures, and such men as Luciano, Lepke, Lansky, Dutch Goldberg, and Waxey Gordon. Here, in the garment center battles, the men of Luciano's organization first came together.

The unions gained even greater recognition after the strike, and the gangsters greater control over the unions. When Orgen was eased out of the garment center in 1925 to perform other services for Rothstein, Louis Lepke was called upon to take his place. Lepke was part of the Luciano organization by now. All the members of that group were partners in the complete subversion of the garment unions, in the complete domination of garment center gambling, loansharking, and whiskey sales. They also took over several clothing factories, becoming both employers and union leaders; ownership of several factories fell to them not by violence, but rather from loansharking—so many clothing shop owners were unable to pay back high interest gangster loans in times of economic distress, and in return for forgiveness of the debt they found men like Lepke and Luciano as majority partners.

To the day he died, Luciano continued to receive an income from several New York, New Jersey, and Pennsylvania clothing factories.

In 1926 Lepke, whose major executive role in the Luciano organization would always be union-industrial racketeering, effectively seized control of the garment center from Rothstein. It occurred because Rothstein had grown so short-sighted in his lust for money that he sold his services to both sides in a strike that began in 1926, apparently being unable to recognize that much more than cash payments were at stake.

That obsession with wealth had been Rothstein's major

strength at first, but now it was a weakness that would lead to his death a few years later. Rothstein's wife, Carolyn, who wrote her memoirs after he was killed, said of him: "When we were married, it was his ambition to have $100,000. Then he raised the limit, first to a quarter of a million, then to a half million, and, finally, to a million. When he had his million, he took off the limit. All he wanted was more."

Blinded by that lust, Rothstein did not understand that Lepke had gained a foothold in the garment center that would bring the racketeers many hundreds of times the amounts Rothstein had been paid by unions and employers. Instead of simply taking a salary from the unions at the end of that 1926 strike, Lepke began to take over the unions. He had a vision: By controlling the unions, he had unlimited millions in dues from the workers at his disposal; by having the power to call strikes, he could extort even greater amounts of money from shop owners.

For Lepke had learned, during the 1926 strike, that he could control the entire garment industry by controlling less than 1,900 workers. That discovery would bring him and his partners enormous riches. And it would, in the future, indirectly lead to a murder that would give Luciano the opportunity to modernize the American Mafia.

It was the structure of the unions that opened the clothing industry to Lepke's pillage. The Amalgamated Clothing Workers is the parent body of many labor unions in the ready-to-wear men's clothing industry. Each distinct craft group within the industry has its own local inside Amalgamated. Lepke one day made the startling discovery that the heart of the industry rested in two of those crafts.

One of them was the local of cutters, who cut out the basic parts of the garment from patterns. There were only 1,800 cutters in the industry. The other vital segment was the truckers' local, which consisted of only about eighty men who delivered everything in the men's suit trade.

Domination of the entire industry could be achieved by gaining leadership over less than 1,900 men.

Lepke moved in on the cutters' local early in 1927. His approach was simple. He went to the local's leaders and said that he and Max Rubin—who testified about it years later—were now on the payroll as organizers, replacing the two men who had filled that post for many years. At the same time, Lepke made the local's business agent, Philip Orlofsky, its manager; Rubin testified that Lepke personally promoted the man.

Once he ruled this key local within the industry, Lepke took over the truckers' local in a similar fashion.

Luciano, in the meantime, was beginning to slip even further away from public view. He was now a business executive, the head of a major corporation which just happened to be engaged in illegal activities. He left his apartment near the East River around 1927 and moved into the very posh Barbizon-Plaza Hotel under the name Charles Reid, businessman. He looked like a businessman, and behaved as sedately as the most cultured executive.

And down on the streets, in the speakeasies and other hangouts, the word was passed—Lucky Luciano's name should never be mentioned in public. It was around this time that a newspaperman was sitting in a bar when a well-known night club doorman (a very important position in those days of illicit drinking) began to tell an anecdote about Luciano. Another patron, "a dark, hard man," interrupted him. "That name isn't talked about," he said. The doorman stopped talking.

Luciano dropped any direct association with the more obvious gangsters. Men like Legs Diamond, for example, who was frequently getting shot and making headlines. Luciano didn't like Diamond because he was too flamboyant and publicity-hungry. Luciano didn't much care for Diamond's wife, either.

"Alice Diamond was the craziest dame I ever knew," Charlie once said. "I told everybody to keep her away from me." Perhaps Luciano didn't care for Alice's morbid sense of humor. Legs had bought a large home in New Jersey, as befit a gangster of his station, and he dearly loved to entertain his gangster friends. Alice, it is said, had one of her large antique chairs electrified, and whenever one of Legs' guests sat in it she would turn on the juice. "I'm rehearsing you guys for the electric chair in Sing Sing," she'd explain. "That's where you're all winding up."

Al Capone traveled frequently to New York in this period for a conference with the boys and probably to catch his breath—so many people were shooting at him that he was forced to ask General Motors to build him a special Cadillac limousine, seven tons of steel armor-plated body and bullet-proof windows. When Capone did come to town he would always drop in at the Club Durant. This popular nightspot in the Broadway area was owned by Clayton, Jackson, and Durante, the entertainment partnership from which Jimmy Durante later emerged as a star. Capone and Eddie Jackson had worked together as boys in a Brooklyn factory, and Jackson had often loaned Capone money for lunch because Al gambled every penny he earned. Now Capone tossed hundred-dollar bills at Eddie as he sang from the Club Durant's stage. "He's a good boy," Capone always explained. "We used to be pals."

Luciano always conferred with Capone when he came to town, either in the Barbizon-Plaza suite, at Johnny Torrio's house in Brooklyn, or in Charlie's headquarters on Broome Street, where Joe the Boss loved to be entertained by Capone's stories of gunfighting in the streets of Chicago. But Charlie would never accompany Big Al on his night club rounds; it just wasn't smart for a businessman to be associated with the likes of Capone.

7

It is somewhat difficult to pinpoint exactly where the feuds which would violently shake Mafia all began. Most "Mafia experts"—including Joe Valachi, the most public informer of them all—have seen and reported on only a small part of the overall picture. From many dozens of sources, and most especially from several men involved with the various factions, men with whom I first began discussing these events a quarter of a century after they occurred, I believe it's possible to present as complete an account as has ever been attempted of the Masseria-Maranzano "wars" and Luciano's eventual domination of Mafia.

What most Mafia authorities have failed to recognize is that the beginning of it all is bound up in two 1928 murders, those of Frankie Yale and Arnold Rothstein.

Yale, you will remember, was the Brooklyn Mafia man who had been placed in charge of Unione Siciliane by Joe the Boss, and who was an old friend of Torrio, Capone, and every important member of the "Italian crowd" in the country. Yale's loyalty to Joe the Boss, to the entire Mafia, had never been questioned. But then, in the spring of 1925, the head of the Chicago chapter of Unione was murdered in one of those gun battles that brought the city such an evil reputation. Another Sicilian who was very much mistrusted by Al Capone walked in and elected himself president of the local chapter. Capone appealed to his old employer, Frankie Yale, national head of Unione, to remove the usurper and replace him with someone more to Capone's taste.

Yale advised patience. Capone, ever impatient, sent some of his gunmen around to a barber shop where the Unione leader was being shaved, and they killed him. Capone then placed his own man in the office.

Back in Brooklyn, Yale grew quite furious that a Neopolitan like Capone should dare kill a Unione leader and dictate the leadership of that pure-bred Sicilian organization; Yale never was able to shake off his conviction that Sicilians were God's chosen, at least in the rackets. And that's when Salvatore Maranzano, ever so cunning and seductive, saw his opportunity to fulfill the destiny which was his birthright—domination of the entire American Mafia.

From the majestic heights of his "Julius Caesar complex," as Joe Valachi called it, Maranzano had long waited for the day that he could oust Joe Masseria and other peasants from Mafia leadership and crown himself *capo di tutti capi*—boss of all bosses. Born on the northwest coast of Sicily, in the town of Castellammare, Maranzano believed himself one of the elite. He was descended from a long line of Sicilian Mafia chieftains whose relatives were entrenched in the island's politics, business, and the Church. He was well educated, spoke at least six languages, and had studied for the priesthood. But his calling was Mafia. When he came to America a year or two after the World War, he too was searching for streets paved with gold. And he found them.

As a Mafia leader from the old country, Maranzano ranked with Lupo, Joe the Boss, and all the rest. He worked with them, in Prohibition, narcotics, in all the rackets which enriched men of the Honored Society.

But he would never deign to appear at the curb exchange to buy liquor. Salesmen must come to him, to his suite of "real estate" offices in the Penn Central Building at 230 Park Avenue. He did deal in real estate and in other legal enterprises which made him quite wealthy. While Luciano, Costello, and the others were attempting to look like businessmen, Maranzano, according to an awe-struck Valachi, "looked just like a banker, you'd never guess in a million years that he was a racketeer." The Masseria types were not for Maranzano; they were peasants and he was a prince of Mafia.

He had been well schooled in Mafia affairs back in Sicily, and he was as wily and ruthless as any man of respect. He was undeniably much smarter than most; not until the day he was murdered did his name ever appear on a police blotter, in court records, or in the newspapers, so well did he hide his activities.

Quite clearly, Maranzano coveted Masseria's title as Mafia boss in all America, and he had been slowly preparing to make a bid for the leadership. For this, the most important of his businesses was no doubt his alien-smuggling operation. Mussolini for years had been chasing the Mafia out of Sicily, and many *mafiosi* made their way to America. Maranzano arranged for the smuggling of hundreds of his Mafia associates and their relatives from the Castellammare area. All of them owed allegiance to him, all knew that to displease Maranzano would bring either death or, worse luck to many, deportation to Sicily. And all were men who would execute a murder commission without knowing or caring why.

When Al Capone had the Chicago Unione president murdered, Maranzano learned rather quickly from his own men in Unione that Frankie Yale considered the murder a grave personal insult. Maranzano had been buying whiskey from Yale, who supervised the landing of cargoes on Long Island for many bootleg gangs in the area. He was quite friendly with Yale. And he began to insinuate that Yale, as a good Sicilian, must get revenge on that Neopolitan, Capone.

Many years later an old friend of my family who was then involved in a clothing manufacturing business with Joe Profaci, one of the leading dons of the new Mafia that Luciano built, sat reminiscing with Profaci about the old days. Profaci, then ill with cancer, let his guard down a bit and began talking about Capone and

Yale. And one of the statements he made was: "All hell broke loose for everybody because Yale threw in with Maranzano and was double-crossing Capone. I know. I was working for Maranzano back then."

The double cross that Profaci mentioned involved the shipment of whiskey to the Capone gang. By 1924 Capone needed larger supplies of liquor than he had been getting from Canada and from Waxey Gordon's Atlantic City shipments. He turned to Frankie Yale, who agreed to ship regular consignments to Chicago by truck. Some time in the autumn of 1927, after Capone had so gravely insulted Yale by interfering with Unione, Capone's trucks began to be hijacked before they even left Brooklyn. Yale sent his apologies, promised to provide greater protection, but the hijackings increased in frequency. Capone, as suspicious as the next bootlegger, finally decided to check up on Yale. He dispatched a spy, James de Amato, to Brooklyn. The spy was discovered by Yale and killed, but not before sending back word confirming Capone's suspicions.

On the afternoon of Sunday, July 1, 1928, four Capone men came to New York. Yale was drinking in a Brooklyn speakeasy when the bartender called him to the phone. He spoke briefly to the man on the other end, then hurried to his car. As he drove along Forty-Fourth Street a few minutes later, a car with four men inside forced Yale's auto to the curb. Using revolvers, a sawed-off shotgun, and a Thompson submachine gun—the first recorded use of that Chicago specialty in New York—they tore up Mr. Yale so dreadfully that the morticians could not quite put him together again and his casket remained closed during the period of mourning.

Yale could not have been murdered by Chicagoans without the approval and assistance of New York Mafia leaders. Capone was vain and violent, but he was on very friendly terms with Luciano, Masseria, and with his old boss, Johnny Torrio. I have heard it said in Brooklyn Mafia circles, by Ernie the Hawk and by others, that Capone had consulted Johnny Torrio about his problems with Yale, and that Torrio conferred with Luciano. After Capone's spy was murdered by Yale, Luciano had contacted his own men within the Yale group, Anthony Carfano (known as L'il Augie Pisano), and asked him to get at the truth. Pisano, it is said, informed Luciano that two Irish kids had been hired by Yale to hijack Capone's trucks.

It is likely, given the circumstances of Yale's murder by four strangers from Chicago, that someone close to Yale made the telephone call luring him to the spot where his killers intercepted him. That man was undoubtedly Pisano, who was both Yale's chief executive and a partner in the Luciano organization. It's not too surprising that Pisano became the new head of the Yale group, giving Luciano even greater strength than before.

And, of course, making an ass—and an enemy—out of Salvatore Maranzano.

The Caesar of Mafia learned these things from his *paisans* within Mafia and the Unione. He learned, also, that Joe the Boss was calling him a trouble maker and was warning everyone to stay away from Maranzano's men. In turn, Maranzano told some of his closest aides that he'd someday be forced to kill Joe the Boss.

"Maranzano sure as hell knew that guys like Charlie and even me, who's on his side, didn't want no war," Profaci told the friend of my family. "We were just interested in business, and in going legit someday so our kids wouldn't have the gangster curse. We didn't really care who was boss."

Younger men like Profaci advised Maranzano against being hasty, advised him to wait for Masseria to start something; should Masseria become the aggressor, the word could be spread that he intended to interfere with all Mafia men, and great numbers would join Maranzano as the injured party in the dispute.

On the other side, Luciano and Costello and any who could get Masseria's ear gave the same advice: Wait until there is greater proof of treachery before committing every Mafia man in the country to an internecine feud.

The advice was heeded for a while, on both sides. Then, a few months after Yale was killed, Arnold Rothstein was shot and the vultures came out to prey. One of the vultures was Maranzano.

By the time of his death, Rothstein's power had begun to wane. The Luciano group was a major importer and wholesaler of whiskey, a business Rothstein abandoned after a couple of years because he was unable to dominate it. Lepke-Luciano controlled a large segment of the garment industry. Costello-Luciano owned an enormous gambling empire. And, thanks to Jimmy Hines, Ed Flynn, and other Tammany politicians, the Luciano group had developed its own political influence. Including such a close working relationship with New York State governor Al Smith that Luciano was able to name several of his political friends to appointed positions in the state government; when one of these appointees dictated by Luciano was discovered to have a criminal record, Gov. Smith replaced him with another Luciano choice.

Rothstein was still a power in some of these areas, but his power was no longer exclusive; he had taught others too well. By this time Luciano's partners were so wealthy that Rothstein was borrowing money from them in order to finance some of his larger deals.

The shooting of Rothstein on a Sunday night in November, 1928, almost immediately came to the attention of those who would be most deeply concerned by his premature death. According to testimony in several court cases years later, the man who was most certainly Rothstein's killer, a gambler named George McManus, telephoned Jimmy Hines as soon as he could get a few blocks away from the scene of the shooting.

Hines, from his Tammany Hall headquarters uptown, instructed McManus to walk to the northeast corner of Fifty-ninth Street and Eighth Avenue, across from Columbus Circle, and wait there. In about fifteen minutes a Buick sedan pulled up and McManus got inside. The driver was Abraham (Bo) Weinberg, at that time the most trusted associate of Dutch Schultz, a relative newcomer to the Prohibition business who had been smart enough to make Jimmy Hines a partner.

While McManus was being rushed to an apartment in the Bronx, from which he would eventually emerge to be acquitted of the Rothstein's murder, both Hines and Schultz alerted those men who would be most interested in the impending demise of The Brain, who was lapsing in and out of a coma in the hospital.

Luciano was most certainly among the first to be called, for it was well known to Hines that Charlie and all the members of his organization had once been Rothstein's employees and were now, at the very least, his partners. Of all the informers who later talked to police under protection of anonymity, or who testified some years later in the investigation of what has come to be called Murder, Inc., no one has ever revealed anything about Luciano's movements in the thirty-six hours between the shooting of Rothstein and his death, so far as is known.

However, it is quite clear that Charles Lucania, "a waiter," was arrested in Rothstein's office with two others a short time after Rothstein died. And, as Luciano himself has said, he had been able to remove from that office all the papers he had gone searching for—papers that made him and his associates the heirs to Rothstein's business interests.

(As a sidelight, the most damning evidence of the total unreliability of the so-called Luciano memoirs, *The Last Testament of Lucky Luciano,* revolves around the authors' handling of Charlie's arrest the day Rothstein died. The writers of that book, Martin Gosch and Richard Hammer, obviously did not know that Luciano was picked up in Rothstein's office, for they have Luciano describing in vivid detail his arrest that day while *participating in a bank robbery!* See Appendix for details.)

The death of Rothstein did not leave a vacuum into

79

which Luciano and his crowd stepped, as many writers have said. Actually, it was a smooth transition; the Luciano men took everything. There were some, however, who did not understand—or didn't want to see—that the Luciano organization had inherited Rothstein's property. One of these men was Salvatore Maranzano.

Months after Rothstein's death, Louis Lepke decided he was ready to bring the Amalgamated Clothing Workers under his complete domination. You'll recall that in 1927 Lepke took over the cutters' local in Amalgamated and installed Philip Orlofsky as business manager.

The parent Amalgamated was headed by Sidney Hillman, still a great idol wherever men worship at the shrine of unionism. For Sidney Hillman would in later years be revered as a great liberal; he would be assigned to a high federal position upon America's entry into the second World War and would be so close to Franklin Delano Roosevelt that the President would often brush aside a problem by shouting, "Clear it with Sidney."

Back then, however, all that Sidney Hillman cared about was saving his job from a Lepke takeover. Early in 1929 Lepke instructed Orlofsky to found a rebel parent organization, challenging Hillman and the Amalgamated. Although Orlofsky didn't know it at the time, his challenge was futile from the start—Lepke was simply using one unionist to create difficulties for another, knowing that eventually Hillman would surrender to him in order to rescue his position and the liberal-political respectability and power he sought.

Hillman's immediate reaction to Orlofsky's rebellion was to seek Charlie Luciano's help in fighting off this Lepke stooge. According to testimony developed at a later trial, Hillman dispatched his union's general organizer, Bruno Belea, to enlist Luciano's aid. Luciano turned him down. "Not a chance," he said. "Lepke and Lansky and Bugsy are friends of mine."

Belea, who obviously knew his way around the upper reaches of Mafia, next went to Salvatore Maranzano for help. Maranzano had never before been involved in labor disputes. But he accepted the contract. It seems likely that Maranzano believed there was indeed a vacuum in garment center criminality because of Rothstein's death, and that he could fill at least part of that void. It appears even more likely, judged by later events, that Maranzano was stepping into the garment center as part of his scheme to remove Joe the Boss and assume control of Mafia—perhaps by using the garment center to force Luciano to align with him in the coming Holy War against Masseria. And so Maranzano went to Luciano in a great display of friendship and frankness.

According to *Murder, Inc.*, written by Burton Turkus, who later prosecuted Lepke and others and heard many details of the rivalry from men who were there, Maranzano said:

"I'm going to take the contract from Amalgamated, Charlie. But there's nothing to worry about. We won't make any trouble. We're just going on for a pay day."

Luciano replied: "Okay. Just remember—those other guys are my pals."

At first, Maranzano lived up to his pledge, but within a couple of months his men clashed with Lepke's men, and several were hurt. Lepke, according to Turkus, complained to Luciano that Maranzano was interfering with the plan to bring Hillman and the Amalgamated to their knees; Maranzano should be taught a lesson. Meaning death, of course.

Luciano refused. He had not warned Maranzano to stay out of the union rivalry that Lepke had promoted and was manipulating to his own ends, simply because Charlie was trying to avoid precipitating a Mafia war that no one wanted. He told Lepke, say Mafia insiders, that Maranzano ultimately would have to be killed but the time was not yet ripe.

Lepke insisted: "When you find you got an enemy, you kill him right away." But Charlie was adamant. To kill Maranzano would mean starting a war that would affect them all, Italians and non-Italians, he explained. He said he would speak with Maranzano, and ask Johnny Torrio to try and reason with him. Maranzano apologized, made more promises, and his men continued to beat and sometimes shoot at union men on Lepke's side.

The troubles with Maranzano were not Luciano's only source of worry. There was also Al Capone, who had so enraged the American public by his Valentine's Day Massacre, in which seven men were gunned to death, that even bootleggers who had supplied that public with its drink were being roundly condemned. Capone was bad for everyone's business.

By all accounts, it was Johnny Torrio who suggested a meeting that would eliminate the Capone problem and bring some order into the bootleg trade. Torrio would come to visit Luciano at his Barbizon-Plaza suite every few days, conducting some business, playing cards, even getting Charlie to listen to opera: Verdi and Puccini, at first, for they were closest to Italian folk music roots. And to talk about that *stupido,* Al Capone.

Talking about Capone led Torrio to reminisce about the early Prohibition years in Chicago, when he had convinced all the gangs to join him in a confederation. It had all worked so well, Torrio told Charlie. For more than thirty months there had been no trouble between the groups, no rivalry.

Why not create such a confederation along the entire East Coast? Luciano and his men were already working closely with every major bootlegger from New England down to the Jersey shore, as was Torrio. All of them had interlocking interests. But there was often unnecessary competition. The men in Philadelphia, for instance, might send more Scotch to New York than was needed, at the same moment that the Providence bootleggers were also dispatching truckloads of Scotch to the same market. Such an oversupply created competition which resulted in lower prices. Or the reverse sometimes occurred, Torrio went on. They might not get enough

Scotch and their retail customers might turn to other sources of supply—from bootleggers who weren't too friendly with Luciano, Torrio, and all those who had a tacit understanding.

What he was driving at, Torrio reportedly said, was the need for a complete bootleg organization which would set prices, establish quotas, and thoroughly control the supply of whiskey in New York for greater benefit of all. Luciano agreed. He later told a federal narcotics informer: "When Johnny tossed out that idea I knew it was a winner. I called Frank and Vito and Meyer, and had Johnny explain it to them."

Torrio, even now that he had given up his guns and had "retired," was a very persuasive man. And so, exactly three months after the Valentine's Day Massacre, a convention was held in the President Hotel, on the Atlantic City boardwalk, over a four-day period from May 13 to May 16, 1929. Every leader of an important bootleg gang on the East Coast, plus representatives from inland cities who would be affected, met to establish a liquor monopoly. Working out the details of an East Coast bootleg cooperative, and joining in a compact, were Torrio, Luciano, Costello, Lansky, and Lepke from New York; Luciano was representing both his own organization and the Italian gang of Joe the Boss. There were representatives from Brooklyn, including Joe Adonis and L'il Augie Pisano, from New Jersey and Philadelphia, from every area of the Atlantic seaboard.

The convention had a second purpose: to deal with the problem of Chicago. Al Capone was there, as were members of almost every Chicago faction. The "sitdown," as the boys called such meetings, was aimed at stopping the fratricidal wars within Mafia and the Unione, and between those Sicilian-Italian groups and gangs headed by Irish, Jews, and Slavs.

At the end of the conference Capone, ever the bigshot and loudmouth who loved to talk to the "newspaper boys," as he so patronizingly called them, said of this meeting:

"I told them there was business enough to make us all rich and it was time to stop all the killings . . . We finally agreed to forget the past and begin all over again, and we drew up a written agreement and each man signed on the dotted line."

But it wasn't exactly as Big Al reported it, making it appear that he had dictated the terms. Capone did not lay down his law by any means. It was Johnny Torrio who decreed that the first step toward peace in Chicago was for Capone to spend a little time in prison to eliminate the abrasion—Capone himself—which was decimating Chicago and had extended to Brooklyn with the killing of Frankie Yale.

Torrio, being ever so diplomatic, first outlined his solution to the Chicago problem, according to several informers who later gave information to authorities. Torrio said that Capone would have to leave Chicago for a time and turn his gang over to cooler heads who would be able to negotiate in good faith. And, he said, those negotiations must include a compact that would return Chicago rackets to the early days of Prohibition—a loose confederation of all the gangs, no encroachment on territories, and no killings without prior discussion of disputes in a conference of all the leaders. Those discussions would have to include Torrio as arbiter.

Torrio got his way, of course. According to information in the files of the FBI and the Narcotics Bureau, Torrio had the support of Luciano, Costello, and every important member of the New York fraternity. There was at least an implied threat—New York and the East Coast gangs with which it was allied could easily withhold liquor and narcotics from Chicago, and also had more than enough troops to enforce its will.

And so, Al Capone went to prison. At seven p.m. on May 16, only hours after the Atlantic City conference ended, Capone drove the eighty miles to Philadelphia where, by prearrangement, he met a local detective with whom he was friendly. After shaking hands with the detective and his partner, Capone went through a formality: "You're a bull, right?" he said. "Well, here's my gun." He handed over a revolver, thereby establishing a charge on which he could be jailed, and he ordered his bodyguard to do the same. Both men pleaded guilty and were sentenced to a year in the County Prison. They served ten months.

And all along Broadway the wise guys whispered that Luciano, Costello, and their organization were so powerful that they could do what no cop had ever done before —send Capone to jail for the first time in his life.

It wasn't too long after this, in fact, that a federal tax agent investigating Capone's huge income and his blatant nonpayment of taxes, wrote from Chicago to his superiors:

"I am advised that there is a man in the East, presumably a New York Italian, named Charles Lucky (spelling of last name uncertain) who has more influence among the criminal Italians than Al Capone ever had. It is said that Lucky is Capone's boss and the boss of all the other Italians engaged in important violation of the law." (It is quite clear from these sentences that Luciano, although perhaps the number one gangster in the country, had succeeded so well in moving into the shadows that his identity wasn't even known to an investigator for the only federal agency attempting to jail important racketeers.)

Two men, both powerful and both even more abrasive to others than Al Capone, were notably absent from the Atlantic City conference. They were Joe the Boss, and Salvatore Maranzano. The Boss had been consulted, but he wanted no part of the conference because he would not sit down as an equal with Jews or any other non-Italians. It had been bad enough to make the concession years before and induct non-Sicilians into Mafia, but to join up with Jews? A sacrilege. Maranzano, on the other hand, had not even been invited.

Their absence, especially Maranzano's, made it clear that the leaders of America's major criminal gangs considered them to be anachronisms—deadly and dangerous ones, certainly, but not worthy of serious consideration. That slap most certainly rankled in Maranzano's breast.

8

Some months after that conference, Charlie Luciano was "taken for a ride" from which he miraculously returned, somewhat scarred and battered by his experience, but still very much alive.

That episode has led to more published garbage—as Ernie the Hawk would still call it were he alive—than any other incident in his life except, perhaps, for his conviction on prostitution charges which wrongfully gave him a reputation as a master pimp.

The basic bit of published garbage is that as a result of surviving an attempt on his life, Luciano forevermore was known as "Lucky." Such writers on Mafia as Sid Feder, Hank Messick, and Ed Reid, each of whom has spent years investigating Mafia and each of whom has published several books, always repeat this particular Luciano myth. Messick, in his book, *Lansky,* so elaborated the original fantasy as to distort it out of all proportion. But it remained for Martin Gosch, who claimed to have tapes of Luciano's reminiscences for the book, *Last Testament,* to come up with such an outrageous story about that so-called murder attempt that his entire book must be considered fiction. (Once again, I'll go into it in the Appendix.)

Actually, as Costello, Luciano and others have said, Charlie was being called Lucky at his own insistence, in the early 1920's. By 1926, when he was studiously avoiding publicity, he had the tattoo of that name erased from his arm and he demanded that "Lucky" be dropped from all lips. "We called him Charlie, or the older Italians called him Salvatore," Costello later said of this period. "Nobody ever called him Lucky any more."

The incident that has led to all the fantasy began, so far as police and the public were concerned, a little after midnight on October 17, 1929. Two policemen cruising in their patrol car along Hylan Boulevard in the wooded and undeveloped section of Staten Island known as Tottenville, saw a figure limping along a road. They pulled up and asked the man if he needed help.

"Where am I?" the man said.

"Staten Island," one of the police officers replied.

"Christ, I thought I was in New Jersey."

The man, who said he was Charles Lucania, a New York businessman, wus taken to a hospital in spite of his protests that he simply wanted to be put on the ferry to Manhattan. He was questioned by detectives, one of whom recognized him as Lucky Luciano, "known gambler." At first, Luciano denied his identity, then finally admitted that much but refused to discuss the beating that had obviously been inflicted on him. After a detective threatened to arrest him on a dozen trumped-up charges, Luciano explained it all.

"Three or four guys kidnap me while I'm walking along Fiftieth Street," he said. "They have guns and they put me into a big, black limousine with curtains on the windows. They put tape on my mouth so I can't holler, and they start to work me over in the back seat. Damned if I know why, they never tell me what they want with me.

"They keep working me over, and I pass out. Next thing I know I'm on a beach and I think I'm in Jersey. Didn't know it was Staten Island 'til the cops told me."

The detectives did not believe him, most naturally. They told reporters, who swarmed all over the hospital when word of Luciano's travel was flashed to the knowing along Broadway, that underworld gossips said Luciano had been taken for a ride by rival gangsters. Luciano said nothing.

When the stories hit the newspapers, embellishments included "gangland information" that Charles (Lucky) Luciano—as the writers called him—had been marked for death because of any number of reasons, which varied from paper to paper, and none of which are important here because none of them were true. But from then on careless writers exploring old newspaper clippings leaped to the conclusion that Charlie had suddenly been given the nickname Lucky because he survived an "underworld attempt to murder him." Only by a miracle did he come back, after being left for dead, they wrote.

Patent nonsense. Although much of the time gangsters weren't very expert marksmen, they would never have botched the job so outrageously had they actually intended to murder Luciano. Had Luciano actually been dumped on the beach by killers, they would have put several bullets into his unconscious body before leaving him.

Charlie, in fact, had been stomped, beaten, and blackjacked. He had not been stabbed and slashed, as all writers have claimed, he did not get a wound over his left eye that gave his lid a definite droop from the use of a knife, as all writers have claimed. He was not assaulted by gangsters.

Luciano was actually beaten by three detectives who wanted information from him which he wasn't about to give them. Charlie said that privately to friends, to members of his family, to visitors in Naples, and to a New York newspaper reporter many years later.

Charlie's story to all of these people, some of whom I've personally interviewed and others whose reports in Narcotics Bureau files have been summarized for me, is that the detectives were searching for Legs Diamond, who was wanted for murder. Back the previous June, four months before Luciano was beaten, Diamond shot a man to death in a fight in the Hotsy-Totsy Club, a place Legs owned at Broadway and Fifty-fourth Street. Legs vanished before police arrived.

For months the newspapers criticized police for their inability to find this killer, and detectives grew desperate. They ran down every rumor. One homicide detective heard that Luciano was hiding Legs somewhere. On the evening of October 16, detectives followed Luciano from the racetrack, where he'd been gambling all day, to a small house that Charlie owned in the Bronx, in which he conducted business with uptown associates and, occasionally, kept a tryst with one or another of the women whom he would not permit into the Barbizon-Plaza suite he considered home.

"I'd just put the car away and was closing the garage doors when these two big bastards popped out of nowhere," Luciano told narcotics agent Sal Vizzini some time in the late 1950's. "I was pretty sure they was cops the minute I saw them. They pushed me up against the garage doors and frisked me, but I was clean. Then a car with two more guys pulls up to the curb. Each one of 'em takes hold of an arm and they hustle me to their car, throw me in face down in back and walk all over me getting into the back seat."

Luciano said his hands were taped behind him, and tape was placed over his eyes. Then the detectives began to demand he tell them where Legs Diamond was hiding, kicking him as they asked their question. Charlie said he hadn't seen Diamond in almost a year. The detectives continued to beat him. They drove around for several hours, kicking and blackjacking him, but Charlie would say nothing. He knew they weren't going to murder him, so he decided to outlast them. Eventually, they took the ferry to Staten Island—although Luciano thought it was a Hudson ferry to New Jersey—and they dumped him on the beach.

Narcotics agent Sal Vizzini, in his book, *Vizzini,* says he asked Luciano whether he had any idea where Legs was hiding. Luciano replied: "Hell, he was right there in my house when they put me against the garage. He got the hell out fast when the news broke about what had happened to me."

As I've said, Luciano repeated this version to dozens of friends over the years. One of them was Johnny Martin, veteran police reporter for the New York *Daily News*, who had known Charlie from Prohibition days. In 1955, shortly after retiring, Martin took a Mediterranean cruise. When the ship docked at Naples, Martin visited Luciano and they chatted for some time.

I was working as a young reporter at Police Headquarters when Martin returned from his cruise and stopped in to tell old colleagues about it. He discussed his visit with Luciano at length, and said that Charlie told him the men who had beaten him were detectives working on the Hotsy-Totsy killings. Said Martin:

"Lucky gave me the names of the cops. guys I know well." Martin named them, but I am unable to recall their names. However, Martin continued: "I checked with one of the cops. Called him up when I got back. He admitted the whole thing."

And finally, as further documentation, attorney George Wolf, who represented both Costello and Luciano, says that this is the true version. Costello heard it from Charlie immediately after the beating, and Wolf heard it later directly from Costello.

As Charlie's bruises and contusions healed, the feudal tensions within Mafia fragmented its members and brought Charlie the involvement he had been trying to avoid. According to Joe Valachi, who joined Mafia at this time and could not have been fully aware of the influence of the Yale-Rothstein killings, the actual shooting war between Mafia factions began in the first days of 1930. And it began with an error in judgment by the greedy Joe the Boss, an error that would doom him.

Joe coveted a very lucrative industrial racket that had been developed by one of his East Harlem underbosses, Gaetano Reina, whose daughter would marry Valachi some years later. Reina, through terror and murder, had formed an association of ice peddlers (a large industry in those days before electric refrigeration was available to the poor) and he had forced every ice peddler and every wholesaler in the city to join and pay him booty, called dues. The income was estimated at about $200,000 a year.

The Boss demanded a share of this lucrative racket. Reina resisted. On the evening of February 26, 1930, Reina was shot to death as he was leaving an apartment on Sheridan Avenue in the Bronx. Joe the Boss took over the ice association.

He also dictated the appointment of one of his stooges, Joe Pinzola, to head the gang previously commanded by the late Mr. Reina. Pinzola was a fat, coarse man, with a handlebar mustache that was always "greasy-looking" as Valachi expressed it. He was one of the old Mustache Petes so much despised by the younger men who had grown up in New York.

By killing Reina, and by assigning one of his own lackies to Reina's high Mafia post, Joe the Boss had abrogated the agreement by which he had succeeded Lupo as Mafia head back in 1920—the pact which had made the uptown branch of the New York Mafia both autonomous and an equal to Masseria's downtown group.

Immediately, the uptown branch decided to kill Pinzola. Which they finally accomplished on September 9, 1930. The victim was lured by men he believed he commanded, but who were loyal to the memory of dear Mr. Reina, to the offices of an importing firm at 1487 Broadway, where he was shot to death. The importing company was owned by Thomas Luchese, a member of Reina's old gang.

Luchese at that time was quite close to Costello and Luciano, working with Costello in whiskey and gambling, and with Luciano in narcotics and in the garment center activities. It is very likely that Luchese consulted Luciano about the killing. If he did not get Luciano's sanction to murder Pinzola, he certainly obtained his promise not to interfere in what then appeared to be an isolated family argument.

What none of them seemed to have known is that Salvatore Maranzano was simultaneously making his first open move against Joe the Boss. Maranzano was shrewdly taking advantage of the dissatisfaction within the uptown group. As Joe Profaci, a Maranzano aide at that time, recalled to the friend of my family: "He (Maranzano) figured by getting rid of some of the old greasers that the Reina men all hated, he could get younger guys like Luchese to throw in with our side. His boys and the uptown boys had a lot of business together, and we all knew what Masseria had done to Reina, so teaming up was a good possibility."

Some three weeks before Pinzola was murdered by his own men, Maranzano's killers shot down Peter Morello in his East Harlem office. Morello, who was in his fifties, was known as the Clutching Hand because of a deformity and because of the terror with which he was held by the Italian community. He and Lupo had been partners in extortion and murder in the first decade of the century, and had gone to prison together on counterfeiting charges in 1910. When President Harding paroled Lupo in 1921 he also paroled Morello, who had returned to the uptown faction of Mafia. Morello was one of the despised old greasers.

Joe Valachi later testified about the significance of the Morello killing: "The way they explained it to me, the Reina boys knew that *they* didn't kill Morello. So they figure somebody else is in trouble with Joe the Boss. They check around and they find out it's Salvatore Maranzano, going out warring against Joe the Boss."

Immediately, the two groups angry with Joe the Boss, for different reasons, joined forces. Maranzano was in command. It was at this time that Valachi and many other young men on the fringes of the Italian mob—burglars, stickupmen, and all sorts of hustlers—were recruited into Mafia to give the Maranzano forces a larger army in the coming war against Masseria.

Two weeks after Pinzola was killed, the newly expanded Maranzano group performed their first joint assassination, the murder of two Masseria men in the Bronx on November 5, 1930. Then followed an attempt to kill Paul Gambino, whose brother, Carlo, was an important Masseria ally in Brooklyn. Carlo was so badly frightened that he and all his men rushed to join Maranzano. Several other men were killed in the Bronx in following weeks, and Joe Masseria himself barely escaped death—again, in the Bronx.

Through all of the "war," as Valachi called it from his rather dangerous position on the front lines, it doesn't appear that any Maranzano soldiers were killed, nor is there any evidence that the battle lines extended below the upper section of Manhattan.

In spite of Valachi's testimony that this was a nationwide war and that between forty and sixty Masseria men were reported killed, no such slaughter ever developed. Luciano, for example, although still Joe the Boss' chief executive in Mafia, was never directly involved. He, Costello, Genovese, and others were prudent enough to stay out of sight as much as possible, but the "war" was in reality between the Maranzano forces and those who still worked closely with Joe the Boss on a daily basis. Luciano's organization was very much a separate entity just barely within Masseria's sphere, and ranking higher than Masseria's gang in wealth, political influence, and probably even in strength in numbers.

Maranzano was wary about moving against Luciano for he was aware that Charlie could bring against him not only his own group, but also the weight of Johnny Torrio and the Capone gang, Jewish groups from New England to Philadelphia and out to Cleveland, and even a new and very vicious power in Manhattan, Dutch Schultz. Maranzano knew, also, that Luchese and many others in the old Reina group were closely allied with

Luciano and would not stand for an attempt on his life. To move against Luciano, at this time, would have meant that all of Maranzano's plans would collapse, and he knew it.

So far as Luciano was concerned, the war was nothing more than a skirmish between a couple of old Mustache Petes who could not keep pace with the times. Yet, since the fighting did involve men with whom he was associated, and because some of these men had been ordered by Masseria to ignore their own businesses and group around the Boss for battle, Luciano believed it absolutely necessary to end the feud.

He spoke with Masseria and sent emissaries to Maranzano, trying to arrange peace. Torrio, Costello, so many others not personally involved, begged for an end to the fighting. Masseria and Maranzano were adamant; it was a fight to the death. Masseria screamed that Maranzano was scheming to become Boss. Maranzano charged that Masseria had vowed to "kill all the Castellammarese"— all the men who had been brought over from his Sicilian town by Maranzano. This accusation, which Maranzano repeated to all who would listen, was a typical *mafioso*-Machiavellian untruth: Through all the history of Mafia, men who sought to expand their power over the bodies of others first raised false charges against them in order to justify the killing. In actuality, as Nicola Gentile said in his memoirs: "The war had been unchained by Maranzano."

Luciano could not convince Maranzano to stop trying to kill Joe the Boss, but others were more successful. Throughout the country, men of the Mafia were watching the events in New York, and were growing more concerned that the feud would actually develop into a national disaster which would interfere with their major aim—making money.

A meeting was called of all the national Mafia leaders, according to Gentile's published report. They convened in Boston and voted to send a "commission," as Gentile calls it, to inform Maranzano that the feud must end immediately. Members of the commission took ten rooms in the Hotel Pennsylvania in New York just after the Christmas holiday in 1930, and sent word to Maranzano that he must come to them, on orders of all the Mafia. Maranzano delayed sending his response, forcing the Mafia commission to wait on the pleasure of the Mafia prince.

As they waited, Luciano called Al Capone and informed him of Maranzano's grave insult to the Mafia's representatives. The next day, Gentile said, Frank (The Enforcer) Nitti arrived from Chicago and sought out Gentile. Capone's enforcer ordered the commission to inform Maranzano that if he did not meet with them immediately then he should tremble because ("of the war we of Chicago will wage, and if it is necessary we will even employ airplanes, because those means are ready and concentrated in a specific place." (The words used are Gentile's formal written Italian. Nitti never said anything so flowery in his life. Most likely he told Gentile: "Tell that bastard Maranzano if he don't make peace we'll send planes to blast him.")

No matter the language employed, Maranzano got the message. He met with the commission and, after much argument and recriminations, was forced to agree to a two-month truce. Maranzano was furious, but he abided by the truce. As did Masseria. But when the two months ran out, both Joe the Boss and Maranzano vowed to renew hostilities.

Before the fighting could begin again, however, Luciano called Frank Costello and Vito Genovese to the garage and offices in Broome Street which he continued to maintain as his downtown headquarters long after the bootleg curb exchange had been put out of business by police. According to Frank Costello, in a conversation years later with his lawyer, George Wolf, the three of them made the decision that Joe the Boss would have to be murdered. Costello didn't spell it out, but it was obvious that by eliminating this party to the dispute, Luciano would then take over the downtown branch of the city's Mafia.

The plotters realized that simply killing Masseria would achieve nothing unless Maranzano promised that the fighting would end with the death of his enemy. When he was approached with the scheme, Maranzano agreed with Luciano's demand that all the branches of Mafia would join together in cooperation once Joe the Boss was dead, and that there would be no more killings.

The story of the murder of Joe the Boss has been told many times and will not be treated in detail here. Luciano, after trying for several months, was able to convince Masseria that it was safe to leave his apartment just off Central Park West, because peace had been imposed. Masseria finally believed that. One day he agreed with Charlie that after the long turmoil a drive out to Geraldo Scarpato's restaurant in Coney Island for lunch and a discussion of the future would be most beneficial to his health. It was not, of course.

On the afternoon of April 15, 1931, Joe the Boss had just finished lunch with Charlie and Vito Genovese, his two most trusted aides, and they had begun to play cards. At about 3:30 a car driven by Ciro Terranova stopped in front of the restaurant and at least two men got out, while Terranova remained behind the wheel. The two, Frank Livorsi and Joe Strachi, Masseria men both, entered the restaurant. Masseria must have greeted them, in surprise at seeing them—before they pulled out revolvers and put six bullets into his body and head.

When police arrived everyone was gone except the owner of the establishment, who had been out for a walk and returned after the shooting, and "Salvatore Lucania" as the newspapers called him. Luciano said he'd been playing a little cards with Masseria after lunch and had gone to the men's room.

"I'm taking a leak," he told detectives, "and I heard a lot of noise. I dry my hands and come out to see what's

97

goin' on. There's nobody around except poor Joe, and he's dead."

Asked why he didn't rush out to help "poor Joe" in his moment of crisis, Luciano replied:

"I don't ever carry a gun, so how could I help?"

By remaining at the scene while all his associates fled, Luciano was signaling to Mafia men across the country that he had personally ordered the murder of Joe the Boss for the good of the society. And, more important, he had publicly notified every Masseria man that the killing was not Maranzano's work but Luciano's, and that he was now in command.

Within hours after he was released by detectives, Luciano instructed members of the national Mafia commission, as quoted here in Gentile's language, to "tell Maranzano that if he should touch even a hair of even a personal enemy of ours we will wage war to the end . . ." From Chicago, Gentile says, Al Capone called Maranzano and threatened him with his "airplanes" if peace didn't descend over all.

Maranzano understood, but he would not be deterred in his drive to control the American Mafia. A new meeting of Mafia leaders was called, convening in Chicago's Lexington Hotel, a Capone fortress. Luciano and Capone tried to revolutionize Mafia by abolishing the concept of *capo di tutti capi,* boss of all bosses, a form of Mafia royalty still in use in Sicily. But Maranzano was too ambitious and too wily to permit that to happen. He threatened some delegates, cajoled others, bribed a few with promises of greatness by his side as king, and had the support of a few important leaders who had always been in his camp against the younger men with strangely modern ideas —such as working in partnership with Jews and the Irishers.

When the convention ended, Maranzano had been elected boss of all bosses.

He immediately proceeded to shake down the entire Italian organization. He announced to the New York Mafia members that he was throwing a banquet to celebrate his crowning as Mafia king, and that each group within Mafia would be expected to buy hundreds of tickets, at six dollars each. He sent a thousand tickets to Capone, who paid his required six thousand dollars; the men in Buffalo purchased the same number of tickets; Mafia organizations all across the country did the same. Between four and five hundred men attended the banquet-extortion that was held in a dance hall in the Bronx, according to Valachi, and Maranzano realized about $115,000 from his little coronation party.

Maranzano loved speeches, and he made a very long one at the banquet. "He started to explain about Masseria and his groups, that they were killing people without justification," Valachi later testified before the TV cameras. "Then he was explaining how the Masseria group did these things. 'Now it's going to be different,' he said. 'First we have the boss of all bosses, which is myself.' "

The new king then set up a table of organization for the New York Mafia, which was eventually adopted by all groups in the country. Through a layer of subbosses and lieutenants, the boss of each of the five families in New York would be carefully insulated from any direct involvement in crime; no soldier, the operator and killer on the streets, could ever talk to a boss without first going through the chain of command. There could be no killings of members without a trial before a commission; peace would now come to Mafia thanks to the benevolence of the new king.

But the kind of peace that Luciano had worked for, and killed for, evaporated rather quickly. Valachi made no mention of it, for he could not be aware of all that was happening from his isolation in the Bronx, but almost immediately after the banquet Maranzano began to test the strength of Luciano and his organization on an old field of battle—the garment center.

While the old greasers of Mafia had been fussing and fighting over the Masseria-Maranzano feud, most gangsters in the country continued to go about their normal business. Especially the Luciano organization, so heavily Jewish and removed from the Mafia nonsense. Lepke was continuing his infiltration of the Amalgamated Clothing Workers—supporting one side so the other would "buy him out" and, in the process, be completely absorbed by him.

And now, Maranzano's earlier promise that he would not make trouble for Luciano's friends in the garment center turned out to be as empty as all his promises were.

One day in mid-July a couple of Maranzano's garment center sluggers, working for the union faction controlled by Sidney Hillman, threw rocks at the windows of a clothing shop that had signed a contract with the union faction supported by Lepke. Visiting the shop at the time was a man named John Ferrari, who manufactured children's coats in a small factory in Brooklyn. Ferrari, almost struck by a rock, rushed into the street with a few other men and began fighting the rock-throwers, who ran off.

Lepke ordered his men to find and punish the hoods of the Hillman faction, and during another melee one of Hillman's business agents was shot in the leg. Hillman, in turn, ordered Maranzano's men to get revenge. Since it was John Ferrari who had started it all, the Maranzano men went to Brooklyn to kill him. They murdered, instead, Guido Ferrari, mistaking him for his brother.

According to the informers who talked about it later in the Murder, Inc. investigation, Lepke once more demanded Maranzano's death. At a meeting of the Luciano organization, attended by Charlie, Lansky, Costello, Siegel, Lepke, and Dutch Goldberg, Lepke insisted that Maranzano would have to be killed because he was planning to absorb every underworld business organization, to dominate every racketeer.

"You think this is a fight in the clothing business?" Lepke is reported to have said. "Open your eyes, Charlie. Maranzano is out to take over everything."

Everyone agreed with Lepke, and Charlie finally consented—Maranzano must be killed. And, with him, every old-style guinea who didn't comprehend that crime was different in America.

When Masseria had been killed, Charlie had made certain that all men of Mafia would understand he had been the killer, or had ordered the killing. This time, however, it would have to be different. Maranzano was too crafty to be lured to a Scarpato's, he would never be foolish enough to meet Luciano or any of his associates except in the safety of his own office. Further, there was no longer any way of knowing, for certain, which of the Italians who might be chosen for the mass killings of Maranzano and all the older men who supported him would be loyal enough to keep the plans secret. Luciano also decided he could not call others around the country, not even Capone, to seek permission in advance, because word would almost certainly leak out to Maranzano.

Meyer Lansky was given the contract to handpick the best Jewish gunmen available in New York to murder Maranzano. At the same time, Lansky was instructed to contact heads of Jewish gangs in other cities and have them kill Maranzano men. The murders must be planned with great caution. There was no need to rush, Luciano said. The only urgency was to work out the logistics so perfectly that Lansky's gunmen would kill the old-time greasers on their lists the very moment Maranzano was killed. The logistics were left to Lansky—he would hire gunmen in each city and pay them to stand by until they got a message that Maranzano was dead. At that moment they were to carry out their murder assignments.

In New York, Lansky assigned the murder of Maranzano to two of his own gunmen and one from the gang of Longy Zwillman of New Jersey. The trio was to be commanded by Bo Weinberg, who had a reputation as the "ace killer" of the Dutch Schultz crowd. As one informer later said: "Bo got the contract because Dutch would've been boilin' mad if Lucky didn't give his troops a crack at that fuckin' Maranzano."

They rented a vacant apartment in a building across from Maranzano's home on Avenue J in Brooklyn, and waited for about a week to get a shot at him. But Maranzano never did come home during that period. The men around Luciano began getting impatient. Weinberg and his team were called back to Manhattan and instructed to try and trap Maranzano between his Park Avenue office and his apartment-hideaway in Yonkers, just north of the Bronx.

Maranzano, meanwhile, had some devious plans of his own concerning Luciano and his associates. A day or two after Lansky's killers abandoned their apartment across from his home, Maranzano returned to his family. Joe Valachi, who had joined Maranzano's Mafia family during the big coronation banquet, went to Maranzano's house that night for a conference. Valachi later testified:

"When I got to his house, he was bandaging his son's foot. I walked in. He greeted me. I waited until he got through with his son. Then he said to me, 'We have to go to the mattress again.' The 'mattress' means we have to go back to war. Naturally, I wasn't too happy to hear that. So he told me he can't get along with Charlie Lucky, Vito—he gave me a list. 'We have to get rid of these people.' On the list was Al Capone, Frank Costello, Charlie Lucky, Vito Genovese, Vincent Mangano, Joe Adonis, Dutch Schultz. These are all important names at the time.

"Now he tells me he is going to meet with Charlie Lucky and Vito Genovese the next day at two o'clock in his office, the last meeting with them." Valachi protested that Maranzano was placing himself in danger, that he should have someone else meet with Luciano, but Maranzano insisted he would personally take care of the matter.

Maranzano obviously didn't believe he was in any danger. He had scheduled the meeting with Luciano and Genovese for two o'clock. He had also purchased the guns of Vince Coll, known as the Mad Dog because he was a pathological killer, a gunman who hijacked bootleg trucks without worrying about the rightful owners, who kidnapped important underworld figures and forced their associates to pay fifty-thousand-dollar ransoms for their release—a killer with a price on his head offered by Luciano, Schultz, Owney Madden, and others.

Coll was scheduled to arrive in Maranzano's office ten minutes after Luciano and Genovese, to kill them. One Maranzano aide privy to the plan later told Valachi: "The boss figured that using Coll, who's crazy and killing everybody anyway, nobody's gonna blame the killing of Charlie and Vito on Maranzano. Just one of those things—crazy Coll came in to kill."

Maranzano's plan seems to have been the worst kept secret in Mafia history. Several Maranzano men—probably scores of them—rushed to tell Charlie about his impending death. Among them, according to Valachi and others, was Tommy Luchese, who didn't intend to jeopardize his close business ties with Charlie and Lepke in the garment center simply to satisfy Maranzano's huge Caesar complex.

At two o'clock on the afternoon of September 10, 1931, the precise hour that Charlie and Vito were scheduled to confer with Maranzano, and to be killed, Bo Weinberg and his gunmen arrived at Maranzano's office. They drew guns, flashed detectives' shields, and ordered eleven men in the outer office and a very frightened secretary to line up against the wall.

Maranzano peeked from his private office to investigate the noise, then turned and raced for his desk. Weinberg and a Lansky man, Red Levine, rushed in after him. Maranzano was seated in his chair, trying to get his desk drawer open to pull out his pistol, when Levine put a hammer lock around his neck and plunged a stiletto into his chest several times. The plan had been to stab Maranzano to death to avoid attracting others in the building with the sounds of gunfire. But Maranzano put up such a vicious fight that they were forced to shoot him, Levine later told Valachi. Four bullets hit Maranzano in the head and chest and he fell back into his chair, dead.

Weinberg took a few moments to complete another assignment. He opened Maranzano's desk and from it drew a file folder labeled "Immigration." He spread the papers in the folder on Maranzano's desk. When detectives began investigating the murder they announced to the press that they had stumbled upon an enormous alien-smuggling ring. Federal officials investigated. Eventually, many of Maranzano's gunmen from Castellammare, all illegal aliens, were located and deported; Luciano never had to worry about them.

By tarrying briefly on this special errand, Weinberg became separated from his men. He lost his way in a stairwell for a time, running from floor to floor. He could hear the police sirens in front of the building, so he hid in a women's toilet. Finally, he emerged into Grand Central Station, which was connected to the building. Worried about the murder gun in his pocket, he mingled with a crowd waiting for a train and dropped the weapon into the topcoat pocket of a homeward-bound commuter.

For months afterward Bo would laugh when he told friends of his misadventures: "I wonder what would've happened if a dame came into the ladies' room while I'm hidin' in there?" he'd say. "And that poor slob on the train, when he got home and found a gun in his pocket?"

Red Levine had an even better story to tell. As he was racing out the front door of the building, after killing Maranzano, several men were entering. "One of them was Vince Coll," Red later said. "He sure as hell was surprised to see me and the boys. I waved to him, 'Beat it, Vince, the cops are coming.' Wonder if he's sore that he's out a bundle on his contract to kill Charlie?"

Throughout the remainder of that day and over the next day, approximately forty Maranzano men in the New York area and in several other cities were murdered in what has come to be known in Mafia circles as The

104

Night of the Sicilian Vespers. Valachi himself was on the death list but he survived by going into hiding and then having someone speak in his favor to Tommy Luchese, who smoothed things out for him. In a short time Valachi joined the Mafia family of Charlie Luciano.

9

"And now there was peace," Valachi said. "Luciano abolished the boss of all bosses system and he put in a group of six *consiglieri* (counselors) to protect the soldiers. That is why the soldiers felt they had a longer life now than ever before."

Luciano, himself a Masseria soldier only a decade before, was foremost a politician who knew what his constituents wanted. The greatest fear of lower-echelon Mafia men under the old greaser system was that the boss and even his lieutenants could order the death of a soldier, for any reason, and no other man could object. The life of a Mafia soldier had always been a perilous one.

But Luciano changed all that by instituting a court that would protect the soldier. Each of the five families in New York and the single Mafia family in New Jersey, Luciano decreed, must appoint one of their number to a special judicial council. These six *consiglieri* would have the duty of listening to charges against any Mafia member, and voting the penalty. Should there be a tie, the boss of the particular family would have the deciding vote, but only after listening to all the evidence. No Mafia soldier could be punished in any way until he was judged by this court.

Every one of the approximately one thousand soldiers in the six families thereafter loved Luciano, and would have given their lives for him. Valachi and the other Mafia men who had been born or raised in America and had always loathed the old country ways adored Luciano even more for another order he sent down. As Valachi explained it:

"In the old days, when you met another member the habit was to kiss him. Charlie Lucky put a stop to this and changed it to a handshake. 'After all,' Charlie said, 'we would stick out kissing each other in restaurants and places like that.'"

With peace and some degree of stability over the Mafia, Luciano turned his attention once more to business affairs. The depression had struck all of Western society, disrupting business everywhere—except for the bootleggers and racketeers, for man must drink and gamble and borrow money at loanshark rates. More urgent than the depression, certainly, was the fact that Prohibition would soon be repealed. More than half the states had ratified the Twenty-First Amendment to repeal the Volstead Act, and it was certain to become a part of the Constitution within a year. Drinking, the manufacture of whiskey and beer, and its distribution and sale, would again be legal. State officials were already creating liquor agencies which would license every company involved in alcoholic beverages, from manufacture to retail sale. Luciano had no fears about his men getting licenses. Although Al Smith was no longer governor, his appointees held important positions inside government and they had always come through for Luciano, Costello, and everyone else who had purchased the leaders of Tammany Hall.

Even more rewarding was the prospect of selecting and having a hold on the next President of the United States. That man no doubt would be a Democrat, for the Republicans were being blamed for creating the depression and Herbert Hoover was bound for defeat. Fortunately, for the New York racketeers, the two leading contenders for the Democratic nomination were the very cooperative Al Smith, who had appointed several of Luciano's choices to state office, and Franklin Delano Roosevelt, who had succeeded Smith as governor and who could be influenced in important matters by Tammany leaders such as Jimmy Hines.

The Democratic convention was held in Chicago in July, 1932. The large delegation from Tammany would be very important in the decision whether to choose Smith or Roosevelt, for both men were New Yorkers, and both were governors. But Tammany Hall was split.

Hines wanted his fellow leaders of the Hall to support Roosevelt. Always a shrewd politician, he believed Roosevelt was certain to get the nomination; Smith had run against Hoover in 1928 and had been badly defeated because he was a Catholic and a product of Tammany. Roosevelt, from an old Dutch family, would not lose the anti-Catholic South nor be tarred with an association with Tammany, for that association had been only minimal on the surface.

Should Roosevelt be elected, Hines argued, it would be wise for Tammany to have supported him from the very beginning, so that Hines and the other New York bosses would be given the federal patronage as usual— the right to select men for federal jobs in New York. Especially the right to name a United States Attorney, an office which, in Republican hands, had brought a young "boy scout" from the Midwest named Thomas E. Dewey roaring into the city "on his goddam white charger," as Hines put it. Dewey had jailed a couple of small Harlem policy bankers who had always been quite liberal in contributing to Tammany coffers and Hines' private fund; he had convicted a vice squad patrolman who always brought Tammany its share of the standard bribes in that business; Dewey had even convicted a Tammany district leader who was a deputy city clerk and ran Tammany's lucrative business in obtaining illegal fees from supplicants requiring licenses from the city.

Most of the old line Tammany leaders, however, were loyal to Al Smith. He was, like they, the product of the Irish ghetto and he had never forgotten his obligations to Tammany even as he pretended to rise above petty politics and thievery. One man, dark, silent, and of growing political power, came to the fore of what was oversimplified in the press as a fight against Hines for control of Tammany. He was Albert Marinelli, who owed his start in politics to Joe (the Boss) Masseria and owed his rise to power to Charlie Luciano.

During the first two years of Prohibition, Marinelli had been appointed by Governor Al Smith to the position of Port Warden of the city, a job in which he greatly aided bootleggers who were unloading whiskey from ships docked in Marinelli's port. Later, Marinelli owned a trucking company which was employed in bootlegging. His company had its offices and garages at Kenmare and Mulberry Streets, directly across from the "social club" in which Masseria had his headquarters and next door to Luciano's own office; there just happened to be a connecting door between the offices of Luciano and Marinelli.

In 1931, a year before the Democrats met to nominate the next President, Marinelli announced he was running for leadership of his Tammany district against the incumbent, Harry C. Perry. The announcement was enough. Perry "resigned." Actually, Perry had simply received word that he should get out of the district and turn it over to Marinelli—that word, it is said, came from two of Luciano's men who walked in on Perry, laid their guns on his desk, and ordered him to sign the resignation. Perry, when later confronted publicly with the story, never bothered to deny it; he told friends, in fact, "I was afraid to stay because they said they'd kill my wife and kids."

As the nominating convention opened in Chicago, the New York delegation was meeting in its hotel, the Drake, to work out strategy. Marinelli, the leader of the Smith faction, shared a hotel suite with Charlie Luciano. Jimmy Hines, leader of the Roosevelt faction, shared his hotel suite with Frank Costello. Other members of the Luciano organization, most notably Meyer Lansky and Dutch Goldberg, floated around among delegates from other states.

No matter who won, Luciano and his associates would

be owed something by a future President. And they would expect payment of that debt when the victor was sworn into office.

Roosevelt became President, of course. While there has never been any documented evidence that Roosevelt bent to the will of the mob—until Richard Nixon, the probity of a man holding the office was never seriously questioned —there were a number of rather suspect actions on Roosevelt's part that makes it possible to suspect that he, too, may have been used by organized crime.

Late in May, 1933, a few months after Roosevelt was sworn into office, the racketeers of the nation held their now famous meeting in a New York hotel (as discussed in the first chapter) from which the modernized American Mafia emerged, with Charlie Luciano as the unofficial President who ranked in his own "secret invisible government," as Valachi called it, as high as FDR in the more socially accepted government. You'll recall that the convention of racketeers established a cooperative in which each important gang across the nation became part of a democratic cartel, each secure against encroachment in its area, and each with a voice in national criminal affairs.

Dutch Schultz, by now a power in New York and New Jersey, was absent from the convention of rackets bosses. Dutch was represented, however; he had given his proxy vote to Charlie Luciano. Dutch could not personally attend because he had been indicted on income tax charges and was "on the lam," as they called it then. He was reported to be in Canada, in Europe, even in Tahiti. But he was in reality hiding in a hotel at Broadway and Eightieth Street that he owned, and from which he continued to direct his enterprises. On May 24, 1933, a few days before the national convention of crime got underway in a Park Avenue hotel, a smaller convention was held in Schultz's hideaway. The details of this meeting came out later, during the Murder, Inc. investigation.

Attending on Mr. Schultz were Dutch Goldberg and Trigger Mike Coppola, both high in the Luciano organization. They told Schultz that Luciano apologized for not meeting personally with him, but that it would have been as dangerous for Luciano to come as it would be for Schultz to take part in the bigger convention downtown. Of course, they said, Luciano had sent them to inform Dutch in advance of his plans, to let Dutch know he was being included in as part of the national combine. And to get Schultz's approval. Dutch, as everyone else would do at the convention later, most certainly approved.

That Luciano would send two of his men to confer with Schultz is striking evidence of the power that Schultz possessed and of the delicate manner in which even Luciano would treat him. For Dutch Schultz was by far the wealthiest and most influential of all the "independents" who continued to operate outside Mafia or the Italian-Jewish group around Luciano. It was Dutch Schultz, more than even Costello or Luciano, who controlled Jimmy Hines and, with that control, practically owned all the greedy men of Tammany.

Schultz had come extraordinarily far in just a few years, and it was his manner of reaching prominence that made all underworld figures wary of upsetting him. Born in the Bronx in the summer of 1902, son of a saloon keeper and livery stable owner, his name was actually Arthur Flegenheimer. He went to school until he was fourteen, dropping out around the time his father deserted the family. In later years, Schultz would always deny his father had abandoned them; "he just died," he insisted. Young Flegenheimer began associating with members of the Bergen Gang, a group of teenage hoodlums who infested the area around Third Ave and 149th Street in the Bronx. He also worked at a variety of jobs, and in his later years as a gangster he'd often display, quite proudly, his membership card in the roofers' union.

In December 1919, as the nation's racketeers prepared for Prohibition, seventeen-year-old Flegenheimer was arrested for burglary and sent to the City Prison. Anxious to demonstrate he was tough, he became so unruly he was sent to a prison upstate. He was caught attempting to escape and additional time was added to his sentence. When he was released around March, 1921 and returned to the Bergen Gang, his reputation had been so enhanced by his actions in prison that his friends called him Dutch Schultz after a locally famous street gang brawler. He wasn't Dutch; his father and mother were German Jews. But the name sounded tough and he wanted to be known as a tough guy.

But he was just a cheap brawler and thief who, according to old friends and policemen who knew him in those days, had less courage than most of the other kids around. Later, those friends and detectives would say they could never understand how he climbed so far. While so many others his age had grown rich in bootlegging by 1921, it wasn't until 1925 that Schultz was more than just another consumer of alcohol. In that year he went to work for an old man with a moving van who was hauling beer from a local brewery. Schultz was a beer delivery boy for three years, but he saved his money and in 1928 became a partner in a speakeasy on Brook Avenue. He acquired three rickety trucks, some drivers, and a few strongarm men. His speakeasy was so profitable that within a year he had acquired a much larger and fancier bar.

This was 1929, the tenth year of Prohibition, a year after Rothstein was killed and Luciano had taken over his business and his political influence. And Dutch Schultz was still a small time saloon keeper in the Bronx.

But now he came into his own. He hired a few very insane gunmen, among them Vince Coll and his brother, Pete, and he expanded his vision. By some inspiration— native business sense and a gift for organization, his admirers said—and through a greater cruelty than most hoodlums possessed, Schultz suddenly became a very big man indeed.

One anecdote will demonstrate his methods. When he decided, in 1929, that he was ready to expand into the wholesale beer business, the biggest of the wholesalers in the Bronx were two brothers, John and Joe Rock. They were the envy of Schultz, at first. Later they were his target. The Rock brothers' trucks began to get hijacked, and some of their men were killed. John Rock sized up his enemy and retired with a big bankroll. He advised his brother to do the same but Joe decided he was tougher than Schultz.

Joe Rock vanished one day, and the underworld buzzed with rumors he had been murdered by the Schultz gang. Two days later he returned alive, a warning to all who would cross Schultz. He was crippled, he was growing blind, and he warned his friends that what had been done to him would be done to others. The Schultz men, he said, had taken him into a cellar somewhere, strung him up by the thumbs and beat him so badly that his legs were like pulp and he would never again walk like a normal man. After crippling him they securely taped over his eyes a strip of gauze that had been smeared with some chemical or infectious matter, and left it in place for many hours while it ate into his eyes. They then tossed him into the street, a cripple who would soon be totally blind.

Rock retired, understandably, and Schultz confiscated his beer business. After that the Dutchman had little difficulty with others who would normally have stood up to him. Schultz's business soon spurted and by the end of that year, 1929, he had enough money to buy political backing: Jimmy Hines and his Tammany partners. Schultz now attracted a very large mob of non-Italian uptown toughs anxious to work for the beer baron of the Bronx.

Schultz concentrated on beer, not competing with the Lucianos and the others in whiskey, and by the end of 1930 he was a gang leader equal to all the others. Through the overlapping interests of all the Prohibition groups, he got into business deals with Luciano, Costello, Lepke, Lansky, even Torrio, and grew friendly with them.

An examination of Schultz's income, documented by

federal accountants at his tax trial some years later, will give a small idea of the sort of income earned by gangsters of the day. According to those documents, Schultz's earnings *from beer alone* were $132,000 in 1929; $202,000 in 1930; $148,000 in 1931. That was net profit to Schultz after all payments to employees, police, and politicans, and did not include income from any other illicit enterprise.

Schultz was such an important factor in New York criminal circles that Luciano thought it wise to obtain his pledge that he would not join the Maranzano side should the Mafia war spread. It was at the height of that interfamily conflict that Schultz made a discovery which would enrich him beyond any fantasy he may have had, making him wealthier and more influential by far than even the Luciano combination. The discovery involved policy, the very popular gambling game in all the ghettoes, but especially among blacks in Harlem. Policy, the numbers game, was and still is the lottery of the poor. Each day hundreds of thousands of the poor, especially the blacks, placed their bets on any three-digit number they favored. The winning number was determined by a somewhat complex formula involving the amount of money bet on each race at the track. If a man's number won, he would be paid off at 600 to one. But the odds were 999 to one against him, so it can be imagined how large the profits were to the bankers of the numbers racket.

It has been estimated, conservatively, that the Harlem policy game was grossing about a hundred million dollars a year at the time Schultz discovered it in 1931, and that the bankers had an income of perhaps ten million a year after all expenses.

Harlem policy had been a matter of rugged individualism until Schultz came along. There were about forty bankers at the top, who provided the capital and took the profits. Beneath them were the foremen of the business, the controllers, who each had a string of collectors.

The collectors took the bets from their customers, and brought to the controller the policy slips on which the customer wrote his number and the cash bet. The controller then delivered the slips to the bank, where they were sorted and totalled, and otherwise arranged for the payoff, in the unlikely event that someone hit the correct number. It was all illegal of course.

One of the largest bankers in Harlem was Henry Ison. His lawyer, Dixie Davis, arranged bail for collectors who were arrested by police, and also arranged a small degree of political protection for the controllers and the banker. Davis was a hustler, a typical Magistrate's Court shyster. But he was young, good-looking and personable, very smart and ambitious, and absolutely without scruple. Had he not been educated, he probably would have become a gangster. With his education, he became the intellect behind Dutch Schultz.

Dixie allied himself with Dutch because Henry Ison came to the lawyer one day with a problem. Some rival policy bankers were not above informing to police about Ison's business, thereby disrupting it, nor did they consider the hijacking of Ison's money to be beneath their station. Did Mr. Davis know someone who could put a stop to all this?

Dixie certainly did. One of his clients was George Weinberg, a minor policy banker who ran a small game among whites on the edges of Harlem. George's brother, Bo, was Schultz's favorite gunman. Dixie didn't mention it to Ison, but he and George Weinberg had often schemed about working their way into the Schultz organization, but they could never come up with an idea to inflame Schultz's imagination and his greed.

Now, suddenly, Dixie saw it—as he later testified so dramatically in court. Schultz's gang could bring order to the very chaotic policy jungle by first giving protection to bankers like Ison, at a stiff fee, then eventually taking over every banker and creating one large bank which would take most of the profits. The reward for Davis?

115

A chance to grow rich as Schultz's advisor, his political contact man, his fixer.

That's how it worked out. Bo Weinberg was introduced to Ison and agreed to protect his bank—in the awesome name of Dutch Schultz—for five hundred dollars a week. Ison now explained that another problem had come up. Henry Miro, a rival banker, was cutting into his territory. Could that be stopped? Weinberg said he'd have to chat with his boss, and Schultz now became personally involved. He met with Davis to learn what this policy business was all about, and Davis explained his grand concept of one dominant policy bank controlled by Schultz. Davis was placed on Schultz's payroll as the mob's lawyer.

Henry Miro was summoned. When Miro got the word one night that the feared Dutch Schultz wanted to see him, the mere mention of that name so terrified him that he was leaving his apartment wearing only silk pajamas and would have gone to the meeting that way had Bo Weinberg not suggested he put on a topcoat and pair of slippers. At the conference he couldn't even look Schultz in the eye; he stared at Schultz's gun on the table between them. And he said he'd be very pleased to join up with Schultz's group.

The Dutchman promptly placed his own men within the Ison and Miro banks, to be certain all receipts were being accounted for and to learn whether Davis had been exaggerating the amount of money being earned in policy. When he understood that Davis had been, if anything, conservative when he threw around figures of a hundred million a year, Dutch informed Ison and Miro that he was now a sixty percent partner in their banks. He quickly moved in on every policy bank in Harlem and put together a central bank which his accountants operated and his gunmen controlled. Records of the Schultz policy bank, discovered after he was killed, disclosed that it was earning almost a million dollars a month.

It was this kind of wealth, plus Dixie Davis' astuteness, that made Schultz so very powerful in the city and state, even though he had come into the rackets ten years after every other major figure. Dixie's contribution was to convince Schultz that a business the size of policy required much greater protection than the simple payoff to politicians. What was needed, said Dixie, was to take into the business as a partner the most important politician in New York, the man who was the power behind the Tammany leader and the conduit through which underworld money flowed to all politicians. Jimmy Hines. The Dutchman's first reaction to this proposal was never disclosed by Davis, but it must have been rather violent considering Schultz's noted miserliness—he was so stingy that he kept an account book of expenses, listing every item down to a one-penny postage stamp.

But Dutch saw the wisdom of Dixie's proposal and by the time every policy bank in Harlem had been merged into the central bank, some time in 1932, Jimmy Hines had been given a share in the operation and he gave to his new employer his total loyalty. Hines received one percent of the profit each year, banking about a hundred thousand dollars annually, by official estimate. "Banking" is the wrong word. "The secret of my political success," Hines liked to boast, "is that I never owned a bank account."

When Luciano and his associates learned what kind of riches and power Dutch Schultz had amassed in Harlem, they most naturally grew envious. Luciano knew that the policy bank for the Italian lottery, downtown, grossed about ten million a year and brought a net profit of about a million. He soon learned from the Mafia men in East Harlem that policy up there was a dozen times more profitable—and he certainly read a careless statement by Dixie Davis that Harlem policy grossed between one hundred and five hundred million a year. The directors of the Luciano corporation decided, quite early, they would have to take that particular racket away from Dutch Schultz.

But they could not simply walk in on Schultz and order him to give it up, for he would fight. Besides, that sort of encroachment would be a violation of the pledge of cooperation that Luciano and Torrio had only just extracted from all the syndicates in the nation, binding them into one cartel. Luciano would have to wait. He was a very patient man.

In the meantime, with the coming of repeal, other sources of income would have to be developed. Besides the slot machines and other forms of gambling that Costello and Lanksy were handling so brilliantly, the most important new field to mine, the corporation decided, was in the labor unions and industry.

In the garment center, Lepke's scheme to take over Amalgamated had begun to move forward after Maranzano was killed. It was to be the model for slicing a piece out of every major industry in the city. A key figure in Lepke's final move to dominate Amalgamated was Bruno Belea, Sidney Hillman's assistant and the man who had called in Maranzano to fight Lepke's faction, headed by Philip Orlofsky. Lepke's climactic manipulative touch was to summon Belea and inform him that he was going to be murdered by Luciano himself, for having introduced Maranzano into the dispute. Belea pleaded for his life, as was natural. Lepke said his only salvation lay in meeting with Luciano, and being quite cooperative. The meeting was held: Luciano, Lepke, and Sidney Hillman's chief aide. When it was over, Belea returned to Hillman and said they would have to make a deal, or be killed. The deal was made; Amalgamated fell into Lepke's hands. As Lepke explained it to one of his aides who later testified about it:

"The deal is for Orlofsky to give up his union. He is out, him and the others with him. We'll see they get a year's pay after the union breaks up." And he explained his reason for dumping Orlofsky in favor of Hillman: "Hillman is a sucker, Orlofsky is a sucker. We'll stay with the sucker who has the most dough."

118

From that point on Lepke dominated the major union in the garment center. Luciano went on Amalgamated's payroll for $75,000 a year, it was later disclosed, and the money was carried to him from Hillman by a hoodlum named Joe Strawberry. Lepke called strikes, dictating policy to Hillman, and he decided when the strikes should be ended—generally, after he had extorted huge sums from owners of struck factories on Lepke's promise to end the strike. Lepke used his power to take over, for himself and the Luciano organization, a large number of trucking companies in the garment center; he already controlled the trucking union. With that lever, the Luciano organization moved in on the other major garment union, the International Garment Workers, and came to also dominate it.

Sidney Hillman, labor leader and associate of killers and hoodlums, would go on to glory as a founder and vice president of the Congress of Industrial Organizations (many of whose member unions would become mob-dominated), and in 1940 he would be appointed head of President Roosevelt's War Production Board. In making that appointment Roosevelt must have known of Hillman's relationship to Luciano, Lepke, and others. It was an open secret in the garment center that Hillman's partners were the nation's major racketeers, and some of the details were published by investigative reporters as early as 1937. Roosevelt made the appointment anyway. Precisely what benefits, if any, the mobsters received by having their man in charge of the War Production Board may not be known until some historian does a close study of that wartime agency. But the board was given sweeping powers over the nation's economic life, assigning priorities in the delivery to industry of scarce materials. Black market activities centered around rulings of the board. At the end of the war a Senate investigating committee found much evidence of favoritism and corruption. Of course.

119

10

At 5:22 P.M. December 5, 1933, Utah became the thirty-sixth state to ratify the 21st Amendment, repealing the Volstead Act. An hour and twenty-three minutes later President Roosevelt signed a proclamation, and for the first time in thirteen years Americans were legally free to drink whatever they wanted—or could find.

They had no trouble finding it. With but a slight shift in gears, the bootleggers went legal. Speakeasies opened their doors, with licenses to operate in the names of relatives or flunkies who had never been arrested and thus were acceptable to state licensing agencies upon payment of a small bribe. The major rackets figures became industrialists, owners of breweries, distilleries, and liquor importing firms, the business they knew best. Johnny Torrio, for example, using the name John T. McCarthy, was a large stockholder and director of Prendergast-Davies, Inc., a major importer and the largest purveyor of wholesale liquors in New York. Luciano and others became hidden partners in similar firms—among them companies that today are listed on the stock exchanges, still run by men who had been bootleggers during Prohibition.

Repeal brought a major benefit, so far as Luciano was concerned. The bootlegging wars which had caused so much killing, and wrote such large headlines, were a thing of the past. Liquor and beer were legal, and the underworld figures became legitimate businessmen in those industries. The other enterprises, gambling and narcotics especially, were hidden under the surface of society;

the agreement between the groups worked out at that meeting which created the modern American Mafia successfully eliminated the sort of friction that had caused murder and notoriety in the past.

Luciano kept pace with the times. He moved out of his Barbizon-Plaza suite and into a larger set of rooms in that more respectable domicile of the very wealthy and very social, the Waldorf Towers. He was known there as Charles Ross, a businessman living in 39-C, and he appeared to be quite wealthy.

As a founder of the national crime syndicate, Luciano was now in great demand for his advice, and for the pleasures of his company. Whenever leaders of local syndicates from Detroit, Cleveland, or Chicago, would come into New York on business, Charlie entertained them at grand dinners—he sometimes cooked Italian dishes himself—and then topped it off with a visit to Polly Adler's house of prostitution, where the most beautiful and the highest-priced whores could be found. Polly was a madam of class, and she ran a class operation. She had known Charlie for years, from his earliest days as a Broadway figure, when he was still being called Lucky Luciano. "I never found him to be other than gentlemanly," she later wrote. "He was always quiet, clean-talking, and considerate of the girls and maids."

Once, Polly recalled, the building superintendant was repairing a pipe under the kitchen sink of her bordello. Charlie came in with some friends. He looked at the middle-aged man, who was by far the most depressed person in the large apartment, and he cracked, "What's this guy doing in a house of joy? He looks ready to croak!" Polly took Luciano aside and explained that the man was ill with leukemia. Charlie was very embarrassed. He gave Polly three hundred dollars for the man and said, "Let me know if he needs more for his treatment."

A show girl who frequently attended gangsters' parties, getting fifty or a hundred dollars for the pleasure of her company and no intimacy expected, told a writer of the

121

era that Luciano often rented a hotel suite to entertain out-of-town gangsters; he'd hire the girls, stock the place with liquor and food, but most often he did not make an appearance himself because, the girl reported, "he didn't like to be seen with gangsters." On one occasion, at a party for members of Detroit's Purple Gang, Luciano did attend. Some of the men from Detroit, not aware of the distinction between party girls and whores, became angry when the girls would not retire to the bedroom with them. It was getting rather nasty when Charlie spoke up.

"Listen," he said, "these girls are show girls. They work for a living."

Charlie, always a gracious host and always protective of women, called Polly Adler and had a couple of her girls sent over to take care of the bedroom end of the entertainment. The party turned out to be a huge success.

Luciano no longer made much personal use of Polly Adler's services, for he had found a young woman who enchanted him and he spent much of his spare time with her. Her name was Gay Orlova, a twenty-year-old chorus girl in Earl Carroll's *Vanities,* one of the more beautiful and mysterious women on Broadway. It was rumored that they would be married. Lansky and Costello were married, and Costello especially often recommended marriage to Charlie. But he would have none of it. "I'll never get married," he told friends, "because then I'd want to have kids. And I'd never have a son of mine goin' through life with the burden of the name Luciano, the gangster." Charlie was to say that several times in his life, but most especially in his last decade, when he actually fell deeply in love for the first time.

Charlie later insisted he never loved Gay Orlova, but admitted she affected him deeply. "She's knocked me right in my head," he told close friends. She was very cosmopolitan, very sophisticated and intelligent, so different from the small-town chorus girls who were provincial, or the local girls who were sometimes as tough as the gangsters.

122

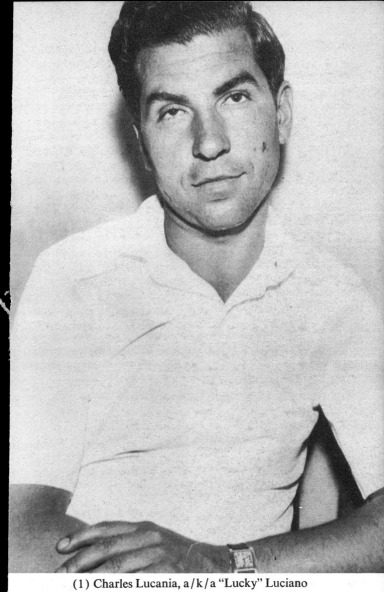

(1) Charles Lucania, a/k/a "Lucky" Luciano

(2) Arnold Rothstein. Until he was shot on November 4, 1928, he ruled New York's underworld.

(3) After his death three men were arrested in Rothstein's office, rifling the files. One of the culprits, a "waiter" named Charles Luciano, somehow managed to steal a document which became his ticket to power in the rackets.

(4) The three lawmen who would be Luciano's nemeses throughout his career in crime, Fiorello La Guardia (being sworn in as Mayor of New York in 1933) and (5) Thomas A. Dewey (being sworn in as Special Prosecutor in 1935). Judge Philip J. McCook swore in both men. By 1936 Justice McCook had Luciano in court and sentenced to 30 to 50 years in Sing Sing.

Legendary figures in the underworld era of Luciano included (6) Alphonse "Scarface Al" Capone, (7) Frankie (Uale) Yale, (8) Guiseppe "Joe the Boss" Masseria, (9) Louis "Lepke" Buchalter. Of the four, only Capone, "Public Enemy No. 1," died of natural causes (brain hemorrhage). Yale and Masseria died in a hail of bullets, and Lepke died in New York's electric chair in 1944 (the only major racketeer ever to be executed).

Other headlined members of the hit parade in the 30's included (10) Jack "Legs" Diamond, (11) Arthur "Dutch Schultz" Flegenheimer, (12) John Torrio, "Public Enemy No. 2," and (13) Benjamin "Bugsy" Siegel.

14 **15**

(14) Gay Orlova, a chorus girl in Earl Carroll's *Vanities,* and Luciano's mistress during his heyday in the mid-30's. She, too, was subsequently deported. (15) Polly Adler, New York's infamous madam, and good friend of Luciano. "He was always considerate of the girls and maids," she said. (16) Jimmy Hines, the best-connected politician in town, and the Tammany-Luciano connection controlled the police and the courts...for a while. (17) Abraham "Bo" Weinberg and "Dixie" Davis,

18 **19**

16   **17**

right-hand men to "Dutch" Schultz. "Bo" pulled the trigger, and "Dixie" fixed any legal troubles. "Bo" later disappeared while swimming in a cement overcoat. (18) Irving "Waxey Gordon" Wexler, bootlegging and blackmarket specialist. (19) Joe (Doto) Adonis, New York gambling czar, later kicked out of U.S. and exiled from Italy. (20) Meyer "The Brains" Lansky, the only non-Italian Mafia leader, a financial wizard. (21) Don Vitone "Vito" Genovese, second only to Luciano as an underworld power.

20   **21**

(22) Sicilian-born Joseph Profaci, Brooklyn crimelord. (23) Joseph Valachi, the first to break the Cosa Nostra oath of silence. (24) Joseph "Joe Bananas" Bonanno, top New York Mafioso and expert at disappearing. (25) Carlo "Boss of Bosses" Gambino, described as the real-life Godfather.

(26) William (Willie Moore) Moretti. Before testifying to Senate investigators in December, 1950. (27) After: October, 1951, shot dead in a New Jersey restaurant. Mafia historians credit a Genovese order for the rubout.

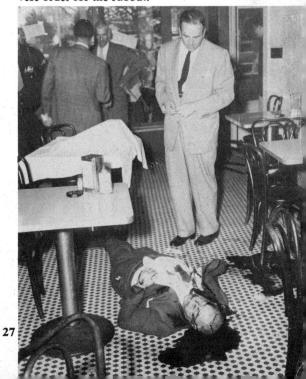

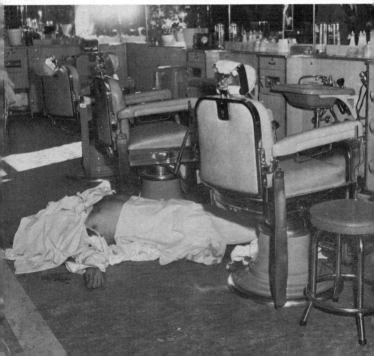

(28) Albert "the Executioner" Anastasia. Before: as he is about to testify before a New York crime commission in late 1952. (29) Anastasia's body after assassination in a Manhattan barber shop, October, 1957. Again, Genovese is reputed to have given the hit order.

(30) Frank (Francesco Castiglia) Costello, a Luciano confidant and dapper Mafia leader while Genovese was in exile. On May 3, 1957, while entering his apartment building, he managed to survive an assassination attempt with only a scalp wound. (31) Vincent L. "the Chin" Gigante. The Genovese hitman who bungled the Costello job.

30   **31**

Luciano and the law, worlds apart but never out of sight. (32) Awaiting a hearing in New York. (33) June, 1936, Luciano is sentenced to Sing Sing. (34) March, 1947, Luciano is asked to leave Cuba, once again exiled to his native Italy.

(35) 1951. Luciano, in Italy, finds himself still a headlined crime figure. (36) Luciano and his good "friend," Sal Vizzini, who later divulged his mission as an undercover narcotics agent for the U.S. government. (37) Lucky and his pet dog, after Naples authorities tag him as a "social menace." (38) 1955. Lucky in business as a distributor of surgical instruments and equipment in Italy. A far cry from his New York days in Little Italy.

(39) Luciano and his lady of Rome, Igea Lissoni, a former ballerina. "She knocked me out the minute I saw her." Marriage was rumored but Lucky never made it to the altar. (40) Igea as she awaits word of Lucky's dispute with Rome police, and possible banishment to Sicily. (41) 1956. Lucky, still Naples' local celebrity, and still pulling underworld strings in the U.S. (42) Shortly after this gay party in Rome Lucky learned that his Igea was dying of cancer. He was never the same after her death.

42

(43) Don Calogero Vizzini (no relation to the U.S. narcotics agent) in a rare photograph. He was the head of the Sicilian Mafia and worked with Luciano in the incredible plan to utilize the Sicilian populace in the Allies' WWII invasion of Sicily in July, 1943. (44) Commander Charles R. Haffenden of Naval Intelligence, who verified Luciano's role in the Sicilian invasion. (45) Vincent Barbi, former boxer and actor, and close friend of Luciano. He talked to Lucky just before he left for the airport meeting with producer Martin A. Gosch. (46) Gosch, who claims Luciano died in his arms.

45   46

(47) January 26, 1962. Charles "Lucky" Luciano collapses and dies of a heart attack at Naples' Capodichino Airport. He was 65 years old. (48) The casket bearing Luciano's body is lifted into the family mausoleum in St. John's Cemetery, N.Y. The end of a man, though his controversial legend lives on.

48

Gay had been born in 1914 in Russia, and had fled with her parents to Paris during the Revolution. She first came to the U.S. in 1926, when she was twelve, accompanied by her mother. She went to school in New York, and got a chorus line job when she was sixteen. A Wall Street broker, Theus Muns, who was four times her age, fell for her and became Gay's sugar daddy, as they so delicately put it back then.

In 1932, after a year with Muns, Gay was in Paris as a model and show girl of exquisite beauty. A young French count she met on the Riviera fell in love with her and they planned to be married. His family objected. Gay lived with him for a year but he could not marry her for his allowance would be cut off. She returned to New York in 1934, on a temporary passport, and was hired by Carroll to dance in his show, *Murder at the Vanities*. And Gay picked up her relationship with Muns.

Unfortunately, Muns was married and Gay needed a husband to remain in America. She was discussing her problem in the theater one night when a young man, Edward Finn, a ten-dollar-a-week usher in the second balcony, expressed his sympathy. Gay became friendly with Finn. One day he announced that he couldn't live on his salary and had decided to go to Texas "where I can make some real money." Gay said: "Why do that? Stay here and marry me. I have rich friends who will support you. That way I can stay in the country and you can stay in New York."

They eloped and were married on March 1, 1934. Earl Carroll sent Gay a congratulatory telegram: "Why, at least, didn't you marry an usher in the first balcony?" Gay left Eddie an hour after the ceremony and the marriage was annulled three weeks later. But she didn't bother telling Immigration about the annulment and was permitted to remain in the country as a citizen.

Earl Carroll had just built the Palm Island Casino, in Florida, and Gay performed in the opening show in the late autumn of 1934. Luciano was there. He, Costello, and several others were guests of Ralph Capone in the house that Al Capone had bought on Palm Island several years before. "Some of the best times I ever had," Luciano would later say, "was when me and Costello would go out fishin' on Al Capone's yacht." But now, in 1934, Al was in prison for income tax evasion and his brother was the host. On opening night they all went over to the Casino, and Charlie met Gay. When the show closed and she returned to New York at the end of the year, her old stockbroker friend leased an apartment for her on East Fifty-Seventh Street and paid the rent for two years in advance. But he didn't get too much for his generosity; Gay was now Luciano's girlfriend and they were seen together a great deal, in the more discreet clubs.

Lee Mortimer, a newspaper columnist, later said that in May, 1935 he was having lunch in Dave's Blue Room on Seventh Avenue, one of Charlie's favorite dining spots, when Gay came in alone. She sat at Mortimer's table. He asked her: "How can you go for that gorilla, Luciano? Muns can buy and sell him twice over." Gay replied: "I love Charlie because he's so sinister."

Though his romance was going well, Charlie had some troubles in other areas. His anonymity was being ripped away from him. In later years he would insist that all his problems flowed from a single mistake—he had become a political activist. His involvement in politics, he insisted, had been for altruistic reasons. As he explained to several friends:

"I never should of bothered with politics. It was the worst mistake I ever made. The funny thing is I got into politics because I wanted to help my people, who were being screwed out of jobs and power. The Irish had it all and the wouldn't let the Italians in."

Charlie's altruistic motives appear to be an afterthought, so far as the record discloses. Luciano involved himself in Tammany Hall to gain protection for his business enterprises. Perhaps he did feel, when he replaced Perry with Marinelli, that a secondary benefit would be

124

to bring greater Italian representation in Tammany. But his motives were always highly personal: Buy a politician for security.

The machinations within Tammany, the strings pulled by Luciano to bring more of his men into power, need not concern us here. The result of those machinations are important.

Fiorello LaGuardia was Italian. He had come up through the Republican Party ranks, and had been assisted by some of Luciano's Mafia associates in East Harlem, but he was not as reliable as Jimmy Hines was. LaGuardia, Charlie often said, "is a snowflake with crazy ideas he calls morals."

The Republican LaGuardia entered the Democratic primary in 1932, hoping to win two-party endorsement in his campaign for the U.S. Congress. This was the Roosevelt landslide year, and though very popular in his district, LaGuardia knew he could be beaten without Tammany backing. All of the Democrats were in favor of endorsing LaGuardia, mostly because the Republicans had raised the cry of corruption in Tammany's New York and, under Republican President Hoover, an assistant U.S. Attorney named Tom Dewey had actually convicted a few racketeers. Tammany leaders felt if they could control LaGuardia by making him obligated to them for their support, they'd have one less reformer to worry about.

Jimmy Hines disagreed, because Luciano didn't trust LaGuardia. Hines overcame the views of all the Tammany leaders, and LaGuardia failed to get the endorsement. He lost the election, and he was furious. He knew—everyone in politics knew, although the public didn't—that Charlie Luciano had ruined his chance for the Congress. LaGuardia vowed revenge.

In the 1933 Mayorality election, LaGuardia ran as a fusion candidate—a combination of Republicans and reformers within the Democratic Party. Luciano and his men did all they could to defeat him, sending "floaters" to the polls to vote fifty and a hundred times. But La-Guardia was a street politician, wise to the ways in which elections are stolen, and he rushed around personally to challenge the floaters. At one election place he began to punch a Luciano goon and raise hell about fraud. Luciano received word and raced to the scene. LaGuardia tried to punch him, but police came between them and escorted Luciano away. LaGuardia promised to "get" him and shouted: "I'll see you in prison."

LaGuardia won the election and took office in January, 1934. One of his earliest acts was to publicly denounce Luciano as "Public Enemy Number One," and then to sally forth from City Hall periodically to lead raids on slot machines owned by the Luciano-Costello partnership. At least once a week there were photos in the newspapers showing LaGuardia personally smashing slot machines with a fire axe, or dumping them from a tug into the harbor. The Little Flower, as the Mayor was called, became the most popular and earthy crusader in the city's history.

Luciano was annoyed, but he could still laugh about it: "The Little Flower's got so many bees buzzin' around him that he's going nuts." Charlie wasn't too concerned about LaGuardia's antics because they had no real effect on the mob's operations. Although the Mayor was now publicly antiracketeer, Luciano through Jimmy Hines was in control of police and courts. Most important, the same election that brought LaGuardia to City Hall put William Copeland Dodge into the District Attorney's office. Dodge was a handmaiden of them all. It was disclosed years later that Dodge had been supported in his election campaign for District Attorney with $35,000 political contributions from Dutch Schultz, about $100,000 from the Luciano group, and a separate $30,000 from Lepke, who wanted extra protection for his garment center activities.

With Dodge in office, Jimmy Hines was usually able to kill any prosecution, even murder. Should Hines be unable to halt an investigation by police and have the evidence destroyed, then District Attorney Dodge could be persuaded to neglect to bring to the grand jury the best evidence found by police. The jurymen, lacking the evidence, would invariably vote not to indict.

Charlie's major concern, in those first few months in 1934 that LaGuardia was rampaging around town with his slot-machine-busting squad, was how to best effect the confiscation of Dutch Schultz's enormous policy bank in Harlem. Schultz had now been in hiding for a year, not wishing to go to trial on the federal income tax indictment which young crusader Tom Dewey had brought against him. Dewey could have been a problem to Luciano and to all men of the rackets, for he not only got the indictment against Schultz but he had also successfully prosecuted bootlegger Waxey Gordon and sent him to prison for 10 years. But immediately after getting the Gordon conviction Dewey resigned from the New York office of the U.S. Attorney's staff, an office which he headed. That resignation, at the end of 1933, was by request—President Roosevelt, bowing to the wishes of Hines' Tammany Hall, agreed that the position should be held by a good party man. He dumped Dewey and appointed in his place a lawyer who would later represent Luciano.

Some time in the summer of 1934, with Schultz still in hiding, Luciano began to move into the Dutchman's policy operations. Charlie held a meeting with Bo Weinberg, who was in charge of the central policy bank, and persuaded Weinberg to place several Luciano men inside the policy business in Harlem. Informers in later investigations say that Weinberg had agreed with Luciano's assessment of the situation: The Dutchman must eventually surrender, and he is certain to be imprisoned for many years; rather than have others try to shoot their way into the policy bank, which would mean Weinberg's death, why doesn't Weinberg join a strong organization, the Luciano syndicate, and bring the Schultz policy bank along with him? What he had in mind, Luciano said, was to quietly place some of his men into the business so that they could learn it all. Schultz, in hiding, would continue to receive his profits and would never learn that Weinberg was making a deal for his own future. Then, after Schultz went to prison, Weinberg would be in charge of the policy business for the Luciano organization.

Weinberg saw the logic in that very peaceful approach, and he became Luciano's man. But before Weinberg could implement the plan, informers continued, Dutch Schultz heard rumors of some kind of sellout. One day, while bringing Schultz his money, Weinberg vanished. The informers say Schultz personally murdered him and had his body dumped into the Hudson River in a large oildrum filled with cement.

Luciano was forced to delay his scheme to gain control of the policy bank by another unforeseen event in Schultz's unusually fortuitous career. Schultz's lawyers, with Jimmy Hines working behind the scenes, informed President Roosevelt's Attorney General, Homer Cummings, that the Dutchman was ready to surrender and stand trial. But there was one condition: Dutch must be guaranteed that the trial would be held in upstate New York rather than in the city, where his name and exploits had made headlines. Cummings agreed. (Whether Roosevelt was personally involved in the decision will never be known; historians don't pay much attention to criminal influence on politicians, certainly not Presidents. But Hines' ability to influence the Attorney General was based for the most part on Tammany's support of Roosevelt in the 1932 nominating convention.) Schultz surrendered in November, 1934, and went on trial in upstate Syracuse.

Schultz moved to that city a month before the trial began, and he established a reputation as a big contributor to local charities and a very sociable fellow in the city's hotels. Among those who socialized with him were Democratic politicians and other local notables. All of his activities were publicized in the local papers, Schultz being treated in such a favorable light that the newspaper readers, from whom his jury would be drawn, understood that he was not such a bad fellow after all. After a two week trial, the jury was unable to agree on a verdict. Dutch was promptly retried in Malone, New York, and his propaganda machine went through the same paces. Schultz was acquitted. "Justice always wins," he said, with not the hint of a smile.

Before Schultz could return to New York, Mayor LaGuardia warned that if he set foot inside the city limits he would be jailed and "mussed up." LaGuardia made such a furious noise, in the newspapers, that Schultz moved to Connecticut to wait for things to quiet down. They didn't, however. Urged on by LaGuardia and the newspapers which found he made marvelous copy, the U.S. Attorney General announced that files in Schultz's case would be turned over to state tax authorities for possible prosecution. And the U.S. Attorney in New York announced that one count in the federal indictment had been held back, and Schultz would be brought to trial in New York City. Luciano, reading it all with much interest, began to hope that perhaps LaGuardia was inadvertently helping him take over Schultz's policy business.

But then, in 1935, the system of protection that Hines had so carefully woven for the benefit of Schultz, Luciano, Costello and all the rest, began to unravel.

The March grand jury had been looking into the Harlem policy business, unaware that it had been forged into one large combination by Schultz and his guns. For two months the jurymen questioned minor policy workers, who didn't tell them much. And the jury began to feel very strongly that District Attorney Dodge's assistants were not asking the proper questions and did not seem all that anxious to inquire about the higher-ups in the policy business. It was clear to the jury that Dodge's office was protecting someone. One day in May an Assistant District Attorney, in questioning a witness who appeared to be friendly and could prove helpful if encouraged, began to bait the witness. The prosecutor behaved so boorishly that the jury criticized him. He shouted: "I'll withdraw if you think you can handle it any better."

The jurymen accepted the challenge, and they became a runaway grand jury—one of those rare bodies that think for themselves and throw off the absolute control of the District Attorney. The grand jury at once demanded that Dodge appoint a special prosecutor from a list of six names it supplied. Dodge struck off all the names on the list, particularly the first one, Tom Dewey, who was now in private practice.

Immediately, the newspapers jumped into the argument and they began to champion Dewey as the man who could "smash the rackets." Editorial writers hinted quite broadly that Dodge was in the employ of the mob. Dodge ignored the press and suggested his own candidate as special prosecuor. The jury rejected him. Finally, Governor Lehman was forced into it by the publicity and agreed to use his executive powers to appoint a special prosecutor. He submitted to the grand jury a list of four names. Dewey's was not on it. The jury declined the four and demanded the appointment of Dewey. After a barrage of quite pointed editorials, the governor was forced to appoint Dewey, and he was sworn in on June 28, 1935. He was 33 years old but looked so much younger that he grew a mustache to give his newspaper photos a little dignity.

Dewey decided his first victim would be Dutch Schultz, who had perverted justice by escaping the income tax case that Dewey himself had put together in 1932, when he was an assistant federal prosecutor. Using as his starting point the grand jury's aborted investigation into policy, Dewey began to dig very deeply into the Schultz policy bank. Surprisingly, he convinced some members of the ring that they would be safe from retribution, that they were not dealing with a man like Dodge, who leaked information to the underworld so that witnesses could be terrorized or killed. And some of them began to talk.

Dutch Schultz, and practically all the gangster-businessmen in New York, grew panicky. Dewey's investigation would have to be stopped. If necessary, Dewey would have to be murdered.

That was considered quite seriously, according to a number of informers. The men who later detailed the exploits of Murder, Inc., the band of killers that was being formalized around this time as the enforcement arm for all members of the national syndicate, and which was commanded by Lepke and Albert Anastasia, told investigators that several meetings were held to discuss Dewey's murder.

The demand for Dewey's death came first from Schultz, who was most immediately affected by the investigation. Schultz was required to discuss Dewey's murder with all the members of the cartel, the informers said, so he convened a meeting of the board. One night in September, 1935, Schultz met with Luciano, Costello, Lepke, Lansky and Siegel, and about a dozen others. The sole item on the agenda was Dewey's murder. Lepke and Lansky were firmly against it, the informers said. Luciano was noncommital, "I want to think it over carefully." Schultz shouted and raved and demanded an immediate vote. Then Lepke came up with a suggestion: "Let's see how tough it's going to be to take Dewey. We get Albert and his boys to stake him out for a few days, see if it's even possible to get a crack at him. Then we meet in a week to hear their report and decide."

Schultz agreed. Albert Anastasia, operational director of the syndicate's new death squad, ordered one of his less offensive-looking gunmen to place Dewey under surveillance. Someone came up with the idea of borrowing a baby and a carriage, and posing as a proud parent walking his infant in front of Dewey's Riverside Drive apartment house. For four mornings this man strolled his "baby," watching as Dewey emerged from his building and followed the same routine—he walked to a drugstore up the street to make some phone calls while two detectives who were his bodyguards waited outside, then after about ten minutes on the phone he got into his car for the ride to his office downtown.

Anastasia's men reported that Dewey could easily be killed. The man with the baby could go into the drugstore before Dewey arrived, and pretend to be selecting from the magazine rack. When Dewey went into the phone booth the gunman could shoot him with a silencer-equipped weapon, kill the druggist so there would be no alarm, then casually stroll out past the bodyguards. It would take the detectives fifteen minutes to realize something was amiss, and by then the killer would have climbed into a waiting car with the baby and be miles away.

The report was presented by Anastasia at the meeting a week later, the informers said. Schultz was ecstatic. "That's settled then," he reportedly said. Luciano and Lepke said it was most certainly not settled. They had all been thinking it over carefully, in the past week, and had concluded that murdering Dewey would create so much official "heat" that business would be curtailed and perhaps ruined. "Kill Dewey and you get ten guys worse than him goin' after you," Lepke said. "Goin' after every guy across the country, and ruining everything." Rather than kill Dewey, Luciano said, they would make certain that all witnesses were killed or bought off.

After a great deal of argument by Dutch, a vote was taken and the murder proposal disapproved. Schultz was livid. "I still say he oughtta be hit," he shouted. "And if nobody else is gonna do it, I'm gonna hit him myself."

The meeting broke up. Over the next several days Schultz remained in New York, despite the tax indictment against him, and he tried to convince others to change their vote. He cornered every syndicate leader he could find, begging each to see things his way. Joe Valachi, a member of Luciano's Mafia family, testified that he went into an Italian restaurant off Times Square one night. Schultz was just rising from a table in the back, at which Luciano was dining. After Schultz left and Charlie finished his meal, he invited Valachi to join his table. Someone in the little group mentioned Schultz and Luciano said: "All the Dutchman can talk about is Tom Dewey this and Tom Dewey that."

Schultz's mania gave Luciano the excuse he needed to confiscate the uptown policy business. Schultz could now be considered an outlaw, a man who defied the wishes of the syndicate by insisting that he was going to murder Dewey in spite of the vote against him. And the only solution to an outlaw problem was to kill the outlaw. With Schultz dead, Charlie knew, there would be no murder of Dewey and no disruption of business from the ensuing public outcry, and Luciano could then rip off Schultz's policy operation.

It was around this time, Valachi said, that he heard from the underboss of the family, Vito Genovese, that Schultz was to be killed on sight. But Genovese was always rather hot-headed and that order was rescinded and three members of Murder, Inc., were specifically given the contract. The three gunmen were Jews. As Valachi pointed out to his biographer, Pete Maas, "Charlie Lucky figured it was best all around that the Dutchman's own kind took care of him."

Schultz was sitting in a sleazy restaurant in Newark, New Jersey, near the hotel in which he'd been living, on the night of October 23, 1935. Two gunmen walked in while a third sat behind the wheel of their car. They shot Dutch Schultz and three of his aides, including the gang's accountant who was murdered as he ran the policy bank's figures through his adding machine. Schultz did not immediately die, however. He lived, in a semicoma for about twenty hours. Part of that time a police stenographer sat by his hospital bed and made a transcript of Schultz's delirious ramblings. Detectives threw questions at Schultz. A part of that questioning reads:

Q. Who shot you?
A. The boss himself?

Q. He did?

A. Yes, I don't know.

Q. What did he shoot you for?

A. I should meet him, boss. Did you hear him meet me? An appointment, appeal stuck.

That's the way it went, for hours. Schultz was apparently naming "the boss himself" as his killer, but then pulling back as he realized police were questioning him. But police and the newspapers said "the boss" might possibly be Luciano.

The killings in the Newark restaurant, and the shooting of a couple of Schultz men in Manhattan, brought terror to everyone associated with Schultz. The moment Dixie Davis heard of the killings he called his girl friend, chorus girl Hope Dare, and ordered her to leave town because "we don't know who's going to get it next. It could be you and it could be me." But, instead of trying to have Davis and his lady killed, Luciano protected them.

"It was one of his cars that rushed me out of town," Hope later said. "He sent a couple of strongarm men to protect me. I didn't know who they were at the time, nor did I know why I was getting the break."

Luciano wasn't being gallant. He needed Dixie Davis because Dixie knew more about the workings of Schultz's policy bank, and the police and political payoffs that were being made, than any man around. He could not kill Dixie. Nor could he permit the lawyer to fall into Special Prosecutor Dewey's hands, for he was certain Davis was a coward who would tell Dewey everything to save himself. So, he helped Davis and Hope to hide out, in various friendly homes around the country. They were not found for three years. By then Luciano was in prison serving what was in effect a life sentence.

11

The arrest, trial, and conviction of Charlie Luciano on charges that he was the organizer and prime beneficiary of a compulsory prostitution ring presents one of the more startling examples of the failure of investigative journalists to dig for the truth. In all the books written about Luciano, in most books about Mafia and organized crime, the official version of how Tom Dewey "got" Luciano has always been accepted as divine truth.

This is the version that has seldom been questioned:

Shortly after Dewey became special prosecutor he heard reports about extortion and "organization" among the city's scores of madams and thousands of prostitutes working for them. Organization had been possible, Dewey was told, because of the structure of the whore's business. Every madam required a constant turnover in prostitutes so that her customers would have fresh faces and bodies from which to choose. To get these girls the madams depended upon bookers, who functioned like actors' booking agents. In the past, in New York, booking had always been rather haphazard. But in 1932 four men had organized it all by making the bookers join a "union" from which the gangsters took most of the profits. Bookers, prostitutes, and madams were forced to share their income with the gangsters. The madams were discouraged, by force, from using girls who did not belong to one of the ring's bookers. In return, everyone received guarantees of bail bonds, legal assistance, and political influence.

That ring had been broken up with the arrest of the

four leaders the year before Dewey became special prosecutor, but it seemed that other mobsters had simply stepped into their shoes. Dewey assigned several investigators to look into these reports, then turned to other matters.

After a few months, the official version goes, Dewey was informed that the new leaders of the prostitution racket were evidently Thomas the Bull Pennochio, Little Davey Betillo, and two other men. Dewey decided to explore this particular racket a little further, by swooping down on all the major bordellos in the city, bringing in the prostitutes and madams, and persuading them to talk in Dewey's "singing school." This is described by the chroniclers of Dewey's career as a secret suite of rooms in which the most modern psychological techniques (but never the unethical "third degree," said Dewey) were employed to make potential witnesses feel safe, to make them believe that Dewey was not like any other prosecutor in the city's history (untrustworthy), and to persuade them that there was more danger in being hit with long prison sentences if they remained silent than there could ever be from confessing. Dewey said he always stressed that the "little people" would not be prosecuted (unless they didn't cooperate), for he was more interested in the higher-ups.

In the early evening of February 1, 1936, a special detail of handpicked plainclothesmen were given sealed envelopes with an address on the outside and orders not to open them and read the instructions inside until 8:55 that night. In this way, Dewey hoped to frustrate those police who were paid for providing information about a raid before it could take place. At precisely nine that evening police raided forty-one brothels in Manhattan and Brooklyn. They arrested one hundred women and seventeen men, among them Pennochio, Betillo, Jimmy Frederico who was known as Jimmy Fredericks, and Abe Wahrman. These four were believed in command of the prostitution racket.

Now, Dewey's official version continues, the little people

in the business were taken to the "singing school" in the Woolworth Building, many blocks from the offices of the regular prosecutor, Dodge, who was so obviously corrupt. All of them, madams, whores, and bookers, were held in high bail as material witnesses so that the ring's bondsmen and lawyers could not afford to free them. Dewey's men questioned them relentlessly, with Dewey taking part in some of the interrogations. For more than a week, however, not one of them would talk about the higher-ups in the racket. As Sid Feder expressed the official tale in *The Luciano Story:* "Something seemed to be sealing the prisoners' lips. Something deadly, like fear."

But then, somehow, one man decided to strike a blow for morality. His name was Dave Miller, who admittedly had never done a moral thing in his life. Miller had been a police constable in Pittsburgh for five years. The job didn't pay much but Miller made a good bit on the side by extorting money from speakeasies and whorehouses. His wife gave him three children, and they had been able to buy a little house from his extralegal income. His ultimate downfall came, Miller said, when he got mixed up in prostitution. It was all Ruth's fault, his wife was to blame because she didn't understand him. One day she walked out on him in the midst of a quarrel. His reaction was to go out and bring home a prostitute. The girl was still there when Ruth Miller came home the next day. After a somewhat frenetic scene both women stayed on in the house, the girl earning her keep by bringing men home. Miller didn't say it, but investigators learned his wife also contributed by turning a trick occasionally. Soon the neighbors complained, and the Millers were arrested for keeping a whorehouse. Miller lost his job as an officer of the law.

Well, with a wife and three kids to support, Miller said he decided to come to New York and try to make an honest living.

They arrived in 1929 and took an apartment in Brooklyn, and Miller began to peddle dresses from door to door. Amazingly, it somehow transpired that some of Miller's growing circle of customers were prostitutes. He didn't really want to do it, but he met a man named Harry Chicago who persuaded him to open a whorehouse on a partnership deal. Ruth Miller became the madam. Soon they had a string of ten houses. Eventually the partnership broke up, and Dave was in business for himself. He was growing wealthy, and was quite pleased with his good fortune when disaster struck one day in July, 1933.

Several men came to him and said a combination was being formed, and he'd better join up. Dave said he wanted nothing to do with it. They threatened him, beat him, fired several shots at him one night. So he packed up and moved his family to California. By March, 1935, he was almost broke, so he returned to New York and decided to become a booker since prostitution was the only business he knew. He checked with friends, and was told he would have to get the approval of "the boys." He was sent to see Jimmy Fredericks, who brought him to see Little Davey Betillo, Jimmy's boss. Betillo had been out in Chicago for five years, where he gained a fearsome reputation as one of Capone's gunmen. Nobody played games with Davey, so Miller joined the combination. He had to pay them fifty dollars a week, and he would have to get every girl he booked to pay in ten dollars a week. After being in the combination for a while, he met Tommy the Bull and the ground rules were changed. From now on, he was told, he would have to turn over every penny and he'd be given a salary of $50 a week. He did not protest, for he knew how to steal from his bosses and make a decent living. Which he was doing until Dewey's men arrested him.

Miller told investigators all this, in very great detail. But whenever he was asked about the bigshots behind the minor figures he had named, he said he didn't know anything about bigshots. Fear sealed his lips, no doubt. But Dewey's assistants were tenacious, and they kept after Miller. One day Miller finally got religion, the tale goes, and when he was once more asked if he knew of any "bigger men" behind Pennochio and the others he suddenly told the truth. He had once been talking to Danny Brooks, he said. Danny was a booker who did some of the ring's accounting work. And out of the blue he told Miller: "Don't let it leak—Charlie Lucky gives the O.K. to run."

And that, said Mr. Dewey, is the first time he and his investigators ever had the faintest inkling that a man like Luciano was the organizer of every whore in the city, sucking riches out of the sweat of their toil, etc. and etc.

The story, so deftly promoted by Dewey and repeated without question for forty years, has it that as soon as Dave Miller opened the door a little he was questioned further and gave another bit of information linking Charlie Luciano to the vice racket. He was taken to a meeting in a Mulberry Street coffee house, he said, where there was a discussion about some problems with another booker. And, during those talks, Jimmy Fredericks told him that Charlie Lucky will take care of all problems.

Armed with that break in the wall of silence, Dewey and his aides now began to employ their brilliant psychological techniques on the women, the prostitutes and the madams. They cajoled, they promised, but most especially they treated their prisoners like ladies: "The girls were being mollified, treated with grave courtesy, called 'Miss,' having chairs, coffee, sandwiches and lights for their cigarettes tendered them," as one of the Dewey-approved stories put it.

And the whores and madams, so pleased were they that Dewey's men were treating them with respect, began to talk. One madam said she was told by Jimmy Fredericks that "Lucky is the big guy behind the combination." Danny Brooks, trapped by Miller's confession, broke down and said he'd also been told by Fredericks that "Charlie Lucky is the boss." And so many more.

But all of their stories were hearsay evidence. What was needed was direct testimony tying Luciano into the racket. And, suddenly, to Dewey's great joy and surprise, two prostitutes gave him the kind of evidence that could bring Charlie to trial and send him to prison.

The first, Cokey Flo Brown, said she had been Jimmy Fredericks' girlfriend. While dining with Jimmy one evening they ran into Luciano. The two men began to discuss a madam who refused to pay up. Luciano said: "You can't talk to them. They're stubborn. Get after them. Step on them." Under further questioning Cokey Flo was able to remember many more meetings with Charlie, and she heard him giving orders and acting like the big boss he so obviously was.

The second prostitute, Nancy Presser, began to talk for Dewey because, the tale goes, she realized she now had an opportunity "to get out of the racket and begin a new life." And she said, quite haughtily, that she knew much more about Luciano's role in the racket than Cokey Flo because she, Nancy, had spent much time with Charlie—she had been his mistress for six months. Luciano discussed with her, personally, the vice racket he was running, and he often complained that he wasn't getting enough money from the madams and bookers. She heard him giving orders to his troops. She knew his every secret—the first few times they were together in Charlie's suite he didn't make love to her because "Lucky just couldn't get it up."

With all this evidence, Dewey had Luciano indicted by a grand jury. All the whores and the others testified against him at a trial, and he and his men were convicted and sent to prison. Luciano was given a sentence of thirty to fifty years. It was a virtual life term, because even if he were to be paroled after serving the minimum of thirty years, he would be almost seventy years old, and his racket days most surely would be over.

The truth about the conviction of Charlie Luciano as the nation's biggest whoremaster is something entirely different from the accepted version. I have pieced together the reality behind the fable from several sources, including the trial record in the Luciano case and, especially, several long neglected books and magazine articles which were written with Dewey's full cooperation and approval. Dewey was running as a candidate for District Attorney, an office he wanted to hold in his own right rather than as a specially appointed prosecutor. He was planning to run for governor the following year, and he needed all the public relations help he could get. He sat for long interviews with the writers, opened his files to them, had final editorial approval over their manuscripts; those books and articles are, in effect, Dewey's own personal story.

That story discloses something rather distorted about the very beginning of the fable that most writers accept as truth. Rather than suddenly learning that Luciano was a master whoremonger when Dave Miller confessed long after the vice investigation had begun, Tom Dewey had decided many months before the first hint of an organization had reached his ears that the only way to get Luciano was to link him with some racket, any racket, in which some of his acquaintances might be involved.

In the Dewey-approved series of articles in the *Saturday Evening Post,* published through several issues in late 1937, Dewey himself told the writer, Forrest Davis, that he had decided to break Charlie Luciano on the night of October 23, 1935, when he learned that Dutch Schultz had been shot and was dying. Mayor LaGuardia and the police had promptly said that Schultz was shot on the orders of nine racketeers who stood to gain by his death. Among them was Luciano. The Mayor conferred with Dewey the next day and said: "I want you to go after that bum, Luciano." The article picks it up from there:

"Dewey's men narrowed (LaGuardia's list) down. Privately, they listed four 'big fellows' . . ." At the head of the list was Luciano. "Schultz had become a small shot when he was rubbed out," the article continued. "Luciano was four times as potent. He was scarcely known to a public which still thought of the Dutchman in big numbers.

"Taking no official notice of the Dutchman's demise,

Dewey made ready for his march into the underworld."

Thus, LaGuardia was finally able to bring an attack on Luciano for opposing him in two election campaigns.

Within a few weeks after Schultz was murdered, Dewey's men began to hear reports that Pennochio was a major figure in the organized prostitution racket. Pennochio was said to have been involved with Joe (the Boss) Masseria in bootlegging; Luciano had been involved with Joe the Boss; therefore, Tommy and Charlie were connected. (No one at this time believed in the existence of Mafia, or of a group of syndicates working in close collaboration; the official thinking was that each gang was a separate entity, working almost in a vacuum and usually making contact when there was a need to shoot it out.)

Now, according to his own personal story (I can't stress that too strongly), Dewey reasoned it all out. He was "morally certain" Luciano was a very big man in all the rackets, so big that he seemed to be "a phantom" behind the scenes. Therefore it seemed likely that Luciano was boss of every illicit enterprise in New York. As Dewey's writer expressed it:

"It was from the fact of Luciano's concealed underworld eminence that Dewey took his departure. He added to what he knew, a hunch. He reasoned this way: If a mob has taken over the unorganized business of vice, creating a syndicate, it must have the authority and patronage of a powerful mob chief; that mob chief must be Luciano, because Lucky is so big that he couldn't brook a rival in control of such underworld territory."

Dewey is quoted as reasoning: "A mob leader cannot control organized crime in a community unless he controls it all, either directly or through alliances where he holds the decisive power and is, in effect, the boss. A mobster's ascendancy and a racket alike rest on the respect and the fear of the exploited. If a racketeer of Luciano's size permitted another racketeer to take over vice, which is at the center of the underworld(!), he would be allowing his

142

power to be whittled away by so much. It might undermine him entirely. A successful rival attracts subordinates and retainers, as well as the minor, semiautonomous racketeers, and weakens the fear which is a top racketeer's stock in trade."

And so, acting on a hunch, and on his very ingenuous reasoning, Dewey set out to prove that Luciano was the head of the vice racket, that "center of the underworld."

Further evidence that Dewey was seeking to dig up something against Luciano long before Miller began to talk comes from Dan Danforth, an undercover agent for Dewey. In his book, *The DA's Man,* Danforth says he applied for a job with Dewey and "one day in the fall of 1935" he was personally interviewed by the special prosecutor. After his background had been thoroughly checked, he was hired. Then, after working a few weeks as a process server, Danforth says he was called into the office of Murray Gurfein, one of Dewey's chief assistants. This was still in autumn, 1935.

"Well, Dan," Gurfein said. "We have an assignment here. Have you ever heard the name Luciano?"

"Vaguely," Danforth said. "I have no knowledge of who or what he is."

Danforth writes: "Gurfein then went on to sketch Dewey's keen interest in Charles 'Lucky' Luciano, who, at the time, was undisputed king of most of New York's rackets."

In 1935, then, Dewey had a "keen interest" in Luciano and had been secretly investigating him, Danforth says. Danforth was then assigned to make contact with Davey Betillo and Tommy Pennochio, by posing as a big brothel-keeper from Boston who wanted to open a few houses in New York, "and to connect, if possible, these men with Luciano." Danforth failed to even meet Luciano, although he became quite close to Betillo, Pennochio, and others. But there was never a sign of Luciano. He was called off the investigation after a couple of months.

In the meantime, Dewey was laying the groundwork for his attack on Luciano. Around the time Schultz was killed and Dewey decided to go after Luciano, he quietly asked the state legislature to pass a new law which would, in effect, make it legal to try a man against whom there was little evidence, and convict him by joining his trial with the trial of his "associates" against whom there was much evidence. The legislation, passed early in 1936, was called the "Dewey Law" for a time, then became know as the "Luciano Law" after its most famous victim.

And now, armed with a theory, and a very questionable conspiracy law, Dewey ordered the roundup of February first, in which the prostitutes and others in the business were arrested. This mass arrest came "before his hunch (that Charlie was boss) was confirmed," the writer of his approved story says.

So much for the fable that Dewey had no inkling Luciano was head of a vice empire until Dave Miller began to talk. The truth is that the entire thrust of the investigation was, from the very start, aimed at sending Luciano to prison.

The second step in the creation of that fable concerns Dewey's "singing school." Dewey, it is claimed, made clear to all the minor figures in the prostitution business that he was after only the "big men" who had organized the racket. His theory was to get the lowest person in the business, the prostitute, to talk about the madam, then persuade the madam to talk about the booker, until the booker was aware that he would be sent to prison as the top man in the pyramid unless he pointed his finger higher up. No force was used, of course, no immoral or illegal persuasion.

A closer look at the techniques employed by Dewey's men is in order here. According to Elmer Irey, the chief tax investigator in the Treasury Department, who commanded tax agents in the cases of Schultz, Gordon, Al Capone, and dozens of other racketeers, and who approved all of Dewey's techniques:

"The only thing wrong with Dewey was his youth . . . he was frightened to death that anybody might accuse him of being a boy on a man's errand. That was the reason for his endless demands for more evidence and still more, past human endurance. He couldn't afford to lose, because a defeat for any other district attorney was just a defeat, but a defeat for a man not yet thirty might well be a career-wrecking catastrophe. Dewey was simply not having his career wrecked."

From Irey, and from many other sources, it becomes very clear that Dewey was a relentless and ambitious man who drove his aides "past human endurance." Many quit, and Dewey was glad to see them go; if they could not give him the evidence he demanded they were of no use to him. And those who remained gave Dewey everything he demanded. Some idea of the techniques that were used can be found in the trial record, some in statements made long after Luciano was sent to prison.

Take David Miller, the hero who—in the accepted fable—first mentioned Charlie's name to a very surprised Mr. Dewey. It has already been seen that Miller was a corrupt cop who pimped simultaneously for his wife and his girl friend, and had come to New York to seek greater self-enrichment.

Miller had been hospitalized for fourteen weeks during the end of 1935 and the beginning of 1936, suffering from a heart attack. During that period his business had been run by his prostitute-wife, Ruth. Only a couple of days after being released from the hospital, Miller and his wife were driving to his doctor's office when they were arrested by Dewey's investigators. Miller felt certain, he said again and again, that he was going to die of a heart attack. He and his wife were in prison. "What's going to happen to our three kids?" he asked himself (by his own admission) as he sat in a jail cell waiting to be questioned. The only chance of saving them all was to tell the prosecutor everything he wanted to know.

Miller, after thinking it out, asked to be taken to Dewey. When an assistant prosecutor came to see him, Miller said he would reveal everything, but only if his wife was released first. Ruth Miller was freed. Then he talked about his troubles with the vice syndicate. He explained how they took away his booking business, shot at him, and ran him out of town. When he returned and agreed to cooperate, he admitted, they put him to work as a fifty-dollar-a-week booker. He gave the investigator all the names; Pennochio, Betillo, Ralph Liguori, and others. He said that's all he knew; there was no mention of Luciano.

Tom Dewey himself now took over the questioning, according to the published article he approved. "Come, Dave, there must have been someone bigger than Betillo, that punk?" Dewey demanded. "I got a bum ticker, Mr. Dewey," Miller pleaded. "Excitement ain't no good for it." Dewey pressed him, "hammering" says the article, at a man afraid that his heart would fail. Finally, Dave Miller said that the "big fellow" was named "Charlie." Nothing else. He did not mention Luciano's name, as the fable has it, neither in Dewey's "singing school" nor during the later trial.

That's not the important point here, for Dewey used hearsay evidence of this kind, repeatedly, to build up in the jurors' minds that "Charlie" was the boss, and the court permitted him to bend the rules of evidence in this fashion. What is more important is that, according to the sworn testimony of many women who were put through the "singing school," Luciano's name was mentioned by investigators again and again *before* any witness made an accusation against him. That name was suggested to all potential witnesses. Everyone knew that Charlie Luciano was the man Dewey was after. Every one of those men and women, each of whom had been arrested dozens of times in the past, knew that to save themselves from long jail sentences—the threat was made repeatedly to each of them—they must furnish Dewey with the "evidence" he demanded—Charlie Luciano as the head of the racket.

Miller is but one example of the tainted evidence presented by Dewey, and of the techniques Dewey employed to persuade witnesses to manufacture evidence for his case. In another such instance, Dewey called the assistant manager of the Barbizon-Plaza Hotel, Frank Brown, to the witness stand. The prosecution expected him to identify several defendants as having visited Luciano's hotel suite. As Dewey began to put Brown through his paces, his case seemed to blow up. Brown said he indeed knew Luciano as a tenant in the hotel, but he could not identify any of the other defendants as visiters.

Dewey was furious. He asked the judge to declare Brown a hostile witness, which was done. Such a declaration permits a prosecutor to cross-examine his own witness as if the man were on trial; more important, it is a subtle device used to persuade the jury, in advance, that the witness is going to lie. Dewey shouted that Brown had "told a different story" when he was being questioned in the prosecutor's office a day earlier, and said he "had identified several photographs of defendants." When Brown was finally able to speak he said:

"I never identified them positively. They tried to force me to identify these men. One of Dewey's men kept telling me, 'You must have seen this one, and this one.' The man persisted in telling me so. He warned me about jail if I didn't tell the truth. There were three or four in the room. They were very insistent about my identifying the pictures.

"When I said I couldn't do it honestly, they threatened me. They hinted that Mr. Dewey was very powerful and could do as he liked."

Dewey later implied that Brown, and others, had been bribed by Luciano's men, or had been threatened with death, which is the only reason Brown testified as he did. That may be so; many witnesses against major racketeers have been bribed, or killed, to prevent them from testifying. But all the evidence available, which shows that almost every one of Dewey's witnesses testified against Luciano because of favors promised or because of threats by Dewey's staff, also makes it almost a certainty that Brown was telling the truth.

12

The trial of Charlie Luciano and nine other men opened on the morning of May 11, 1936, before Justice Philip J. McCook in the County Courthouse, Manhattan. It took two days to select a jury from a special blue-ribbon panel of veniremen. Then Dewey paraded his witnesses to the stand. The first of them testified about the activities of various defendants, but none mentioned Luciano. Then, on the fifth day, David Miller told his story to the jury. He swore the other defendants were actively engaged in the prostitution racket and that two of them had said "Charlie" was the boss. Despite the later accounts of his testimony, Miller never did say it was Charlie Luciano. But Dewey, of course, made it clear there could be only one Charlie, and Judge McCook permitted him to get away with hearsay evidence.

Danny Brooks, the next witness, testified that while working for the vice combination he had been told by Jimmy Fredericks, on two occasions, that "Charlie Lucky is behind this" and was protecting everyone from arrest and prosecution. Danny made a good witness for Dewey. But his testimony is quite suspect. Danny, according to the records in the case, had been serving seven and a half years in Sing Sing for compulsory prostitution, a conviction in the original vice racket case the year before Dewey decided to go after Luciano. Danny had been brought down from prison upstate to Dewey's "singing school," where for seven weeks he insisted he didn't know anything about any new organization because he had been jailed the year before.

During his eighth week as Dewey's material witness, Danny was promised that in return for his "full confession" Dewey would "write the governor and tell him what I did for the people in this case" (the words are Danny's) and ask the governor to grant him parole. Danny Brooks, sensing his opportunity to get out of prison, then came up with his story placing Luciano at the very top of the vice combination.

(Incidentally, that original vice ring in which Danny admitted participating had been broken up by District Attorney William C. Dodge. This man, you'll recall, was elected with the financial assistance of Luciano and others, and he was Jimmy Hines' puppet. Had Luciano been head of the vice racket, as Dewey's witnesses now claimed, then Dodge would never have investigated so deeply that he secured a conviction against several Luciano men; Luciano would have forced Dodge to quash the investigation, as he had done in several other cases. Which brings up another very curious fact. In all the stories approved by Dewey and in the first indictment voted against Luciano, it was said that he became leader of the vice racket only after the original heads of the ring were jailed by Dodge in 1935. Before Luciano's trial began Dewey got his grand jury to bring a second indictment charging Luciano had been the leader of the racket since 1932. Which opens up another can of worms. Did Dodge, perhaps, jail "Luciano's men" in the original ring but permit Charlie to go free? It's unlikely he would have annoyed Luciano by disrupting a racket which Dewey claimed was "at the center of the underworld." But suppose it did happen, suppose Dodge needed a few convictions to satisfy the grand jury or the newspapers, and he stopped just short of the top—Luciano. Then, certainly, Danny Brooks and other witnesses would have known of this. Why didn't Dewey explore this aspect of the case? Dodge was a Democrat, beholden to Tammany. Dewey was a Republican and a reformer. Certainly, if there were evidence that Luciano had been running a prostitution racket since 1932 and Dodge had protected him, Dewey would have brought it out. The only logical explanation is that there was no such evidence—that Luciano was not involved in the first vice ring as all the witnesses seemed to imply he was. With that, Dewey's entire case must fall.)

An even more vital witness was Joe Bendix, who also happened to be serving a prison term. Bendix was in deeper trouble than Danny Brooks. He had been sentenced to fifteen years to life as a fourth felony offender. Dewey put Bendix on the stand and got him to swear that he had given up burglary—his normal profession—and was looking for a job where "the boss" would protect him. Naturally, he thought of Charlie Luciano. He had, you see, known Luciano since 1929, having been introduced to him because both hung out a great deal on Broadway. To quote one of Dewey's approved books, *Ninety Times Guilty,* by Hickman Powell, Bendix said that after the introduction "he often did business with Lucky, meeting him on the sidewalk in front of the drugstore near Forty-Ninth and Seventh Avenue. Lucky, according to Joe, at that period was a very active fence. Besides being a narcotics runner, a bootlegger and all around mobster, Lucky was a fellow who would never turn down a chance to make a quick profit. Joe said that when he had a nice piece of jewelry Lucky was always ready to take it off his hands quick for a fraction of its value. According to Joe, Lucky had an interest in three drugstores around town which he used not only to push dope, but to get rid of stolen perfume and cigarettes."

That, in sum, was the early part of Bendix's testimony. He then swore that when he decided to seek a safe occupation he went to see Jimmy Fredericks, whom he knew as one of "Lucky's boys." He asked Fredericks for a position in the prostitution business, and was told to go that evening to the Villanova Restaurant off Times Square. When Bendix arrived, Fredericks was waiting for him.

"Charlie Lucky will be out in a few minutes," Fredericks told him. "He wants to look you over." Sure enough, Charlie came out of a back room (perhaps he'd been peddling stolen macaroni), and he sat down at their table. And, Bendix swore: "Lucky said that Fredericks talked to him about me. He understood that I wanted a job as a collector in some of these houses of prostitution and he understood that I was a little too high hat for the job, and what's the idea of my looking for that as a job, that it only paid thirty-five or forty dollars a week.

"I said, 'It is better than going back to stealing. I would rather work for forty dollars a week than go out and face the Baumes Law, which I was as a fourth offender.'

"He said, 'If you are willing to work for forty dollars a week, it is O.K. with me. I will tell Little Davie to put you on. You can always meet me here, you can always see me here. I will see you here in a few days.' "

Bendix, under gentle questioning by Dewey, testified that he had returned to the restaurant four or five times, but never did find Luciano. He didn't go to work for the organization because he wasn't certain that he had actually received Luciano's approval. Two weeks after that first meeting he finally saw Luciano. He was told to report to a man in a nearby hotel-whorehouse who would "take care of you," Charlie said. Unfortunately, Bendix testified, he tried for several weeks to see the man Charlie referred him to but could never find him at his hotel, so he never went to work for the mob. About a month later he was arrested on robbery charges and sent to prison.

Dewey knew that Bendix was a barely believable witness; in his summation he told the jury that it faced two choices about Bendix—either the Dewey office was corrupt and coached Bendix to lie, or Bendix knew from his own knowledge about the men involved in this case, the restaurant Luciano used as his vice office, the hotel where Bendix was sent to begin work. The jury, clearly, chose to believe in Dewey's honor.

Yet all the evidence points to "corruption" in Dewey's

152

office—a case against Luciano manufactured from top to bottom. The witness, Joe Bendix, helps prove this quite strongly.

Bendix, by his own later admission in an appeal for parole, would have done anything to get out of his fifteen-year-to-life prison sentence. Three weeks before the raids in which Dewey's men began their drive against Luciano, Joe Bendix had been arrested on burglary charges. Knowing he faced a possible life sentence as a fourth offender, he told Assistant District Attorney Morris Panger that he had information about a $500,000 bond theft, and would become an informer if Panger would get him leniency in his own case. Panger agreed. Bendix told Panger several stories which sent investigators chasing down leads which proved to be valueless, and Bendix sensed that Panger "was growing cold towards me."

Luciano had by now been indicted and Dewey was preparing his case for trial. As he sat in the Tombs, Bendix began considering his fate. And the Luciano case. Bendix then wrote a long series of letters to his wife, Muriel, but he sent some of them by mistake to Panger. Those letters, introduced by Luciano's attorney, make it plain that Bendix had decided to lie in order to get out of a mandatory life sentence. The letters suggested that Muriel go to Dewey's office and tell him that Bendix was willing to talk about his relationship with Luciano. In one of those letters Bendix wrote: "Try to think up some real clever story which will prove of interest to Mr. Ariola (a Dewey assistant), anything to show your willingness to help him. The chances are he may not need it, but it will help nevertheless."

There can be little doubt Bendix invented his story hoping Dewey would help get him out of prison. There is much internal evidence in Bendix's own testimony which brands him a liar. I'll go into only two of these.

One is Bendix's assertion that Luciano was a fence of stolen property and was "peddling dope" in Times Square in 1929. That's plainly absurd. Rothstein was killed in

1928. By the following year Luciano was one of the most important crime figures in the nation, a partner with every major racketeer in the city, known in the Chicago crime fraternity as even more influential in Mafia than Al Capone. Dewey knew this, he said time and again that Luciano had for years been the "phantom" boss behind all racketeers. Yet he never blinked at Bendix's patent lie, and he convinced the jury that Bendix was telling the truth.

The second reason that Bendix's testimony can't be believed is, to be fair, something that not even Tom Dewey could have been aware of in complete detail. The fact is that since the death of Maranzano, Luciano had been extremely careful to insulate himself from direct involvement in crimes. The structure of Mafia families set up by Maranzano and still in effect today made it almost impossible for the soldier in the street to deal directly with the head of the family in any discussion of criminal activities. There was then, and is today, a buffer system to protect men like Luciano.

Joe Bendix, as an outsider, not a member of Mafia, could never have held those conversations with Luciano. In fact, in 1935, around the time Bendix claimed to be getting Luciano's personal approval to become an employee, Joe Valachi was seeking approval to place slot machines in select outlets in the Bronx. He knew he could not directly approach the head of his family, who was Charlie Luciano. He went instead to his lieutenant, and was told to come to a building downtown to discuss it with the captain, Vito Genovese. When Valachi arrived for the appointment, at the offices of Genovese's legitimate front, a scrap metals firm in Little Italy, Luciano happened to be there. Both Valachi and his lieutenant were surprised to see him in the office. Luciano, annoyed at the interruption, asked the lieutenant what Valachi wanted, never even speaking directly to a soldier in his own family. Told that Valachi wanted permission to get into slot machines, Luciano said, "Give him twenty." Again, he

154

wouldn't give his approval directly to Valachi, for that was against Mafia protocol. That personal approval from Luciano was purely accidental, Valachi has said, a rare occurrance that came about simply because the family lieutenant did not know Luciano would be in Genovese's office. Never before that, and never again, did Valachi ever discuss illicit business directly with the head of his family. After Luciano went to prison and Frank Costello became acting head, Valachi had no business contact with him; all dealings went through the lieutenants.

Bendix, non-Mafia, a cheap burglar and sneak thief, would never have commanded more attention than Valachi.

Cokey Flo Brown next took the stand. Once she had been the classiest of madams, running a high-toned house, but in recent years she'd been a two-dollar whore, addicted to drugs. She was a small and very pale woman, cheaply dressed as she sat in the witness chair. Her nerves were twitching from morphine withdrawal, she seemed ready to collapse before the first question could be asked. Judge McCook ordered an attendant to bring her small doses of brandy, so that she could begin and continue her recital. And Cokey Flo swore that she was Jimmy Fredericks' girl friend. Jimmy, she said, had introduced her to Luciano in a midtown restaurant. Almost immediately, Luciano started discussing a madam who had refused to pay the sydnicate's fees. Charlie said: "You can't talk to them, they're stubborn. Get after them. Step on them." Sipping brandy occasionally, Cokie Flo swore that she was present at several meetings, in restaurants and even in a garage, during which Charlie expressed his disgust with the prostitution racket "because there wasn't enough money in it," she said. And she quoted Charlie as saying, at one of those meetings: "We could syndicate the houses on a large scale, like the A&P. We could even get the madams on a salary or commission, so we could keep all the profits. It'll take a little time, but we can do it."

Her testimony was very damaging to Luciano. Once

155

more, however, a "star witness" for Mr. Dewey becomes, on closer examination, a perjurer. The truth is that Cokey Flo manufactured the story that Dewey wanted to hear because she was suffering from withdrawal pains in a jail, and feeling totally abandoned by Fredericks and everyone else in the world.

Flo had become a booker herself sometime in late 1934, because she was so addicted that she had lost even her two-dollar customers. She met Jimmy Fredericks and agreed to pay him ten dollars a week for each whore she booked, in return for lawyers, bail money, and other assistance in case of arrest. She soon went to live with Jimmy. In January, 1936, just two weeks before Dewey's men went out on their massive roundup, Cokey's place was invaded by vice squad cops and she and her girls were arrested. She was charged not only with maintaining a disorderly house, but also with possession of drugs—police found her opium pipe, hypodermic syringe and morphine.

Jimmy helped her raise bail, through his combination, and she and her girls were released. Flo decided she'd better get cured of her addiction before going to trial because she was certain to be convicted on drug charges and she knew a cure in prison was tough. She checked into a sanatorium on Central Park West. She also jumped her bail by not reporting to court when required.

While taking the cure Flo read in the papers about Dewey's raids and she knew that Fredericks had been picked up and was held in very high bail; the newspapers carried full details of the arrests on the afternoon of February 2, the day after the raids.

About three weeks later, Flo left the sanatorium. She was still an addict, because a friend had smuggled morphine tablets into her room. Once out on the street Flo scrounged around a bit, soliciting a few customers, shoplifting, and hiding out from Dewey's men who were still arresting whores and bookers. After a time her doctor got her a job as a companion-nurse to an elderly invalid, and she moved into the woman's hotel suite. She worked at it for two months, being paid $25 a week. Her morphine habit was building up again, and the $25 wasn't even enough for the dope.

Flo then rented a basement room around the corner from her employer's place and began picking up customers again. She was so doped out of her head much of the time that one night she made the beginner's mistake of propositioning a plainclothes policeman. She was arrested again, quickly convicted, and placed in the Women's House of Detention. Once more she went on the cure, but jail wasn't any considerate private sanatorium. It was the torture of total withdrawal.

For two weeks she was so ill she couldn't eat much more than a few spoonfuls of milk and cereal each day. Many of her friends from the trade were in prison, many of them were material witnesses for Dewey and were being treated grandly even in prison. They suggested that if she wanted to help herself out of her serious trouble as a bail jumper in the narcotics case, she should see Dewey's men. The Luciano trial had by now begun. Cokey Flo read it all, and she realized quickly enough that her boy friend, Jimmy Fredericks, was doomed. The evidence against him was overwhelming. But, so far, there had been no testimony against Luciano. And Cokey Flo, in prison, going through a cure for addiction without any medical or psychiatric support, and knowing that the only person in the world who had ever cared for her was going to be convicted, decided to save herself "by giving testimony for the state so maybe I can get a break from the judge when I'm sentenced," as she later admitted.

She wrote a letter to one of Dewey's assistants, whose name was given her by another prostitute in the jail. In it she said she knew Luciano and was willing to "tell you the truth about what you want to know." She was immediately questioned in a private room in the jail, and she reeled off names, dates, meeting places with such conviction that the prosecutor's men believed her completely. She was rushed

157

to the witness stand on May 22 because Dewey felt her testimony was so damaging to Luciano.

Dewey and his aides must have known that Cokey Flo had seen the newspapers, and had been hearing much information from other witnesses in the jail. Nothing which Cokey told the prosecutor, not one piece of solid fact such as the name of a restaurant or a hotel in which meetings were held, came from Flo's lips. Every fact that could have been investigated for verification was a repitition of what other witnesses had said. Her account was suspect on the surface. To give Dewey the benefit of the doubt, he may not have known that a few days before Flo was arrested on her latest prostitution charge she had gone to the office of David Siegel, who was Fredericks' defense attorney, to inquire after Jimmy's health in prison. During that visit Flo saw a copy of the indictment against Luciano and the rest and spent more than an hour making notes of the girls' names listed in it and the various places in which Charlie was supposed to have held his meetings with the vice combination. Flo's remarkable ability to confirm the places named by others as Lucky's hangouts, where all the business was conducted, made a great impression on the jurors. They could not know, of course, that everything she said undoubtedly came out of the indictment and the newspapers. Further, Cokey Flo admitted that when she went to visit the lawyer's office he asked her what she knew of Luciano, his client's co-defendant, because the lawyer knew only what he read in the papers. And Flo responded: "I don't know the man at all."

While the trial was still going forward Cokey Flo and Mildred Harris, another madam and addict who testified she'd been told "Lucky is the boss," received from Dewey's office what would be called a reward in some circles and a bribe in others—it's unethical, no matter what it's called. The editors of *Liberty Magazine* were permitted, by Dewey, to sign Flo and Mildred to a contract for their published memoirs about whores and the underworld. They were paid fifty dollars a week for ten weeks with an additional payment of five hundred dollars each when the interviews were completed. The writer was permitted to visit them in prison even as the trial was going on. The girls received their payments from Frank Hogan, then an assistant to Dewey and later New York District Attorney for many years. Flo also got her $1,500 forfeited bail returned to her, through Dewey's intervention with the court.

It is no longer possible to learn whether these deals were suggested before the witnesses testified, and it can never be claimed that the girls were actually paid by Dewey himself. They were, nonetheless, bought witnesses. And it has long been axiomatic in law that the testimony of paid witnesses is so badly tainted as to be totally valueless.

Another "star witness" always cited by Dewey and his writers as being vital in the conviction of Luciano, in actuality supports the real evidence—that Luciano was convicted on perjured, manufactured testimony. That witness was Nancy Presser, who told the most fantastic tale of all, and who was in reality such a poor witness that Dewey and the judge had to come to her rescue. During Dewey's later summation, however, Nancy was cited as "an important link in the chain of evidence" against Luciano. The jury ignored what they had seen in the courtroom and believed the prosecutor.

Nancy testified that some time at the end of 1933 or early 1934 she was in a midtown restaurant when Luciano asked her to join him at his table. She had known Charlie casually for a few years, she claimed, so she was not just a cheap pickup. While dining with him that day she played up to him and slipped her telephone number to him. In spite of the fact that she was the mistress of Ralph Liguori, a pimp and gunman of whom she was deathly afraid, she soon became Luciano's mistress. She visited him regularly at the Barbizon-Plaza and dined with him often as he made the rounds of the spots "where his vice men hung out."

And she heard many intimate details of the organization, she swore. One day she heard a conversation between Charlie and Dave Wahrman, one of the defendants. Wahrman reported that he was having trouble with madams who didn't want to join up and pay their fees. One of the more recalcitrant of these madams, he said, was a woman known as Dago Jean. Upon hearing this, Charlie said: "Go ahead and wreck her joint."

Nancy claimed that she was Luciano's mistress for about six months, visiting him even after he moved into Suite 39-C of the Waldorf Towers. Most of her visits were well after midnight, when none of the staff were on duty, and she'd just slip upstairs to see her lover, Charlie. It was during one of these many visits to the Waldorf, she claimed, that she heard Charlie shouting angrily at someone on the telephone. When he hung up she asked him what was wrong, as any good mistress does. "He told me it was Betillo on the phone, that he couldn't depend on him, and Charlie would be better off if he went on the thing himself." The "thing," of course, was wrecking the places of madams who would not pay, and torturing the poor women until they became more pliable.

Prosecutor Dewey led her through several hours of testimony in which, as he later said in his summation, "Nancy Presser ripped the mask off Luciano, this monster fattening on the profits of the bodies of women."

Well, hardly. In truth, Nancy's glib story of intimacies with the vice king at the Waldorf began to fall apart the moment Luciano's lawyer started his cross-examination. Asked how it was possible for her to sneak up to Luciano's suite many dozens of times without ever being seen, since the Towers entrance on Fiftieth Street had a doorman, receptionist, and elevator operator on duty twenty-four hours a day, Nancy said it was just one of those fortunate breaks. She could not say whether there was a piano in Charlie's living room, or a phonograph, or whether there was a refrigerator in the kitchen. She could not in any way describe the suite or its furnishings. Not even the bedroom, in which she spent so much time with Charlie.

Asked the kind of beds in the apartment—whether twin or double—Nancy said she couldn't remember. Luciano's lawyer then said:

"Come, Miss Presser, just describe as any woman would, this bedroom you visited so often."

"Oh, I'm sure I can't," said Nancy. She then turned to Dewey and said, "I'm feeling sick. I need a little air."

That very convenient sickness brought an adjournment of five minutes. But Nancy never did return to the stand that day. Dewey announced that she was too ill to testify for at least a couple of days. When she recovered, Luciano's attorney decided not to question her further and risk the possibility that she was now more thoroughly coached than before and might have all the answers.

It is so very strange that all of these people, like Nancy Presser, who testified that they had talked to Luciano personally about the prostitution racket, had been able to find him in various bars and restaurants all over town. Because Dewey's undercover investigator, Dan Danforth, never saw even a glimpse of the man. In his book, Danforth recounts how he visited almost nightly a bar in West Fifty-Seventh Street that was headquarters for Betillo and Fredericks. Posing as a master pimp from Boston anxious to open a few bordellos in New York, Danforth eventually wormed his way into their confidence and was actually getting advice from them on the prostitution business in New York. Yet, through all these many weeks and dozens of meetings with "Luciano's men," Danforth never once met Luciano. Dewey would have us believe that Luciano met with bookers to give them his personal approval for work, met with addicted two-dollar whores and discussed his most private affairs with them, was generally available to every pimp and whore in the city including a cheap burglar like Joe Bendix, and never bothered to meet Danforth, a man accepted by Betillo and Fredericks as a major figure in Boston prostitution circles.

At the beginning of the trial Luciano seemed to be certain that he would be acquitted. But as the witnesses were paraded before him, relating their fantastic stories, Charlie realized that it was growing rather serious. When Dewey rested his case, Luciano insisted he must take the stand in his own defense, "because I'm innocent and I gotta get them to believe me," he said. It was a mistake, for Charlie simply reinforced the jury's impression that he was an evil gangster. He was that, most certainly, but he knew he had nothing to do with prostitution and he was determined to set the record straight.

During a battering four-hour cross-examination by Dewey, the only real defendant in the trial was trapped in so many lies about his past, about his criminal record and his gangster associates, that he left the jury with the feeling he would lie about anything—including his role in the prostitution racket. The most damaging of the several attacks made by Dewey concerned Luciano's denials that he knew any of the other defendants or ever called them in the restaurants some of the witnesses had named as being gathering places of the ring's leaders. Dewey produced phone records to show that calls had indeed been made from Charlie's suite to those places. Toward the end, Luciano was so uncomfortable under Dewey's assault that he answered most questions with "I don't remember."

When it was over, Charlie told his lawyer that he still believed he'd be acquitted, or at least win a hung jury, because no juror with any intelligence at all would believe witnesses who were so plainly lying about him. But Luciano misjudged the temper of the times. The gaudy era of Prohibition had ended. The nation, and the world, was being strangled by an economic depression more severe than any in modern history. Corruption of police and perversion of the political process by racketeers such as Luciano was slowly becoming a part of the public's consciousness because of the investigations by Dewey and others. Dewey, indeed, represented a morality that had been missing in American affairs since the end of World War I. Dewey would not lie. He would not manufacture

162

evidence, as Luciano's defense claimed. Dewey represented Good destroying Evil.

There was something else, also. Frank Hogan, Dewey's aide, admitted in 1972, "I sort of doubt that Luciano could be convicted today." Back then, during the Luciano trial, American courts did not protect the rights of defendants as they have been doing for more than a decade. A confession could be beaten out of a man and, even if the court agreed a beating had occurred, that confession would still be used as evidence. In Luciano's case, he was at a very great disadvantage because a defendant in a criminal case had no right of discovery—the requirement that a prosecutor reveal the names of his witnesses and even, on a court order, reveal some or all documents in the prosecutor's possession. Back then, because there was no right of discovery, Dewey could spring his surprise witnesses and Luciano's lawyers had no time to investigate the backgrounds of those witnesses and determine whether one of them, for instance, might have been in California at the time she testified to events in New York.

The jury was given the case for deliberation on June 6. After discussing it for only six hours the jurors returned and announced that all nine defendants were guilty as charged. Luciano did not react. "We'll beat this bullshit in appeal," he whispered to one of his lawyers. The lawyers asked that the jurors be individually polled to verify their verdict. As each juror was asked how he had found, one of them wept. Reporters who questioned him later said he had voted against conviction, at first, "because Dewey didn't prove it," but the others convinced him to change his vote to guilty.

Less than two weeks later, Luciano and the other defendants were again brought before Justice McCook. When the clerk of the court asked Luciano whether he had anything to say before sentence was imposed, Charlie leaned over and held a whispered consultation with his lawyer. Then he straightened up and said:

163

"Your honor, I have nothing to say outside the fact that I want to say again that I am innocent."

The judge then addressed Luciano. "An intelligent, courageous and discriminating jury has found you guilty of heading a conspiracy or combination to commit these crimes," he said. "This makes you responsible, in law and morals, for every foul and cruel deed performed by the band of co-defendants."

Then he imposed a sentence of "30 to 50 years in State Prison." Luciano's eyelids quivered slightly on hearing the sentence, but he quickly recovered his outward calm and followed his guards out of the courtroom with almost a bounce in his walk. Years later he would tell friends:

"He could of sentenced me to the chair and I wouldn't have been more shocked. I was in a fog, really. All I could think was that I was thirty-eight, and thirty years meant I'd be sixty-eight before I got out—I'd be an old man, or I'd be dead by then. I didn't even think about time off for good behavior, or beating the rap on appeal—just that old man of sixty-eight, walkin' out of prison."

One more point must be made about the evidence against Luciano. During the three years or so that Dewey's evidence "proved" Luciano was the leader of a syndicate extorting money from madams, prostitutes, and bookers, Polly Adler was running the finest, most expensive and most profitable whorehouse in town. In her book, *A House Is Not a Home,* Adler says this about Dewey's charges:

"I was astonished to learn that Dewey was seeking to link Charlie Luciano with the prostitution racket. It was inconceivable to me that any such connection could exist. For one thing, I used to supply the girls when Charlie Lucky entertained in his plushy hotel suites, and it hardly seems logical that if he had the alleged tie-ups, he would patronize a madam outside the combine. Of course it was no secret that Charlie Lucky was mixed up in all sorts of rackets, and his activities were openly discussed by the men who were 'too light for heavy work and too heavy for

164

light work.' But not once was it ever even implied that he derived any part of his income from prostitution.

"Certainly I believe that in the many years I was associated with prostitution if there had been even a hint of a rumor of a tie-up between Charlie and the combination, I would have heard of it."

I interviewed Polly Adler in 1955, when she returned to America after living in Europe for a couple of years. Her book had been published some months earlier, and I was curious about her remarks concerning Luciano. I asked her about the vice trial and she said: "I knew some of the girls who testified and I knew people who were friendly with them. And every one of those girls later said, quite specifically, that Dewey and his staff put words into their mouths and gave them all the information they needed to tell a convincing story. Those girls lied because they'd been threatened by Dewey, they admitted that quite freely. I couldn't write it in my book because of libel laws."

I'll leave to others any moral judgments they care to make. Luciano, by his own admission, was a killer and a lot of other things, none of them good. The state could never prove murder against him, nor any of the dozens of other crimes he most certainly committed. But it was "proved," through what can only be called a frameup, that Luciano was guilty of prostitution charges. The moral issue is clear: Does the state have the right to pervert the law? In a nation that prides itself on being one of the most civilized nations in history because of the equal application to all of law and Constitution, is it moral to twist that civilizing law in order to put into prison any man who is *suspected* of crimes, against whom no legal proof has been discovered?

13

Luciano and the others convicted with him were sent to Sing Sing Prison. After three weeks it was decided that the group should be broken up. Luciano, Betillo, and a couple of others were transferred to Clinton State Prison at Dannemora, known as the Siberia of the prison system because it is in the far north of the state, where snow lies on the earth from October through May and the winds make it impossible to keep warm.

Charlie's lawyers began to work on an appeal. Some of the women had been sent by Dewey to Europe, all expenses paid by his office—another unethical reward, or bribe—but the defense attorneys were able to locate others. Some of them were persuaded to tell the truth, to change their stories. Dewey fought the appeal, claiming witnesses like Nancy Presser and Joe Bendix had been frightened into denying their earlier testimony. The courts upheld the original verdict.

It was only then, when he lost his appeal about a year after conviction, that Charlie understood for the first time that he would be in prison for many years. His lawyers were going to appeal all the way to the U.S. Supreme Court, but Charlie was now certain he would lose. So he summoned Frank Costello to see him, and Costello was permitted to visit (as so many other Luciano associates would be) in spite of a rule that a convict could see only lawyers and nearest relatives. Costello was told that he was now in charge of the Luciano Mafia family, and of

Luciano's interests in the larger combination they had all formed.

Costello didn't want the position, for he much preferred to remain in the background, the legitimate businessman with marvelous political connections. But he had no choice. The only other possible candidate, Vito Genovese, had sailed for Italy a few months before. Vito had opened his newspaper one morning and was rather astonished to read that Tom Dewey had said, "Vito Genovese has taken over for Lucky Luciano," and had added that Genovese was his next target. Vito decided to go on a little holiday. He packed his finest clothing and, according to his wife's testimony during her suit for separate maintenance many years later, he filled a suitcase with $750,000 more or less, just in case his trip might turn out to be an extended one. With Genovese gone, Costello was placed in charge of all Luciano's interests.

He and Meyer Lansky were also given the far more important task of finding a way to get Luciano out of prison, "even if it takes a million bucks," Costello later told friends. It would be rather difficult, however. Herbert Lehman was governor and could not be easily reached for a pardon or parole. And Jimmy Hines would not be much help because Dewey had begun to look into the policy business put together with Hines' political aid, and the old Tammany man was being very cautious.

The day Luciano arrived at Dannemora with Little Davey Betillo and forty-six other prisoners, July 1, 1936, was a big day inside the walls, for Luciano was considered a king of men. John Resko was there, and he remembered that all the talk was of Luciano's impending arrival. Resko had been sentenced to death in 1930 for killing a man during a robbery. He was nineteen at the time. After two years in the Death House his sentence was commuted to life. In Dannemora he discovered a talent for painting and eventually gave art courses to other prisoners. He was an unusual felon—artistic, intelligent, rehabilitated in prison when most inmates learn only how to refine their criminal

167

techniques. After he was released in 1949, Resko wrote one of the best books about the trauma of prison and a man's struggle against institutional brutalization, *Reprieve*.

Resko wrote that when Luciano arrived, a great number of friends were waiting for him. Immediately, Charlie had his own "court"—a name for both the piece of territory in the recreation yard that a clique has appropriated for itself, and the members of that clique.

"Life in prison picked up tempo after the arrival of Luciano and his partners," Resko wrote. "Cons and guards were constantly planning accidental meetings with Lucky. Involved were curiosity, a desire to enhance prestige, or a plea for aid. Everyone around Luciano was approached at one time or another to intercede, to introduce, to pass on information . . . Among the inmate population he was always referred to as "Lucky." The guards were about evenly divided between "Lucky" and "Luciano." His friends called him Charlie.

"Though other convicts, with less influence and less cash, availed themselves of special privileges, wearing outside shirts and tailor-made trousers, having special meals in their cells and hired help, Luciano for one reason or another refused all such favors. The psychology was excellent. He was never pointed out as a big shot because he wore a white shirt or had a guy cleaning out his cell. He was one of the boys. Just another con . . . Among his fellow cons Charlie was highly regarded, respected, and defended with ardor.

"They told the story of the gray, old convict who had no money and no friends and hardly any hope of seeing the outside again, who came to the court to see Charlie. He explained to Luciano that he was in prison on a bum rap and that only the week before he had contacted a witness who could clear him. All he needed was a lawyer and briefs. All he needed was seven hundred dollars.

"About one month later the old man was back on the court—for the last time. He was saying good-bye. He was

168

on his way home and he had come to thank Charlie for helping him."

Leo Katcher, who would later write the Rothstein biography, went up to Dannemora to interview Luciano for the New York *Post* at the end of 1938, to get his reaction to the news that the Supreme Court had turned down his last possible appeal.

"Yeah, I heard about it," Charlie said. "I didn't expect much. My lawyers told me not to expect much, just to hope. That's what I been doin' for a couple of years. Hoping."

Katcher said he thought Luciano was looking good. Charlie replied: "Why shouldn't I? Lots of work, lots of exercise. No late hours. Just what the doctor ordered. God, how I hate it."

He'd been working in the laundry, Charlie said, and displayed the calluses on his palms to prove it. He didn't mind working because it kept him from thinking. What did he think about? Katcher asked.

"What does anybody think about when he's in the jug? About getting out. That's all anybody thinks about. He thinks about streets that you can't see the end of. He thinks about people walking in all directions. He thinks about autos going where they want. He thinks about places without walls. He thinks about getting out."

Asked about the witnesses who testified against him, Charlie surprisingly said he understood why everyone had lied, and he sounded as if he could even forgive them.

"They lied to save themselves," he said. "They just lied because that was the way out for them. Look around this jail. You'll see two thousand guys. There ain't one of 'em —and I guess that goes for me—who won't swear to anything so he can get out of here. There ain't one of 'em won't send his grandmother to jail if it means that it cuts his bit."

"They got radios in the rooms and we get radio programs," Charlie said, his voice beginning to rise. The guard in the room with them seemed a little apprehensive because Luciano was getting upset. "Sometimes when you

169

hear music and singing and hear people laughing, you want to grab your headphones and throw them on the floor and step on them and then kick them all around the room and break them into little bits so you'll never hear people laughing again."

He stopped speaking for a time. When he calmed down, after apologizing to Katcher and the guard, he considered the next question carefully—whether he would get out of prison before his time was up.

"I don't know, I hope so," he said. "One day somebody who lied is going to tell the whole truth. Then somebody else will. Then the whole lot of them will. Then I'll get out. When I do, watch me.

"I'll follow the horses from Saratoga to Belmont to Florida to California. I'll sleep with my windows open so I can reach out and hold the air in my hands. I'll never lock a door again. Wherever I hear a noise I'm going to go in and look at people and watch them. I'll watch women laughing and dancing. I'll laugh and dance, too. When I get out, I'm going to be free."

The guard announced that time was up. As Katcher rose to shake hands, he asked: "Anything I can do for you?"

"Yeah," Luciano said. "Don't close the door as you go out."

Still, he seemed to know how to "do time" quite easily. Costello and Lansky came up to see him regularly, as did many others in the organization who should not have been permitted as visitors. His sisters and brothers visited as often as they could. And Charlie was revered by most other convicts. He was even liked by a group of inmates who declared they hated the power of "the Italian gang that thinks it's boss in here," and who began to fight Davey Betillo and a group he kept around him.

For months, according to another convict who wrote a book about his prison experiences, a "mob war" between the two groups raged on, men from each faction being stabbed or beaten. Then one day in the recreation yard Luciano told Betillo it was time to stop the fighting. Betillo refused. Luciano commanded. Betillo picked up a baseball bat and came at Luciano with it. Another convict fought Betillo off, punching him to the ground. Betillo was placed in solitary for a while, and a truce was declared which lasted as long as Luciano was imprisoned there.

Christmas, 1941, was an especially dreadful time in prison, Resko wrote. Pearl Harbor had been bombed less than three weeks earlier. The usual Christmas packages sent by philanthropic organizations were being channeled to the armed forces, and charity packages of that kind were the only reminder of Christmas for many prisoners whose families wanted nothing to do with them. The prison's Catholic chaplain asked some convicts whether they had any suggestions for helping the prisoners who would not be getting packages this year. Several suggested Luciano.

"Charlie gave Father Hyland several names and telephone numbers," Resko writes, "and on Christmas Day three trucks arrived in Dannemora after an all-night drive from New York City. They carried maximum loads. Loads of fruits and candies and cigarettes. It was not a bad Christmas."

As Luciano told Katcher, getting out of prison is the only serious thinking most convicts do. With the coming of war, Luciano and his friends outside began to work on a scheme which would open the prison gates for him. The plan had actually started years before, underworld sources and some investigators say, although the specific direction it took could not have been foreseen.

Only the governor could pardon a state prisoner. It had been obvious as far back as 1936, when he indicted Luciano, that Dewey wanted to become governor. He ran for, and won, the Republican nomination in 1938. An election campaign takes enormous sums of money, as every gangster knew from personal financing of Tammany candidates and even support of Republicans, to cover all bets. It is said, not only in Mafia circles but among law enforcement officials who later investigated, and by Luciano himself in conversations with friends, that Costello and Lansky raised a secret fund of $250,000 and contributed it to Dewey's gubernatorial campaign through intermediaries—some of Costello's very respectable friends in Republican politics. Should Dewey win he would be obligated to Costello and Lansky and he would later find some very good reason to commute Luciano's sentence: Perhaps because Luciano was suffering from an incurable illness and should be permitted to spend his remaining days with his brothers and sisters.

Dewey lost the election by a very narrow margin, however. He returned to the District Attorney's office and now began to concentrate on building his image further by convicting more racketeers. Especially Louis Lepke, the industrial gangster, and Jimmy Hines, the protector of them all. And, it has been said by Mafia informers and by the men who testified in the Murder, Inc. investigation, both Lepke and Hines were betrayed by Luciano, scheming to get out of prison.

Lepke had been indicted in 1937 by a federal grand jury for violation of the Sherman Antitrust Act, the first attempt to use that law to imprison a racketeer. The specific charge was "interfering with interstate commerce." While out on bail, Lepke learned the federal government was about to indict him again, this time on a narcotics smuggling conspiracy involving the international organization Arnold Rothstein had set up some fifteen years earlier. If convicted on the narcotics charges Lepke faced a possible fifty years in prison. He also learned, around the same time, that Dewey claimed to have so much evidence of Lepke's racketeering "that I can send him away for five hundred years." Lepke jumped bail, on July 6, 1937, and went into hiding.

He was living in an apartment in Brooklyn, protected by Al Anastasia and his men, and successfully eluded discovery for almost two years, in spite of a daily manhunt by a special squad of city detectives and a million wanted circulars that were distributed across the country by the FBI. While in hiding, Lepke directed Anastasia to oversee the assassination of every possible witness against him. Anastasia and his men killed at least eight potential witnesses, including several unionists. They failed to murder Philip Orlofsky, who had been used in the takeover of Hillman's Amalgamated Clothing Workers, only because the killer squad shot someone else by mistake.

The official version of events is that FBI Director J. Edgar Hoover decided his band of manhunters must find Lepke before Dewey did, so that Hoover could look heroic and live up to the billing that "the FBI always gets its man." Hoover, therefore, sent word to Frank Costello that unless Lepke came out of hiding, every Italian mobster in the country would be picked up and harassed. So frightened was Costello over this ultimatum that he told Lepke: "You surrender, or else." That threat was enough to send Lepke flying into the arms of J. Edgar himself, surrendering to him personally in August, 1939.

The true story, developed from various official investigations, is that Lepke was sacrificed to Hoover and to Dewey, who was more feared by Lepke. Luciano began thinking about it quite seriously when he learned the Supreme Court turned down his appeal. In conferences with Costello and others who visited him in Dannemora, a scheme was developed to assist Dewey.

Lepke, quite obviously, was going to be captured eventually, and sent to prison for the rest of his life. Why not hasten the inevitable and place Dewey in Luciano's debt? Lepke would not surrender to Dewey, of course. But suppose Lepke could be convinced that a deal had been made with Hoover, a guarantee that he would be tried on Federal charges and not turned over to Dewey. Then get Dewey to understand that Lepke was surrendering on Luciano's advice . . . that he would only surrender to Hoover because he was deathly afraid of Dewey . . . and that as soon as the federal courts were through with him, Dewey would get him . . . in plenty of time to build his reputation as a "rackets buster" even further for the 1942 gubernatorial campaign. And all that Luciano would expect was "an honest break" from the new governor who certainly knew how innocent Charlie was of the prostitution charges.

Costello and his associates agreed that the scheme was a good one, especially when coupled with further mob financing of Dewey's election drive. But the major drawback was that Lepke trusted no one. He would never believe Anastasia, or Costello, or any other ranking member of the syndicate should they come to him and tell him a deal had been made with Hoover. Still, there was one man Lepke did trust—Moe Wilensky, known as Dimples, a long-time Lepke associate in the garment center and in gambling, a man who adored his boss. Precisely how Dimples was persuaded to do it, whether he'd been bribed or threatened, or simply accepted the lie, won't ever be known. There are some who say that Dimples was called into Dewey's office and told about the deal by the District Attorney himself; but that is later rumor and is not the hard information supplied by the men who confessed their roles in Murder, Inc. In any case, the informers say that Dimples visited Lepke in his Brooklyn hideout one day, fairly bubbling with excitement:

"A deal is in with the feds," he announced. He said he'd been told by the most reliable sources in the world that Hoover had agreed to accept Lepke's surrender, have the federal prosecutor send him to prison for a spell, and then refuse to turn him over to New York officials until he'd completed his prison term. "The deal is you get 10 to 12 years tops," Dimples told him, "get out in about seven, and by that time Dewey is governor or president and he's not thinking about you any more." Lepke went for it, especially after it was pointed out that while he was living in a federal penitentiary, witnesses against him in the state cases would suffer loss of memory, could be made to vanish or be killed by Anastasia's gunmen, and the cases would collapse.

Lepke, conned by Luciano's scheme, surrendered to

Hoover. That's the way Murder Inc. informers told the story. They weren't boasting about it—they were quite angry that their Lepke was double-crossed by "that bastard Luciano."

Unfortunately for Lepke, he was indeed turned over to Dewey after being convicted on the federal narcotics charge. Dewey convicted him on racketeering charges and thereby won himself another large amount of glory. Then Dewey turned his prisoner over to Brooklyn authorities to stand trial on murder charges growing out of the Murder, Inc. case, and he was convicted and sentenced to the electric chair. Now some bizarre events unfolded, which would lead some newspapers to charge President Roosevelt with "protecting" Lepke and cause *The New York Times* to state in an editorial: "Knowledge Lepke has of an old murder involving labor leaders said to be close to the present national administration is said to be one of the factors in the long involved negotiations." The *Times* was referring to Hillman but was unable to use his name because of the libel laws. And the "negotiations" mentioned in the editorial are what made the Lepke case take such a weird twist.

In sentencing Lepke to death, the judge said the execution would be carried out "subject to any legal impediments." What he meant was that, because Lepke was still a federal prisoner, it was possible he could not be executed unless Lepke were given a federal pardon so that he could be turned over to the state; there was precedent in an older case. The Brooklyn District Attorney's office wrote to Roosevelt's Justice Department and requested the pardon. After two months Justice said the Lepke case was "not a proper case" for pardon. Further requests from the DA's office were turned down. In September, 1943, Tom Dewey, now governor, demanded that Roosevelt pardon Lepke so he could be executed. After many further demands went unanswered, Dewey implied that Roosevelt was protecting Lepke—and he quietly fed to the newspapers the complicity of Sidney Hillman in the murder of a Brooklyn clothing manufacturer a decade earlier. Finally, more than two years after Lepke had been sentenced to death, the federal government agreed that Lepke would be pardoned to enable him to be transferred to state control. By then Dewey was an announced candidate to run against Roosevelt and, as the newspapers noted, the government gave in "because the case is too hot to handle in an election year."

Lepke was executed in February, 1944, the first and only major rackets figure to suffer such a fate, and he went to his death blaming Luciano and Costello for betraying him.

Dewey, while he was still District Attorney, attained even greater reknown for his indictment of Jimmy Hines as the political protector of the Dutch Schultz policy ring. And in that trial hangs another Mafia story, sworn to as truth by men who insist they know; including my old friend, Ernie the Hawk, who spent some time in prison with Hines and some of his associates.

Dixie Davis, Dutch Schultz's lawyer, had been in hiding under the protection of the Luciano organization since the Dutchman was killed in 1935. Schultz's policy bank was confiscated by Luciano men, and Dixie had been kept alive at first solely to assist in making that takeover go smoothly, the gossip in Mafia and enforcement circles has it. There was actually no longer any reason to protect his life. In reality, with Dewey investigating Jimmy Hines and his connection with the Schultz policy ring, Davis was a danger to the men who currently owned that policy bank. Prudence should have dictated his death.

And yet, somehow, "acting on a tip from an undisclosed source," police arrested Dixie and his girl friend, Hope Dare, in their Philadelphia hotel in February, 1938. Davis was persuaded to talk. He talked about Schultz, he talked about the takeover of the black policy banks by the Dutchman, he talked at such great length about Jimmy Hines' role in protecting that bank and participating in the profits that Hines was actually convicted by Dewey and sent to prison.

But in all the hundreds of thousands of words he spoke, Davis never mentioned Luciano publicly. He never said a word about Luciano's associates in East Harlem who were running the policy bank even as Davis was testifying, men who were instructed by Davis. He spoke only about underworld history that was quite ancient, in the telescoped time span of mob events. There was no evidence that he was ever asked about the new policy barons. Dewey certainly knew what was going on; the newspapers of the day were publishing enough information about "Lucky's mob in Harlem policy," as one story put it, that Dewey should have expressed even a passing curiosity. But, nothing.

And underworld sources began reporting to several agencies that some kind of a deal had been made: Luciano and his associates had sacrificed Jimmy Hines to feed Dewey's quest for the reputation which would make him governor, and then president. I first personally heard this gossip, this Mafia theory, from Ernie the Hawk when I sought him out in 1957 for information about the shooting of Frank Costello. We again talked about Luciano. Ernie was a member of the Luciano-Costello family, and he swore he knew what he was talking about. "Dixie Davis was surrendered as part of a deal," Ernie said. "Dewey could look good by getting Hines and Tammany, but he had to lay off the guys running the policy business after Schultz was hit. He agreed to that, and Charlie Lucky handed him Dixie Davis. Even Hines knew it. He used to run around telling everybody, 'I wish I was a guinea, I'd kill that bastard Luciano.' But there wasn't nothin' he could do 'cause he was posin' as a guy framed by Dewey."

I've heard similar reports from several investigative agencies specializing in Mafia affairs. I don't vouch for their accuracy. I know only that later events in the careers of Tom Dewey and Charlie Luciano may possibly be explained, in part at least, by this information.

14

America's entry into the Second World War not only provided Luciano with an opportunity to show his fellow inmates in Dannemora how thoughtful he was in having truckloads of gifts sent up at Christmas, but it also gave him the lever he'd been seeking to open the prison gates.

In February, 1942, less than three months after Pearl Harbor, the luxury liner *Normandie* was burned and destroyed in its pier on the Hudson River, where it was being overhauled for use as a troop ship. There were immediate scare headlines about sabotage, reports that German U-boats had dropped espionage agents ashore, and veiled hints that Mussolini sympathizers among the longshoremen, many of whom were Italian-Americans, may have been responsible.

It was the duty of Naval Intelligence in New York to detect espionage and prevent sabotage. The head of Naval Intelligence in the area was Lieutenant Commander Charles Haffenden, an old Navy man from the First World War, later a businessman and a press agent for business associations. Through the entire period between the two wars Haffenden had been in Naval Reserve Intelligence, and he was called back into service just before the Japanese attacked Pearl Harbor. For all his background with the Navy, and all his years in New York, Haffenden knew very little about the waterfront or the dock unions and rackets controlled by mobsters. When the *Normandie* was burned, he asked his aides for suggestions about convincing dock workers to remain faithful to flag and country; especially the longshoremen of Italian descent. No one had any really brilliant ideas, at first, until someone (it has never been disclosed precisely whom) suggested that a man named Joseph Lanza might prove helpful.

The next day Lanza, best known as Socks, was seated in Haffenden's office, sympathizing as the commander spoke about security problems on the New York waterfront. Socks Lanza was then under indictment for racketeering on that waterfront. He dominated several dock locals and used his power to extort money from stevedore companies, shippers, wholesalers, even the commercial fishermen who unloaded their catch at the city-owned wholesale market on the East River; Socks was known as the Boss of the Fulton Fish Market. He was very well connected. One Tammany district leader was married to Lanza's sister while another, Marinelli, was dependent on Lanza's goons for certain political jobs. Lanza was a member of Charlie Luciano's Mafia family, a relationship that not even the most naive would call coincidental in this case.

After learning the details of the Navy's fear that the war effort would be greatly hampered unless the docks were cleared of potential saboteurs, Lanza said he was a patriotic American who "hated that bum Mussolini." He would do anything in his power to help the government in this crisis. But Commander Haffenden must understand that his, er . . . unions, Lanza's union members, worked only a small section of the East River waterfront. If the entire harbor, Manhattan, Brooklyn, Staten Island, and over to the New Jersey docks, was to be swept clean of guys like the rats who burned the *Normandie,* then a man with more influence than he, Lanza, would have to be consulted.

Was there a man with so much influence? Haffenden asked.

There sure in hell was, Lanza replied, but only one.

And who might that man be?

Why, good old Charlie Luciano. The only problem is, good old Charlie was serving a long prison sentence way up in Dannemora, and he couldn't very well assist the war effort from so far away. Poor Charlie had been sent to the slammer by Tom Dewey, Socks explained, and it was just a strange coincidence that some of Dewey's old assistants were now serving with Haffenden in Naval Intelligence. The record does not disclose whether the Commander asked the racketeer how he knew who was on the Naval Intelligence staff.

Haffenden promptly consulted those assistants, and they and the captain in charge of the Navy District agreed that Lanza's suggestion should be further explored. Within hours Haffenden's captain and a junior officer who had worked on Dewey's case against Luciano were in consultation with District Attorney Frank Hogan and the chief of his rackets bureau, Murray Gurfein—both of whom had by some coincidence also worked on the Luciano case.

And that's when what has come to be called Operation Underworld in Navy jargon started to move rather quickly. Lanza, the racketeer, was called in for consultation by Gurfein, the rackets bureau chief. After being warned that whatever help he gave to Naval Intelligence would not be a bargaining point should he be convicted of racketeering, Lanza said he'd make certain his section of the waterfront remained patriotic. (Lanza, in fact, was convicted and sentenced to fifteen years on extortion charges and was released by Governor Dewey's Parole Board after serving only seven years, in spite of a record that spanned three decades and ranged from murder to robbery.)

Once more, Lanza repeated his assertion that only Luciano could guarantee the safety of the entire harbor. It has never been very clear precisely when Governor Dewey was first told about these meetings, but knowing the protocol among prosecutors who had worked through a major investigation together, and most especially the close relationship between Frank Hogan and Tom Dewey, it's a safe bet the Governor was notified of the negotiations the moment Hogan knew of them. And it is even more of a certainty that Hogan would not have proceeded without Dewey's very positive approval. Now, after hearing Gurfein's report of his conversation with Socks Lanza, the District Attorney suggested that Luciano's lawyer be consulted.

Luciano was no doubt fully aware of what was happening. Frank Costello telephoned him almost every day, in violation of regulations, and Luciano took those calls in the warden's private office. Costello, according to informants, was simply keeping Luciano apprised of latest developments; Ernie the Hawk and others have said they were told, within the Mafia family, that Luciano knew all the details of the request by Naval Intelligence that he assist the war effort because the idea was Frank Costello's in the first place. Costello simply planted it in the mind of a "friend" in Haffenden's office. "I heard it was an old Coast Guard guy, from Frank's rumrunning days out at Montauk," Ernie once told me.

In any event Luciano's lawyer, Moses Polakoff, was called in and informed of the country's desperate need for his client's services. Polakoff went to see Luciano in Dannemora. On his return he told rackets bureau chief Gurfein that Charlie might possibly cooperate, but on two conditions: His old friend, Meyer Lansky, must be a party to any conferences and negotiations; and Luciano must be transferred to a prison closer to the city. Naval Intelligence, when informed, insisted the conditions must be met because Luciano's aid was so desirable.

Almost immediately, and most certainly with the approval of Governor Dewey, Luciano was transferred to Great Meadow Correctional Institution, which is known as the "connections can" because convicts there led an easier life than in any other state prison.

And then the strangest part of the entire affair occurred. The Corrections Commissioner of the state, at the urging of the District Attorney and Naval Intelligence, and most definitely with the approval of Governor Dewey, agreed that anyone could visit Luciano so long as his lawyer was present. The only person required to sign the visitor's book was Moe Polakoff, the lawyer, who was permitted to sign as "Mr. Polakoff and two guests," depending on the number involved. Beginning in May, 1942, and continuing right up to V-E Day in May, 1945, among those guests were some of the elite of the East Coast syndicate: Lansky conferred with Charlie at least ten times, Lanza four, Mike Liscari of New Jersey, Longy Zwillman's partner, nine times; and Costello, Willie Moretti, and Mike Miranda, the *consiglieri* of the Luciano family, at least once. Those are minimum estimates, based on the memory of prison officials who were questioned many years later and who relied on memory because no records were kept.

Polakoff attended every conference. As a member of the bar he was considered a "representative of the state," a man who could vouch that nothing illegal was being discussed by such important underworld figures. Most of the time, however, Luciano and his visitors carried on their conversation in Italian, a language Polakoff did not understand. Once, asked what he did during these conferences, Polakoff is reported to have replied:

"Me? Oh, I just sat in a corner and read a newspaper."

At the beginning of 1943 Luciano decided he had done enough to help the Navy guard against sabotage, and now wanted his reward. He asked his lawyers to move for a reduction in sentence, so he would be eligible for immediate parole. The motion was made before Judge McCook, whose own bias had been so evident when he presided at Luciano's trial. McCook could not believe that the world's greatest whoremaster could have assisted the government in any way. He privately questioned Murray Gurfein, DA Hogan's assistant who had helped prosecute Luciano and had become involved in Operation Underworld. When they returned to the courtroom from the judge's private chambers McCook announced that, although it seemed that Luciano had indeed helped his country, that he'd been informed there was no sabotage on the New York waterfront since Luciano's help was sought, that wasn't enough reason to release him. He castigated Luciano once more for his role in the prostitution racket. But then he added: "If Luciano continues to cooperate (with the Navy) and remains a model prisoner, it may be appropriate at some future time to apply for executive clemency."

The door was officially opened, a record created on which a later, more favorable ruling, could be given legal justification.

Luciano did continue to cooperate, for he wanted out very badly. The next event in this curious saga that seemed to be leading Charlie closer to freedom every day, and bringing the men who had put him in prison closer to the brink of scandal, arrived in the person of Commander Haffenden. A short time after McCook's ruling, Haffenden visited Charlie in prison with a new problem, one even greater than potential espionage. It had been decided to liberate Italy very soon, he said. The first step was an invasion of Sicily. Would Luciano assist once more by consulting with his Sicilian-American friends, and ask them to identify those Sicilians who would help Allied forces once the landings were made? Even, if possible, use his contacts to get for the Navy a list of Sicilian partisans who could be enlisted as espionage agents to soften up the enemy and lower the loss of American life?

Luciano said he was certain he could help. Many of his friends still had relatives in Sicily, and it would be a simple matter to determine which of them hated Mussolini and Hitler. Haffenden asked him to begin working on it immediately. Charlie called in Frank Costello and informed him of the new assignment. Word was delivered to Joe Adonis, Vince Mangano, Joe Profaci, and many others, ordering them to get together the list of names the Navy requested. It would be a surprising list.

At the very moment Allied forces invaded Sicily in July, 1943, reconnaissance planes flew over the island dropping packages to "partisans" who had been radioed to expect them. In these bundles were flags with the letter "L" (for Luciano) embroidered on them. When the invaders arrived the populations of entire towns, headed by men waving the L-flags, turned out to greet them. The island was completely in Allied hands within a month, and the men with the L-flags were rewarded with important positions in local governing bodies by the Occupation Forces.

It was not by accident, certainly, that every one of those "partisans" was a member of the Sicilian Mafia. Most of them had been under virtual house arrest since Mussolini vowed to destroy the Mafia, others had been in prison or exile. All turned up with the L-flag. One man, Don Calogero Vizzini, was the *capo di tutti capi* of the Mafia. His reward for helping the invading forces was to be made mayor of his town, Villalba, and an "honorary colonel" in the U.S. Army. An American tank patrol had made a dash from the coast to Vizzini's estate to protect his honored and very corpulent body from the enemy. When Vizzini was later returned to his town, at the head of an American Army column, the entire populace turned out, shouting, "Long live the Allies! Long live the Mafia!"

On that day in May, 1945, that Victory was declared in Europe, Charlie Luciano moved to cash in the promissory notes he held from Naval Intelligence. He officially requested that Governor Dewey pardon him or commute his sentence to time served, because of his "considerable assistance" to the Navy during the war.

Dewey, as required by law, turned Luciano's petition over to the State Parole Board for review and advice; according to the cynics, who speak knowingly of a deal, "Dewey was trying to make it look like any ordinary pardon request, going through channels." On the surface, at least, it appears that the Parole Board performed

184

its duties: It investigated, questioning Gurfein, Polakoff, Lansky, Costello, and others, and getting a letter from Commander Haffenden, who was in the Pacific, which said that Luciano had provided assistance to the Navy. The board ruled, at the end of 1945, that Luciano had indeed been a wartime patriot and should be released. But, it added, since Luciano had never become a naturalized citizen his release should be contingent upon his agreeing to voluntary deportation. Luciano agreed and on February 2, 1946, Dewey signed the commutation papers and Charlie was taken to Ellis Island to be held for the next ship to Italy.

Behind the scenes, under the surface of that official story, some rather unusual events had occurred, if Luciano and many others can be believed. Luciano himself told U.S. agents in Italy, and some of his many visitors, that more than his aid to the war effort freed him. What Charlie said, in conversations on many occasions, is pieced together here in continuity, as one long explanation in his own words.

"Dewey and all those politicians claim I got out because of my efforts to help the Navy," Luciano said. "That wasn't it at all.

"Sure, I did everything I could when those Navy guys got suckered into coming to me. But I was looking out for *numero uno* first. The Navy was gonna get me out.

"See, I been around in politics for a long time and I know politicians. I been in court in my life, I know how things work. Dewey was gonna free me, I knew that. But he needed an excuse, something for the record they call it, so the papers wouldn't jump on him and say he sold out to me. The stuff about the Navy was the excuse, to make it all legit for the papers.

"But I didn't trust Dewey. He wanted to be president so bad he would have framed me on a murder charge if he figured it could help. No way could I trust the bastard. So, I told some of my friends to get together a big, fat book on Dewey. Startin' with the money my friends gave him to run for Governor. Stuff on how he let some of my friends run wide open gambling joints in Saratoga while he was governor. Stuff on the money he got to run against Roosevelt durin' the war. Stuff on how he . . . well, stuff about the Hines case.

"Why do you think Meyer and Frank came up to see me so much? To play cards? No, to get the stuff together for the book, to get me out. So we got the book together and one of my friends took it to Dewey. He put it down on his desk and he said to Dewey: 'If Luciano isn't released, this book will be published.'

"I had no trouble with Dewey, just had to wait till the Navy bullshit story could be told. Actually, the real trouble was with that bastard Moran, head of the Parole Board. He wouldn't go along. I don't know if he was too clean and honest or if he just figured he wanted no part of Dewey's deal. Dewey had to put pressure on him. Moran's time on the board had run out and Dewey kept him around, but didn't reappoint him. He let Moran know, this was told to me by a guy in Dewey's office, that he wasn't getting no appointment until he fell in line. Moran sure did, but that cocksucker is the guy who insisted that Dewey deport me. It was the big rage to deport Italians. By this time it's maybe eight months since I ask for release, and I want out, so I tell them I'll go along with deportation.

"Shit, I figured I'd get back in after a few years. Just buy us a president—maybe Dewey himself, he sure looked a winner."

And so Tom Dewey, the rackets buster who sent Luciano away for fifty years on manufactured evidence, used his power as governor to release him after ten years. It may be total coincidence, but one month before Luciano was released Commander Haffenden was appointed New York City Commissioner of Marine and Aviation by Mayor William O'Dwyer, that good friend of so many *mafiosi*. A recounting of all the benefits accruing to the mob during O'Dwyer's years as Brooklyn district attorney and as mayor would require another full book; suffice it to say that Albert Anastasia escaped prosecution for his role in Murder, Inc. because O'Dwyer's men permitted the chief witness against Anastasia to be thrown from a window to his death while under police guard.

A couple of days after being placed in a guarded room in the Ellis Island complex, Charlie was permitted to slip ashore to attend a farewell party in his honor. It was all top secret, of course, for it was quite extra legal. The party was held in the Village Inn in Sheridan Square, Greenwich Village, a club owned by Luciano and several others in his organization.

Robert Slatzer, author of *The Curious Death of Marilyn Monroe,* now a Hollywood producer, director and writer, but back then a young reporter from the Midwest, was taken to the party by comedian B. S. Pulley. Slatzer was introduced to such *mafiosi* as Joe Adonis, Willie Moretti, Tony Bender, Johnny Robolotto and, eventually, to Charlie Luciano himself.

"You're a newspaper man?" Luciano asked.

"Yes, just breaking in," Slatzer said.

"You here professionally?"

"No, socially."

"That's good," Luciano said. "I don't care much for newspaper men."

But Charlie was gracious and charming. When he learned Slatzer was in town on such a slim budget that he couldn't afford to see any Broadway shows, Charlie ordered one of his men to get Slatzer tickets to the Schubert and St. James theaters. And he made no attempt to hide the fact that he was receiving, from Mafia men, judges, and politicians, bon voyage presents consisting of thick envelopes obviously filled with cash. It was, Slatzer says, the most stunning example of mafia power he's ever witnessed.

Now occurred the most astonishing part of the entire Luciano affair, a brazen display of hoodlum power marshalled to protect the boss from the intrusion of the press.

On February 9, two days after the party, Luciano was taken by Immigration officials to a pier in Brooklyn and placed aboard a Liberty ship, the *Laura Keene,* for the voyage back to Italy. Newspaper reporters had been invited by federal officials to a shipboard press conference with Luciano, and dozens of writers and photographers turned out. Accompanied by Harry Ratzke, the Immigration Bureau's assistant chief of security, the group approached the pier entrance.

In front of them was a wall of fifty longshoremen, members of Albert Anastasia's union. Equipped with bailing hooks, they would not permit anyone on the pier. Luciano arrived at about three P.M., greeted by an outburst of cheering from the dock workers. They created a small opening for him and he went aboard the ship; the opening closed behind Luciano and Ratzke and the reporters again came up against the wall of longshoremen.

"Nobody goes on the pier," the head of Anastasia's goon squad announced. "Somebody might trip and get hurt. We gotta be careful of lawsuits."

Ratzke said that was ridiculous, that he represented the U.S. government and he was taking the reporters aboard. The longshoremen surrounded Ratzke, asking him to try to get past them. Ratzke backed down. "Is it all right if I go aboard alone and talk to Luciano?" he asked. That was agreeable, and Ratzke went aboard. He returned a few minutes later and said that Luciano had decreed: No press conference, no pictures.

"I want you fellows to know it wasn't Immigration that kept you off this boat," Ratzke lamely said.

By then it was clear that a greater authority than the government controlled the piers. As reporters stood there, helpless, they could see dozens of men being passed through the longshoremen's screen, and baskets of lobster, cavier, champagne, and other delicacies; Charlie

Luciano was being given a bon voyage party. Among the well-wishers recognized by newsmen were Costello, Adonis, Anastasia, Lansky, several Tammany leaders and at least one judge of the State Supreme Court. Charlie later told friends that "the boys brought me a million bucks that I had stashed away, so I wouldn't go hungry in the old country."

"The cause of this celebration and expression of loyalty," George Wolf, Costello's lawyer, later wrote, "I was not to discover until late that same year. That's when I heard Luciano was coming back to power. He would set up his headquarters in Cuba . . . where he would issue orders to his underlings in America."

Wolf undoubtedly did not know Charlie's complete plans. The base in Cuba would be a temporary expedient. From Havana, Luciano would be directing the campaign to return him to the U.S., legally.

"Dewey was gonna be president, that's for sure," Luciano later told friends. "There was no way he could lose in 1948, because after the war things were swinging over to the Republicans. And I still had that big book on Dewey. When he's president, he's gonna figure some way to get me back in."

15

Upon his arrival in Palermo Charlie was met at the pier by Don Calo Vizzini, Mayor of Villalba and Mafia king of the island, who was accompanied by a number of the highest-ranking *mafiosi*. All had come to thank Charlie for helping restore them to power. After spending several days in a Palermo hotel noted as a Mafia resort, Charlie went to visit his parents' birthplace. Then he traveled down to Villalba to consult Don Calo privately. Exactly what occurred between the two men will never be known, but, as Luciano later put it: "I needed a passport, so I got into Sicilian politics."

The Italian Communist Party's growing strength in northern Italy immediately after the war began to trouble American Army intelligence experts and the State Department. In Sicily, a Separatist Party had once more been formed, after being suppressed for two decades by Mussolini. The Separatists promised Sicilians either complete independence, or autonomy as an American colony. American officials encouraged the Separatists, for a while, on the theory that should mainland Italy go Communist, the American forces would have an independent Sicily as a base in the Mediterranean.

Don Calo Vizzini also encouraged the Separatists; should Stalinists gain control of the Italian government the *mafiosi* might be shot without trial or other legal niceties and the great estates they controlled would be divided among the peasants.

Several months after Luciano arrived in Sicily the Separatists held a convention in Palermo to recreate the old party and plan strategy for secession from the Italian state. Don Calo was housed in his regular hotel suite, receiving visitors who sought his support and blessings. In an adjoining suite lived Charles Luciano, who sat by Don Calo's side during the formation of the party. It was said, among Sicilians and some American Army men of Sicilian descent, that part of the deal in which the U.S. War Department had gone along with the L-flag ploy which brought the Mafia great political power, was that Luciano would guarantee the Mafia would support a Separatist movement.

Luciano shortly became a folk hero in Sicily. At that time the bandit, Salvatore Giuliano, a combination Robin Hood and Pancho Villa, was believed by most Sicilians to be the sole salvation of the island. Giuliano fought the Mafia (at first), he fought the Communists, and the landowners. He was then seduced by Don Calo into joining the Separatist Party. His bandits were to be the army which would fight the Communist conspiracy. Giuliano was loved. And there were many Sicilians who believed quite sincerely that Giuliano the bandit was a disguise adopted by Lucky Luciano so that he could pursue his new aim in life: to free the Sicilian peasants from centuries of near slavery. Giuliano's sister, Maria, knew that was not true: "Luciano is a lieutenant in the United States Navy," she told American correspondent Michael Stern. "He was decorated for bravery during the war." When Stern expressed his doubt, Maria Giuliano said she knew it was true: "Luciano told me himself."

He was all things to all men in Sicily. But he was not a Sicilian, he was American and he wanted to return. Early in October, 1946, he flew to Rome and paid a call at the Cuban Consulate. Waiting there for him, with the personal regards of Cuban Senator Edouardo Suarez Rivas, were visas to be attached to the two Italian passports that Don Calo had given Luciano in Sicily. Both visas permitted entry into Cuba; to one of them was appended papers which would permit Signore Salvatore Lucania to stop in Mexico, Brazil, Colombia, Bolivia, and Venezuela.

Luciano soon boarded a plane for the West. Rather than fly directly to Havana he took a more circuitous route, stopping first in Brazil and then Venezuela. Then, after a brief stopover in Mexico City, he landed at Camaguey, Cuba, in mid-November. He was accompanied by fourteen men and women, each of them having arrest records in the files of the FBI. Cuban officials welcomed them.

"I had the police chief, a couple of senators, and even the president himself in my pocket," Charlie told friends years later, after Castro had come to power and it didn't matter much any more. "The president was a guy named San Martin. All the stories about it say Batista was president, but they got it wrong. It was this San Martin. But Batista was the big shot behind the scenes. The whole thing was set up for me by Meyer Lansky."

Cuban political leaders had been accustomed to cooperating with American entrepeneurs, at a price, since at least as far back as the early Prohibition days, when Charles Stoneham was running the Havana casinos and race track and helping Arnold Rothstein and the others to smuggle liquor into the U.S. Through the years, no matter which dictator or reformer was in power in Cuba, the color of the American gangsters' money was irresistible. Lansky had gained control of Cuban dictator Fulgencio Batista in the mid-1930's, paying a large royalty on sugar that Lansky was buying to produce untaxed alcohol even after repeal. Eventually Lansky was running all the gambling in Cuba. His partners, of course, were Luciano, Costello, and several other members of the Luciano syndicate (and Batista). Luciano would later claim that he owned twenty-five percent of the casino in the Hotel Nacional, and would continually curse "that cocksucker Castro for ruinin' it all."

That influence in Cuban affairs is the major reason

Luciano accepted deportation with equanimity. He knew he would be greeted warmly in Cuba, only ninety miles from the U.S. And he was. He leased a lavish penthouse apartment atop the Nacional, and a pilgrimage of mainland *mafiosi* soon got underway. They came from every major city in America to pay their respects. And they came to assure him they would do all in their power to use their political influence to get Charlie back into America. Dewey was certain to run against Harry Truman in 1948, and he and the Republicans were overwhelming favorites to capture the White House and the Congress. The Mafia men were going to work even harder to buy enough Republicans to legitimize, if necessary, the action that Dewey was certain to take under the pressure of blackmail—permitting Luciano to emigrate to America.

"The plan was really beautiful," Luciano told friends years later. "You see, I was really a citizen. My father took out citizenship papers and listed all the kids, and that's enough to make me a legit citizen. I started to fight the deportation idea when I'm in Dannemora, but then I figure I'm stuck in the can another couple of years fightin' the bastards and maybe get deported permanently, which happens when you fight Immigration. So I took voluntary deportation, meaning I have the right to apply to come back in. That was a laugh, Dewey sayin' he did the whole country a favor by deporting me. That cocksucker knows we was settin' it up so's I could get back.

"I figure with Dewey as president, he's gonna make his Immigration people say it's all a mistake, I'm a citizen, I'm rehabilitated, I'm a war hero—all that bullshit. And I'm back in New York with my friends, maybe six months after Dewey's president."

Vincent Barbi frequently visited Luciano in Italy through his exile. Barbi had fought in the New York area in the early 1930s as Kid Barry. He was managed by Damon Runyon and had met all the Broadway sporting crowd, including Luciano, with whom he became friendly. By the time Charlie was living in Naples, Barbi

193

had become an actor, screenwriter, and film producer. He recalls:

"Charlie told me the deal was all set up when he was still in Dannemora. He said his lawyers met with Dewey's assistants, and they worked it out. Charlie promised to take deportation, live in Italy a couple of years, and stay out of trouble—and when Dewey is President he'll let Charlie come back to America under another name. His real name; Salvatore Lucania. Part of the deal was that Charlie promised to stay out of New York City, live in a small town out on Long Island or up in Connecticut. That was Charlie's deal with Dewey."

Luciano's plans never did work out. A writer for a Cuban newspaper, *Tiempo de Cuba,* was told that Luciano "has paid big money" and was living in the Nacional. His story was bannered across the front page in late February, 1947. Luciano, the article said, had been in Cuba for four months, with government approval. Not only did he occupy the Nacional penthouse, where he conferred with all sorts of tough-looking gangsters from America, and where he entertained the city's most beauteous show girls and prostitutes, but he had also leased a large home in fashionable Miramar, a suburb overlooking the Caribbean.

That story didn't generate too much excitement in government circles. But it was read by an agent of the U.S. Narcotics Bureau, sent to Cuba to infiltrate a gang smuggling heroin and cocaine to Florida. He forwarded it to his superiors in Washington, and asked for instructions.

Within hours after Henry Anslinger, head of the Narcotics Bureau, received the article a dozen narcotics agents arrived in Havana. Their mission was to keep Luciano under close surveillance, for two purposes: to see whether he had any connection with Cuban narcotics smuggling, and to gather evidence that might indicate whether Luciano was still in control of his Mafia organization. (It must be said here that while FBI Director Hoover and

194

most police officials in America were denigrating the possibility that Mafia actually exists, the Narcotics Bureau was the only investigative agency that believed there was a Mafia.)

Narcotics agents watched Luciano for months, and filed almost daily reports on his movements and his visitors. One of those reports discussed in detail a convention of the mob boys that was held in Luciano's penthouse in March. Lansky was there, he had been in Havana since Charlie arrived. From Chicago came Al Capone's cousins, Rocco and Charley Fischetti, plus Tony Accardo, the new head of the Capone syndicate. From New Orleans, where Costello still ran the slot machines that had been installed with the approval of Louisiana Governor Huey Long shortly before he was assassinated in 1935, came Mafia leader Carlos Marcello. From New York came Costello, Pisano, Mangano, Tommy Luchese and a dozen delegates from the Mafia families. From Cleveland, Pittsburgh, Buffalo, and every major American city came at least one member of the crime cartel. Many of them were Jewish, which brought enormous confusion to the Mafia watchers in the Narcotics Bureau.

In the files of the Bureau is an extensive report about that week-long convention, which broke up for visits to the gambling casino, the track, and to a couple of select local whorehouses. In the report is a short paragraph:

"Purpose of these meetings could not be determined with certainty. Sources indicate that a major topic of discussion was Ben (Bugsy) Siegel, said to be building a hotel and gambling casino in Nevada."

It wasn't until more than a year later, when Bugsy Siegel was murdered in the plush home he had bought for his girl friend, Virginia Hill, that the pieces began to fall into place. Siegel had been sent to Hollywood by the Luciano organization in the late 1930's, to investigate the possibility of establishing a union racket in the film industry along the lines of the garment center rackets which Lepke had put together. Bugsy did just that, winning complete control of workers at most Hollywood film studios.

Some time during the war, Bugsy had a dream: Gambling was legal in Nevada, so why not build a huge gambling palace in Las Vegas to which every sucker in the country would flock, to lose their money to the organization? Bugsy ran around telling all his associates about it, and convincing Lansky, Costello, and the others that his dream could become reality. Mafia men, Jewish members of the national syndicate, everyone with gangster connections was sold a share in the business. They were dubious at first, but when Frank Costello said that he was buying in and could not see how it could fail, the others contributed millions of dollars.

Bugsy, however, was not a businessman. He decided that his Flamingo Hotel must be more luxurious, more gaudy and flamboyant, than anything ever built before. The cost was originally estimated at about two million, but construction costs skyrocketed immediately because Bugsy wanted nothing but the best. It was war time, and copper was impossible to get. Bugsy bought it in the black market, paying outrageous prices; the plumbing bill alone came to more than one million. By early 1946, Bugsy's demands for more and more money were ignored—except for Costello, who sent what he could—and Bugsy began holding back the share of the Hollywood rackets that was to be paid to his gangster partners in Chicago and in the East.

Finally, the hotel was completed—many millions of dollars over cost. The grand opening was December 26, 1946, and Bugsy had convinced all his many friends in Hollywood, including the biggest stars, to attend and to bring the place worldwide publicity. The night of the opening, however, a heavy fog fell over Los Angeles and Bugsy's guests could not fly to Las Vegas. The opening was a disaster. The worst thing of all is that the casino lost money—$500,000 in the first two weeks because there weren't enough customers to cover the overhead.

"The Flamingo's a washout," the boys across the country started saying. And they were quite angry about the money they had lost in Bugsy's fiasco.

Some of the investors had traveled to Havana to complain to Luciano that they had been misled by Siegel and Costello, and they demanded the death penalty for both. Luciano refused. The pressure mounted, however, and Charlie was forced to reconsider. According to Costello's lawyer, George Wolf, Luciano called Costello to come see him in Havana. He told Costello that he'd have to get up the money to pay back all the other investors who had gone into the Flamingo because of his advice, "otherwise I can't hold them back." Costello said he would raise the money. Luciano told him: "Meanwhile, you retire as head of the commission. Genovese takes over . . . But I told the boys, and they agree, as soon as you get the money back, you take over again. I want *you* there."

"What happens to Bugsy?" Costello asked.

"Him I can't help," Luciano said.

(Siegel was murdered in June, 1947.)

By the time of the large convention of American racketeers at the Nacional, the decision had already been made to kill Bugsy. The more important purpose of the meeting was, as Luciano himself later told friends, to plot his return to America.

Narcotics agents kept Luciano and his guests under surveillance for several weeks, a chore which consisted mostly of making a list of his visitors, the most famous racketeers in America. It was a rather boring assignment for the agents, except for the occasional titillation provided by the arrival of an unusual guest. The foremost of these was Frank Sinatra, the idol of American bobby-soxers, who stayed at the Nacional for a while and was frequently seen in Luciano's company. Years later, when Italian police searched Luciano's apartment for evidence that he was involved in a narcotics ring, they discovered a gold cigarette lighter with the inscription: "To Charlie/

197

From His Pal/Frank." It is said that Sinatra gave him that lighter during the visit to Havana.

The Narcotics Bureau did not want news of Luciano's presence in Havana to be published, because it was felt that much information could be obtained by secretly watching his conferences. But then newspaper columnist Robert Ruark happened to fly to Havana for a vacation and one day, quite by accident, he saw Luciano in a restaurant with a New York society woman who had recently been divorced. Ruark investigated, then began to write a series of articles about Luciano's presence in Havana, pointing out that the increased use of narcotics in American cities was undoubtedly connected with Luciano's residence so near to the U.S.

Now that the news was out, the Cuban government reacted with great calm: Officials simply pretended they couldn't read. After many demands from Anslinger that Luciano be deported back to Italy, demands that were ignored by Luciano's political protectors in Cuba, the U.S. government announced that because Luciano was a long-time narcotics wholesaler, an embargo on all shipments of medicines and narcotics into Cuba would be immediately effective. Luciano's friends continued to try to help him, but Cuban medical authorities demanded that Luciano be deported before Cuban hospitals ran out of medical supplies. After much hand-wringing and stirring speeches in the Cuban Senate in defense of Charlie Luciano, he was forced to leave. Immigration police placed him on the Turkish freighter *Bakir,* bound for Genoa. And in Genoa the chief of police announced that Charlie would be thrown into prison for "clandestine departure without proper credentials."

Charlie was furious that his plans to use Havana as a springboard for re-entry had been ruined by Anslinger (Charlie always called him Ass-slinger from then on). But he could laugh about the whole thing in later years. "That cop in Genoa was a joke," Charlie told friends. "By the time my boat arrived he was kissin' my ass because he got word from Rome, from the guys who got me my passports, that he better be nice to me, or else. So these charges didn't amount to nothin'. But to keep up the game for the newspapers, they announced they were sending me back to Palermo, where I'd be thrown in jail and questioned. They gave me first class to Palermo. The head cop in Palermo visits me in my hotel, asks me if I've broken the law and I say I sure as hell didn't. He tells me to please stay out of trouble and don't get my name in the papers. So we have a drink on it. I keep out of sight for a couple of months, repairing my political fences like they say in the papers. Then I fly off to Rome to live."

16

From the moment he arrived in Rome Luciano began to cultivate Italian politicians, industrialists, and the heirs of the late dictator, Benito Mussolini; it had been reported that Mussolini's daughter was for a time Luciano's mistress. All of Italian "society" knew about Luciano, especially that he was known to be wealthier and more powerful than Vito Genovese, that he was in fact Genovese's superior in their joint American "business" enterprises. And Genovese was remembered quite fondly by the Italians.

Through all the war years in Italy, Genovese had been close to the seat of power through his alliances with Mussolini's son-in-law, Count Ciano. He had been so generous with his contributions to the Fascist Party that Mussolini expressed his gratitude by conferring upon Genovese the title of *Commendatore,* the highest civilian award in Italy. When Italy surrendered and Mussolini was killed, most Italians of substance, and Genovese, promptly jumped to the Americans and denounced Mussolini as a Fascist pig. Genovese himself was placed on the staff of the American Military Government, as an interpreter, through the good offices of Charles Poletti, a former acting governor of New York who was in Italy as a U.S. Army colonel. Genovese used his position to establish a black market operation, utilizing Army trucks and American soldiers, to steal Army supplies and foodstuffs. The black market made him so wealthy that he shared his income with his Italian friends who might prove helpful to him in the future.

Genovese needed all the help he could get, at that point, for he had heard through the Mafia communications network that he'd better not return to New York after the war. It seemed that Ernie the Hawk had turned state's evidence and, now that District Attorney O'Dwyer was in the Army and could no longer help Brooklyn *mafiosi,* Genovese faced a murder charge. Ernie later told me that he had confessed only because he thought Genovese was dead, in Italy; "I would have never squealed if I knew he was alive, but figurin' he was dead I'd thought I could talk myself out of jail," he once told me. So he said that it was Genovese who had given him the contract to kill a Brooklyn man in 1934.

An arrest warrant went out for Genovese, and he was discovered alive in Italy and sent back to America to stand trial for murder. Ernie, in his confession to Brooklyn authorities, had given them the name of a man who had heard the murder plot but had not been directly involved. Without his corroborating testimony, under the law, Ernie's testimony was worthless. This witness, Pete LaTempa, was put in jail for safekeeping, where he was promptly poisoned "with enough strychnine to kill eight men," said the autopsy report. Genovese was released. And, says Ernie the Hawk, Genovese got word to him that he wasn't angry, he would not have Ernie killed. "I gotta thank you for gettin' me back to New York," Genovese told him.

All the Italians in power who had so greatly admired *Commendatore* Genovese, now welcomed Luciano. No matter what had been said of him in those scandalous newspaper stories, *Signore* Luciano was obviously a wealthy American businessman, and a gentleman. Charlie soon used his social contacts to establish business relationships with the owners of several pharmaceutical houses, which would supply American *mafiosi* with many hundreds of pounds of narcotics.

Although he denied to the day of his death that he was involved in narcotics, and insisted that "Ass-slinger watches me so close that he would've busted me if he could pin a dope rap on me," the evidence is overwhelming that Luciano was a major source of the narcotics which has flooded the United States since the war. An idea of the size of that torrent can be seen in a single statistic. Between 1951 and 1963 Italian authorities and the Federal Narcotics Bureau seized almost eleven *tons* of heroin, opium, and morphine base that was destined for shipment from Italy to America. It is axiomatic in smuggling circles that no more than five percent of the narcotics is ever seized, a rule of thumb which makes clear the amount of narcotics smuggled into America.

It is not surprising, in fact it is most logical, that Luciano in exile should have been involved in narcotics. His first underworld assignment of any stature, and his first arrest, stemmed from dope peddling. It was Luciano who had suggested to Arnold Rothstein that narcotics be shipped into America along with whiskey. It was from that suggestion that Rothstein developed an international purchasing and shipping organization, sending his men to buy from the source and ship the narcotics back to Rothstein's organization. And it was Luciano who took control of that organization when Rothstein was killed in 1928. Indeed, it would have been more surprising had Luciano stayed out of the international narcotics business.

One of Luciano's first acts, upon his arrival in Sicily in 1946, had been to repair the narcotics pipeline that had been virtually destroyed by the war. According to Italian and Sicilian sources and the Narcotics Bureau, Luciano broached the subject with Don Calo Vizzini, the Sicilian Mafia chief. Vizzini and the religious, old-fashioned men of honor like him, condoned the use of murder as an instrument of power. They corrupted the aristocracy, the government, and the Church, but they believed there were two things that were *infamita,* two pursuits to be shunned by an honorable man. Prostitution was first. Narcotics was a close second. Luciano agreed about prostitution, according to informers, and he explained that he had been framed by a man who wanted to be president. But Charlie persisted about narcotics.

He pointed out to Vizzini that America was deporting scores of racketeers who had been born in Sicily and Italy. Most of them were younger men who had been corrupted by their contact with American customs and did not wholly believe in all the tenets of the Honored Society. These men dealt in narcotics, for narcotics was an enormously profitable business in America. They would continue to deal in narcotics in Sicily and on the mainland, to supply their American associates. Should the honorable *mafiosi*, honorable men like Don Calo, ignore this business, then some day the younger men in Mafia, not only Americans but also young Sicilians in Palermo who were being similarly corrupted by contact with the deportees, would gather enough wealth and power to challenge Don Calo's right to rule Mafia.

Don Calo got the point. He sent word to all *mafiosi* throughout the island that narcotics was now an acceptable trade, to be run under the beneficient protection of Don Calo himself. Luciano and Don Calo became partners in a narcotics operation in Sicily, importing the raw opium from the mid-east and refining it into heroin in clandestine factories on the island. It was Luciano, according to Sicilian legend, who hit upon an invention that would eliminate some risk in smuggling heroin from Sicily to mainland ports from which it was shipped to America. Sicily is an enormous producer of oranges. Much of the crop is sent to the mainland. Luciano conceived the idea of counterfeiting oranges from wax, and filling them with heroin. For several years, whenever a shipment of oranges was made, every crate contained at least one of those wax oranges, filled by syringe with one hundred grams of heroin.

Over the years the Federal Narcotics Bureau always maintained that "Lucky Luciano is the head of a multimillion-dollar international narcotics operation." Repeated annually, that statement created a mental image of Luciano sitting at his desk, moving pins on his map like a wartime general keeping track of his troops, the pins marking Luciano's heroin factories, poppy fields, ships in transit, and so on. That's nonsense. On the evidence available Luciano remained as completely detached from actual criminal involvement as it was possible to become. His business was patterned after Rothstein's: Luciano was financier for some of the major narcotics purchasers, advancing money to buy the crude opium in Turkey and other countries and getting a large share of the profits when sold to the refiners; he was the contact man, the politician so to speak, who worked on the greed of owners of major drug houses in Italy, so that these men would divert large amounts of heroin into the illicit market; and, finally, he established the distribution network to bring narcotics from Italy to his friends in New York City and in Canada.

Only in the very early years, when he was first establishing the contacts and the narcotics network, did Charlie come even near to personal involvement. At that time Italian officials would not consider dishonoring Signore Luciano by placing him under investigation and, perhaps through some misfortune, discovering evidence against him. When the Federal Narcotics Bureau did set up an office in Rome, in 1950, Luciano had by then stepped back from even the minimal involvement that had been necessary in the early years. The only evidence ever turned up by federal narcotics agents was that Luciano seemed to be on very close terms with everyone involved in narcotics, from visiting American *mafiosi* to the president of Italy's largest and most respectable pharmaceutical house.

The first indication that Luciano was one of those engaged in narcotics in Italy came in 1948, when customs agents at the Rome airport searched the luggage of a New Yorker named Vincent Trupia and discovered he was trying to bring three kilos of heroin back home with him. Italian police notified Henry Manfredi, of the American Army's Criminal Intelligence Division. He began to check on Trupia's movements. He discovered that Trupia had flown into Rome a week before his arrest. He immediately checked into the Albergo Quirinale, where Luciano was living, and called Luciano's room. Trupia then placed calls to two men in Milan who were suspected of being major narcotics wholesalers.

Two days after Trupia arrived in Rome, another New Yorker checked into the same hotel. He was Joseph Di Palermo, known to his Mafia associates in East Harlem as Joey Beck. Joey was a member of the Luciano family, and he was a veteran dope importer. (He and Vito Genovese would be sent to prison together years later on charges of operating the largest heroin-importing syndicate in America.) Joey Beck then went to Milan, where he apparently examined the heroin and made arrangements for it to be delivered to his hotel in Rome. Before delivery was made, Luciano visited police headquarters and reported that he was leaving that day for a brief vacation in the country; two businessmen with great political power stood by Charlie's side and said they were going with him. The heroin was then delivered and paid for. Joey Beck flew home the next day. Two days later Trupia started home, and was seized by the customs guards. Luciano, meanwhile, was still in the country on his vacation.

Rome police agreed there seemed to be something suspicious about all this. They arrested Luciano and the two men from Milan, and jailed them. Luciano was asked to explain the phone call from Trupia. He said he had never heard of the man, never spoke to him in his life, so it must have been a wrong number or an error by the telephone operator. Charlie was released and the police announced he had been barred from Rome forever and ordered back to his home town in Sicily. Charlie went to visit some other friends in a country villa, graciously permitting photos to be taken of him on the way to "exile." He returned to his Rome apartment two days later and wasn't troubled again for a couple of years.

In 1950, Federal narcotics agent Charles Siragusa was sent to Rome to open an office from which, it was hoped, the men under his command would infiltrate the narcotics operation in Italy and destroy it. Most of all, they hoped to prove that Luciano was the mastermind. Siragusa tried, and he and his men arrested many dozens of wholesalers and confiscated tons of narcotics. But there was never any direct evidence against Luciano. They came close, many times, but never close enough. The best their reports could do was to inform Anslinger that Carlo Gambino, for example, visited with Luciano in a Palermo hotel, and immediately after that the Gambino family in Brooklyn began to deal in dope on a large scale. Or that Joe Biondo, a close associate of Joe Adonis and a member of the Luciano organization from its founding in the mid-1920's, visited Luciano and was introduced by him to the president of a highly esteemed pharmaceutical house in Milan.

That visit, incidentally, had wide repercussions in Italy and provided evidence of how Luciano operated. The owner of that medical company was himself a *Commendatore,* and one of the members of the Italian aristocracy. An investigation disclosed that the *Commendatore* had diverted several hundred kilos of legal heroin to the illicit drug-smuggling market. Proof was also found that the *Commendatore* had been attempting to convince other drug houses to produce illicit quantities of heroin and sell it to him. The firm was shut down and the *Commendatore* was indicted. He never went to trial. And Luciano? Evidence was developed that Charlie had introduced dozens of American "businessmen" to the *Commendatore.* When the man's niece was married she and her groom spent their honeymoon in Charlie's villa in Capri. There was no further evidence. The *Commendatore* was untouchable. So was Luciano.

But that case brought investigation of other drug houses,

and it was discovered that several of them were also diverting their legal heroin production to the illicit market. Some of them had, in fact, manufactured enough heroin to last a hundred years in legitimate medical channels, and had been selling it to *mafiosi* who just happened to be old friends of Luciano. One of the biggest firms of all was discovered to have clandestinely produced about 770 pounds of illicit heroin from 1948 to 1951, all of it apparently going to Luciano associates.

Further evidence of Luciano's involvement in narcotics came many years later, when Valachi began to talk about Mafia. One of the men he discussed was Eugene Giannini, a narcotics importer. Giannini was also an informer, feeding information to narcotics agents, including information about Luciano. Giannini was arrested in Naples in 1950 and sent to prison on narcotics charges. From the Naples jail he wrote to narcotics agents for their help in getting him out because "I've given you a lot of information." Receiving no help from the agents Giannini grew more desperate, and he committed the ultimate indiscretion. "I once gave you information on Charlie Lucky and his connection man, Joe Pici," Giannini wrote. "I know also Charlie's other connection man and where the stuff comes from . . . I have now the information that can link Lucky to all these affairs."

Giannini was released after serving twenty months, and he returned to New York in April, 1952. Some time after that Valachi was called to a dinner meeting with the captain of his family, who came right to the point: "Gene Giannini has been squealing to the junk agents. The old man (Vito Genovese) has got the word personally from Charlie Lucky. Charlie says Gene is the smartest stool pigeon that ever lived. He has been talking to the junk agents for years. He has got to be hit, him and anybody with him." Giannini was murdered by Valachi and two other men on September 20, 1952, shot through the head several times on a street in East Harlem. Valachi said he felt proud to be doing it for a guy he really respected, Charlie Luciano.

17

While living in Rome, and journeying frequently to Milan to mingle with drug company industrialists and in Milanese society opened to him by the *Commendatore* who appears to have been his narcotics supplier, Luciano met Igea Lissoni. She was then twenty-six, almost half Charlie's age. He later would tell friends, "She knocked me out the minute I saw her." Igea was darkly beautiful, but she had the clear blue eyes of northern Italians. Her soft brown hair was dyed a honey blonde back then. "Not the cheap peroxide blondes I used to know on Broadway," Charlie said, "but blonde with real class." Igea has often been described by journalists as a B-girl, just a cut above the whores they said Charlie had beaten into forced prostitution; the stories about Igea are just as absurd as the stories about the whoremaster Luciano.

Igea was Milanese, the daughter of a middle-class merchant who stressed culture and artistic development. She learned to speak French fluently as a child, and was very young when she was sent off to ballet school. As her talent developed she was accepted in the ballet course at La Scala Opera House and soon was dancing in La Scala's ballet company. "She's a lady to the tips of her toes," Charlie used to say of her, and his old New York friends who met her agreed, and were enchanted by her.

When she was about twenty, Igea gave up ballet. She explained to one of Charlie's American friends: "I realized I could never become a prima ballerina, that I did not have enough talent. So I began to dance in night-clubs, hoping I could some day dance in films and perhaps become a star. My family was scandalized, of course, but I would wrap Papa around my finger."

She was introduced to Luciano in Milan in early 1948, at a rather formal dinner party. Luciano was, as he later said, "too scared to make a play for her." But he learned she was scheduled to open in a nightclub in Rome the following month, and he was at a ringside table on opening night. Someone introduced them again, and Charlie asked her for a date. She turned him down. He kept after her, and after a time she agreed to go out with him. They dated many times over the next few months and, in June, 1948, she moved into his apartment. Igea's father disowned her when she first told him of her relationship with Luciano, but after a couple of years her family came to accept him.

"She's the only girl I ever loved," Charlie often said. "There was something about her that was special. If all broads were like her the world would be a terrific place."

Igea wanted Charlie to marry her, but he refused, although they did exchange wedding bands which they wore until their deaths. "That's the one thing I couldn't give her, marriage, and I feel bad about that," Charlie told a friend after Igea's death in 1958. "I knew that if I got married I'd break down and I'd give her kids, a lot of them, like she wanted. But I didn't want no kids. I didn't want no son of mine to go through life as the son of Luciano, the gangster. That's one thing I still hate Dewey for, making me a gangster in the eyes of the whole world. Dewey and that cocksucker Ass-linger, they're why I never married Igea."

After they had been living together for two years, Italian authorities ordered Luciano to leave Rome. They said, quite frankly, that the order had come as a result of pressure from Siragusa, Anslinger, and the U.S. Ambassador, Claire Booth Luce, on the Italian government. Luciano protested that he was being persecuted by Anslinger, but he and Igea quietly moved to Naples. He soon was giving out interviews, cursing at "that cocksucker Ass-slinger who runs the Italian government with his bullshit about dope." Charlies' favorite expression to describe someone he particularly loathed was "cocksucker." But he never used it in front of Igea, nor when any respectable woman was within hearing. "He had an old-world attitude toward women as he grew older," one friend who visited him often in Naples said. "He was very respectful towards women, very charming. He'd rise when they approached his table, he'd hold doors for them, light their cigarettes, that whole charming Continental manner. He wasn't trying to impress anyone. It was how he just naturally felt about women."

Another friend remembers: "It was funny. He'd talk about 'broads' and 'whores' when he was with a group of men, playing that wise-ass Broadway type. But whenever there was a woman around he'd be all manners. I began to understand he was playing the tough guy, the man who had no use for women except to screw them, whenever he was with his crowd of boys. As if it was expected of him and he couldn't let the boys down. But when he was with a woman, the real Charlie showed through."

Luciano was fifty-four when he moved to Naples. His hair was turning grey, just enough to give him a respectable, distinguished look. He dressed very conservatively and was always immaculate when he went out for breakfast, or sat for hours in the San Francisco Bar and Grill, which he owned and in which he would receive a steady stream of visitors—from New York *mafiosi* to American sailors whose ship had just come into port. For several years Charlie was the favorite attraction for American tourists, and he probably signed several thousand autographs. The sole bit of flash in Charlie was a stickpin with a small diamond and a pinky ring with a diamond only slightly larger.

He and Igea lived at first in the Hotel Mediterraneo,

which Luciano reportedly bought. He would house visitors from America in the hotel, where they were treated by the staff as if they were royal guests; they could never pay a bill or even get a tip accepted. "Signore Luciano has taken care of it," his visitors were always told. Igea told Charlie she wanted to find a proper home after a few months of hotel living. They moved into a large apartment on the top floor of Via Tesso 464, a brand new five-story building high on the famed Vomero that overlooks the sea and Capri, with a stunning view of Mt. Vesuvius. Luciano, it is said, bought the building with $150,000 cash.

Igea, settled into a routine now as Charlie's wife, which is what he often called her, let her hair revert to its natural brown. Almost as an antidote to the stories about this American gangster and his B-girl mistress in the American papers they both read, Igea "started looking like a society woman," as a friend described her. "She dressed perfectly, very conservatively, very Peck & Peck socialite style." But she never lost her fire. "My Sharlie," as she pronounced it in English, loved her very much but his love didn't stop him from sampling other women. Especially when American guests were in Naples, and expecting to be entertained as Charlie had entertained them with girls from Polly Adler's years before.

Once, according to Neapolitan gossips, Igea was alone in their apartment when a woman called and asked for Charlie. Igea said Signore Luciano wasn't in. The woman expressed surprise, saying that when Charlie left her apartment last night he said he'd be home all the next day, so she decided to call and invite him for dinner that evening. Igea, recognizing both a bitch and a competitor, slammed down the phone. She dressed rather quickly and ran over to the San Francisco Bar. As she ran in, the hoods around Charlie, who attained great stature by becoming known as his bodyguards, melted out of her way. Igea began shouting at him about his perfidy. Charlie,

211

quite embarrassed in front of lunch guests, slapped her on the butt and told her to be quiet.

Igea drew from her handbag a cute little .22-caliber item Charlie had given her, and she said: "OK, my friend. If I ever see you even flirt with another girl you'll get this." Knowing she could never come up with a better exit line than that, she turned and quickly left.

Luciano, it is said, behaved himself for quite some time.

Charlie was very wealthy, by all accounts. He was receiving money from his varied legal investments in the Naples area, including bars, clubs, restaurants, hotels and other real estate, all of which gave him an income permitting a lavish style of life that could not be said to be the fruits of the narcotics traffic. Charlie also had an income of about $60,000 a year from what he like to call "the administrators of my estate" in the U.S. At least a part of that "estate" was a men's suit manufacturer; during the Second World War, while Charlie was in prison, that firm received millions of dollars in military uniform contracts from the War Department. Another company contributing to Charlie's upkeep in Naples, and which also managed to receive large military contracts while Charlie was imprisoned, was an optical supply house in New Jersey which Luciano owned in partnership with a very respected member of his community.

From quite legal sources alone, it would appear that Luciano was receiving upwards of $100,000 a year.

There were also the illegal sources. It sounds glib, and is certainly impossible to prove, when one reels off such industries as narcotics, gambling, labor-industrial rackets, and then claim that Charlie was getting his share. Yet it is undoubtedly true. One New York friend, a respectable businessman whose family background includes Mafia members but who never became involved himself, frequently visited Luciano in Naples in the 1950's. He recalls that once, as he was preparing to fly back to New York, he asked Charlie: "Is there anything I can do, anything you need?" Luciano replied: "No, I'm okay. Meyer's boys come back and forth to bring me my money." And he talked about Lansky, as he'd often done:

"I always liked and admired Meyer. We never have any fights, there's never any feeling he's cheating me or competing with me. He's always straight ahead, always does things in a businesslike manner. Always stuck by me, always went to bat for me more than anybody else."

Luciano often expressed warm feelings about Costello, also for helping in all the machinations to get Charlie out of prison, and for his honesty. "Frank never tried to cheat me," he once told a friend. "Sometimes I used to send word to him that he was sending me more than he should of." Narcotics agent Vizzini, posing as an Air Force major, was with Luciano one day when a courier from New York arrived and handed him a thick envelope. "That's from Frank Costello," he said. "You better count it, Charlie. Frank says there's seventy big ones ($70,000) in there." Luciano said: "I'll count it later because I guess it's there if Frank says so."

Luciano did not have the same respect for several others who had been a part of his combination. Especially Vito Genovese and Carlo Gambino. Narcotics agent Vizzini reported to his superiors that the same courier who brought Charlie the $70,000 from Costello asked, before leaving, whether there was anything he could do when he got back to New York. Luciano took off his gold watch and his diamond tie pin and handed them to the courier.

"See that Vito and Carlo get these," he said. "They gave 'em to me as presents when I was kicked out of the States. Tell 'em to hock these things for me. I'm runnin' out of money." Later, informers said that Vito and Carlo, upon getting the message, returned their gifts with apologies, plus the installments they owed Charlie, and two extra payments in advance.

Luciano seems to have accepted the fact that he might never return to the U.S. "I didn't give up until a few

213

years after Cuba," he said. "I figured maybe Dewey would make it in '48, but Truman beat his ass off and then Eisenhower comes in and you can't fix that cocksuckin' general with all the money and all the pussy in the world. So, I'm stuck in Italy. It ain't so bad. Igea makes it pretty O. K."

Some time in 1956, however, Charlie began chafing again at his exile, insisting to some friends that he had to get back to America "before it all gets fucked up." Those who did not know of events in the Mafia were puzzled. Insiders, including some who passed information to the narcotics bureau, understood perfectly. Vito Genovese, it seemed, was intent on becoming the *capo di tutti capi,* determined for the sake of his ego to tear down all that Luciano had so assiduously constructed and return Mafia to the days of the old greasers.

Since 1951, because of various state and federal investigations, Costello had been in and out of prisons and courtrooms and had been unable to manage the affairs of the old Luciano Mafia family. Genovese, as next in line, became the acting boss. And Genovese, possessed of a Byzantine mind, began a move to dominate all the American Mafia as soon as Costello was sentenced to five years for income tax evasion in May, 1956.

While out on bail, Costello received word that Anastasia wanted to see him. They met in a midtown restaurant. Anastasia complained that Genovese had been telling everyone that as soon as Costello goes to prison then he, Genovese, would become the head of the commission—an unofficial boss of all bosses that had been Luciano's role, because he was the natural leader, and was then handed to Costello as Luciano's representative; the intention being that Luciano would resume the role on his return to America. But now, Anastasia said, Genovese had the mistaken belief he would inherit the role as part of his inheritance of the Luciano family. Anastasia did not agree that it should go to Genovese automatically, nor that it must necessarily remain in the Luciano family. The position must be earned, he said. As boss of his own Mafia family in Brooklyn, Anastasia had as much right to the role as Genovese. Only a vote of the commission could decide the issue.

Costello agreed, and he said he would talk to Genovese about it. Genovese listened to Costello's talk—that the role of chairman of the Mafia commission would be put to a vote, that Genovese was just one of many contenders—and he said he agreed with that. Costello went off to prison, but a new head of the commission was not selected because it was possible that Frank would be freed on appeal. The Supreme Court agreed to hear Costello's case, and ordered him freed on bail. When he returned to New York, Albert Anastasia came to him once more. According to Costello's lawyer, George Wolf, Anastasia complained that "Genovese is bad-mouthing me" by claiming "I'm muscling in on Cuba," meaning the gambling concession which was owned by the Luciano-Lansky partnership. Costello asked: "So?" And Albert said that Genovese didn't give a damn about Cuba, he had something more sinister in mind.

"I'll talk to him," Costello said.

Anastasia was silent for a time. And then he said, in the typical Mafia understatement which Costello immediately understood: "I don't think that's a good idea, Frank."

And, says Wolf, Costello "knew he had just heard his own death warrant."

Very cautiously, Costello sent word to Luciano about his suspicions, and fear, that Genovese planned to kill all who stood in his way. Luciano began telling everyone that he must return to New York, but he could not explain what was troubling him. Even Igea, from whom Charlie kept his Mafia business secret, noticed a great change in him. "There's some kind of trouble in America," she told a friend, who told another, until the statement ended up in Narcotics Bureau files. Igea continued: "Charlie keeps cursing Vito—Vito this and Vito that, he's destroying everything. I don't know how to help Charlie."

On the evening of May 2, 1957, Costello entered the lobby of the Majestic Apartments, where he and his wife had lived for many years, and barely noticed a heavy-set man standing off to one side. As Costello walked toward the elevators, the man said: "This is for you, Frank." Costello turned, and the man fired a single shot at him from a few feet away. The bullet hit Costello in the head and he went down. The "hulking man," as police described him, believed he had fulfilled his contract and he ran out. But Costello wasn't dead; the bullet had only creased his scalp. He was taken to a hospital and released the next morning.

Costello would never officially identify the man who had shot him, even after a stupid goon named Vince Gigante, one of Genovese's favorite messenger boys, was arrested and placed on trial. But he had recognized Gigante, he later told his lawyer and others, and he knew Genovese had assigned him the murder contract. Costello went off to prison, and was probably quite happy to be out of Genovese's firing range.

The day after Costello was shot and it was clear he was not dead, Vito Genovese retreated to his mansion in New Jersey and ordered all the lieutenants of what was the Luciano-Costello family to come to him. They all did except for L'il Augie Pisano, who sent word to Costello that he would remain loyal and dispatched a courier to Naples to tell Luciano what was happening. (Pisano would be murdered by Genovese a couple of years later.) At that meeting in Genovese's home on the Atlantic Highlands, he told all the men assembled that he had tried to kill Costello because Costello was planning to kill *him*. Further, he said, Costello was completely disinterested in the affairs of the family members. Therefore, Costello was out as family boss and any member found even talking to him would have to answer personally to Genovese. And, of course, Genovese was now

216

boss of the family. As Joe Valachi later put it: "Who was going to argue?"

Genovese had already set up the next stage of his scheme. He had brought to Carlo Gambino, underboss of the Anastasia family, a proposition Gambino could not resist: Kill the boss and you will become boss in his place and preside at my right hand as chief assistant to the new *capo di tutti capi*. Gambino, a Sicilian of the old school and one of those who had been on Maranzeno's side during the 1930 fighting, readily agreed. On the afternoon of October 25, 1957, Albert Anastasia, the man who had been called the Lord High Executioner of Murder, Inc., walked into the barber shop of the Park Sheraton, the same hotel under a new name in which Rothstein had been shot in 1928. As he sat in his chair, with towels over his face to prepare him for a shave, two men walked in and began shooting him in the back of the head. Anastasia was thrown from the chair with such force that he broke the footrest. His killers continued pumping bullets into his body long after he was obviously dead; they were not going to fail this assignment as Gigante had done in the shooting of Costello.

In Naples, Luciano was livid when he heard of Anastasia's murder. "Vito's crazy, that cocksucker's crazier than Maranzano," he shouted to many Neapolitans, including some who made a good living feeding such tidbits to police. "Fuckin' Maranzano was a Caesar but this cocksucker Vito is a Borgia."

But there was nothing Luciano could do, for the present. Days after Anastasia was killed, three New Yorkers flew to Palermo separately, and Charlie slipped down to join them in the same hotel where Don Calo had helped create the Separatist Party. The three were Carmine Galenti, who was very close to Genovese, Joe Bonanno, head of his own small family in Brooklyn, and Bonanno's underboss, John Bonventre. The three, according to Mafia insiders, had been sent by Genovese to explain the reasons for ordering contracts on Costello and Anastasia.

They also told Charlie that Genovese had convened a meeting of the Mafia's national commission, before which he would explain his actions and ask them to confirm him as head of the commission. The word in Mafia circles is that Luciano's sole message to Genovese was: "Good luck."

Luciano knew that his visitors were not being totally frank. From what he had learned in messages from Costello, Anastasia, Pisano, and others, Genovese intended to do what Maranzano had done in a ballroom in the Bronx a quarter century earlier: crown himself boss of all bosses. And Luciano felt strongly that none of the other Mafia bosses would have the stomach to stand up to Genovese. As he once said in an interview, in another context: "When you got the whole town in your vest pocket, what can go wrong? It's peaches and cream as long as it lasts and some of the time it lasts so long everybody gets soft and careless." The men of the Mafia, Luciano felt, had grown so soft that Genovese would step all over them. And he was very depressed over it all.

The gloom ended less than a month later, and Charlie began to laugh, quite heartily, when he opened his newspaper one afternoon. Right there, on the front page of the *International Herald Tribune,* Charlie read that a State Trooper sniffing around a hick town called Apalachin, in upstate New York, had raided the home of Joe Barbara and arrested fifty-eight of the top Mafia bosses in the country. Including *Commendatore* Vito Genovese.

"Vito's party sure got fucked up," Luciano said to friends some time later. "I'll tell you, if I was still in New York there wouldn't be no Apalachin. There wouldn't be no cocksucker named Vito."

But Charlie insisted that such problems in America no longer concerned him. He had more serious concern at home. Igea had not been feeling well for several months and, shortly after the raid on the Mafia convention in Apalachin, she had gone to a doctor for a checkup. He discovered lumps on her breast. After a series of external

218

treatments failed to dissolve the lumps and restore Igea's normal high spirits, a biopsy was performed. The tumors were malignant and Igea's left breast was removed.

"I knew she was gonna die," Charlie later told a close friend. "My whole fuckin' world was comin' apart around me—the woman I loved more than anything I loved before, or since for that matter, she was gonna die. And the thing I'd put together over there was being ruined by that fuckin' Genovese. I even thought of puttin' a contract out on Vito."

Luciano did not try to have Genovese killed, however. He was too wrapped up in Igea's last months. The cancer had spread through her lymph system, and the specialists said there was nothing that could be done for her except relieve the pain when it grew much worse, which would be soon. After suffering for several months, and lapsing into a coma in her last days, with Charlie constantly by her side, Igea died at the end of September, 1958. She was 37.

Charlie and several friends rode on the train with her casket, bringing her body home to be buried in Milan. As her casket was lowered into the grave, Luciano cried. His friends, among them deportees from Prohibition days, told reporters it was the first time they'd ever seen Charlie crying. Several of them were crying as they spoke to newsmen.

18

Charlie was still dressed in mourning, wearing the traditional black tie and black armband, when a process server handed him a summons ordering his appearance in the Naples Appeals Court on December 10. The city's prosecutor announced that an investigation the previous March by a special magistrate's commission had, in clearing Luciano of all accusations that he had been trafficking in narcotics, neglected to consider his sources of income. How, the prosecutor demanded, could Luciano be living in an expensive apartment, eating in gourmet restaurants, frequenting the track almost daily, even paying for his girl friend's funeral—on the small income he'd been reporting to tax authorities?

"Shit, nobody pays all their taxes in Italy, not even that fuckin' prosecutor," Charlie later told a journalist. "That Ass-slinger set the whole thing up. He got the American Ambassador in Rome to pressure the guys in Naples, because Ass-slinger was sore that the Italian papers were real nice to me about Igea dying. I got some sympathy, that's all that rap was about." The investigation amounted to nothing, of course. All charges were dismissed.

Back in America, meanwhile, some unusual things were happening to Vito Genovese, the new dictator of Mafia. About six months after the Apalachin meeting Genovese and three dozen others were arrested and indicted on charges of operating a major narcotics importing ring. It seemed inconceivable, but the boss of all bosses had fallen only a few months after securing his crown. Genovese was convicted and, in 1959, was sentenced to fifteen years in prison.

It has always been said that Genovese fell because one of the very minor members of the ring, who had the improbable name of Nelson Silva Cantellops, had been arrested for peddling dope on the street and had begun to talk about his very personal contacts with his boss, Vito Genovese. Cantellops had languished in prison for several months, the story goes, neither Genovese nor any of his associates coming to his aid. After Genovese was being harrassed by grand juries and investigating commissions because of the Apalachin meeting, Cantellops decided no one would ever remember him, so he began to talk to narcotics agents. It was his testimony, primarily, which convicted Genovese and helped send him to prison.

However. After Genovese died of a heart attack in Atlanta Penitentiary in 1969, I interviewed a number of active and retired agents of the Federal Narcotics Bureau for a series of newspaper articles about Genovese. His conviction had always been suspect, for Cantellops was a cheap dope peddler and, most important, he was not Italian and not Mafia. Genovese, so caught up in Mafia tradition, would never have permitted an outsider to get as close as Cantellops claimed to have been. I asked those agents I interviewed whether my suspicions were correct. One of them, during some ten years of a journalist-source relationship, would always tell me very specifically when some information I had was not accurate; he would refuse to comment if the information was accurate but he could not admit it even off the record. When I asked him whether we had the whole story about the Genovese conviction he said: "Cantellops didn't do it alone. We got information from a guy whose name you'd never believe, and that helped us break down Cantellops and get a lot of other proof." I asked if the informant had been Luciano, and the agent replied: "No comment."

A year or so later I received a letter from a relatively

221

well-known *mafioso*, who was in prison and who asked me to help him write his memoirs "like Valachi did." Among the anecdotes he listed, to demonstrate that his memoirs would make good reading, was this sentence:

"I can tell you how the Big Boss in Europe helped dump Genovese."

The book project never came to be because the *mafioso* thought better of it. It is impossible to state, with any degree of certainty, that Luciano did indeed pass information to the Federal Narcotics Bureau so that Genovese could be imprisoned. But it perhaps did happen that way.

What is certain is that immediately after Genovese was indicted, Charlie seemed to grow more carefree, to be more relaxed than at any time since Genovese had begun to reach for total power. It was around this time that Luciano was introduced to Barnett Glassman, a Hollywood film producer who was about to go off to Spain to make a film with Samuel Bronson. Luciano took a liking to Glassman, entertaining him in Naples and on Capri. Some time in 1959 Charlie agreed to permit Glassman to produce *The Lucky Luciano Story,* then the working title. Luciano signed a contract with Glassman. "The first time in my life I ever signed a contract," Charlie said.

Luciano had been thinking about filming his life story for some time—he quite frankly said he wanted the world to know that he was not the evil whoremaster he had been portrayed by Dewey and the press. His message, in a film script which he had himself written a few years earlier, was that he was just a middle-aged gambler who'd been wrongfully imprisoned years before and who, in Italy, became known and loved for his philanthrophy. He wrote that script because he'd been so anxious to get his message across that he wanted to have a complete package to offer a producer—script, financing, and even Igea to play the feminine lead. He asked Italian producer Paul Tamburella, whose film *Shoeshine* had won an Oscar, to make the *Luciano Story,* and for a time it appeared ready to go before the cameras. "I want Marlon Brando to play me," Charlie said.

But that deal had fallen through before Glassman met Charlie, and they began all over again. Luciano's script was terrible, and Glassman hired a professional screen writer. Two other scripts were eventually done, both rather vapid, and Charlie finally agreed he would get a little closer to the truth. A film about Luciano would have to discuss the very obvious events in his life as a racketeer in America. But it would be "fictionalized" from old newspaper stories; Charlie was not about to tell anyone about Mafia and the actual events under the surface of the headlines.

Now another problem came up. Charlie had been feeling ill for some time and he had an extensive medical examination in late 1959. The doctor told him he had a mild heart condition and a serious case of ulcers. "He says I gotta take it easy, no smoking or drinking or late nights," Charlie told New York columnist Leonard Lyons. "And no screwing. Those other things I can give up, but not the broads." By now he was living with a twenty-four-year-old Neapolitan shop girl, Adriana Rizzo.

Luciano's ulcers were causing him more distress than his heart. Vincent Barbi recalls:

"The doctors all told Charlie he should have an operation for the ulcers, but Charlie refused. He was afraid of the knife. I remember one time that I visited him up in Santa Marinella, a villa he owned outside Rome, next to Ingrid Bergman's villa. Joe Adonis had come up. And we both tried to talk Charlie into having the operation. He kept saying, 'No, no, I'm not going to let anybody cut me open.' He really thought he'd never come out of the operating room alive."

Charlie was trying to follow his doctor's orders, trying to relax and to pull back from business interests that caused him anxiety. But he was unable to do so. He seemed to sense that time was running out for him. He

223

was sixty-two and ill, and he was anxious to get the film project underway. He talked about it to Barbi, to visiting journalists, to all who would listen. "A pity Humphrey Bogart is dead," he said. "Boy, that would have been the man to play Luciano. Now, maybe, George Raft —the only tough type left."

The plans for the film went forward, but slowly. Glassman went to Spain to work on another film, and the Luciano project was put aside for a while. In Spain Glassman met a man named Martin Gosch, who would later write the alleged Luciano "memoirs."

"I liked the guy," Glassman said. "He was a hustler, and he didn't have any credits, he never did much except put movie deals together and get his piece, but I liked him." One day, after they had grown friendly, Gosch said:

"Barney, you're really busy on this film. Why not introduce me to Luciano and I'll help get that project together."

"I hired Gosch as my assistant, and I introduced him to Charlie," Glassman said. "Gosch saw Charlie a number of times in the next couple of years, but Charlie never talked to him about his mob activites or anything like that. You couldn't get twenty words out of Charlie unless he really trusted you, and he didn't care much for Gosch. All their conversation was about things in the script, a few things that had nothing to do with the Mafia or anything like that. Gosch was in London a lot, writing a script with John Cresswell, mostly fictionalizing things from newspaper clippings."

Vincent Barbi confirms Glassman's account. Says Barbi: "Charlie didn't like Gosch, and he didn't like his script. He told me Gosch was just a fly-by-night asshole movie guy bluffing his way through Europe, a fucking phony—those are the words Charlie used. He said he got taken in by Gosch, that he thought the guy was on the level at first but he made the mistake of not checking him out. He said, 'I didn't have any way of checking him out, here in Naples. It would have meant a lot of calls to people in New York and Hollywood, and I had so many other problems that Gosch wasn't worth the trouble. The biggest mistake I ever made.' "

Barbi adds: "Charlie was never doing a book with Gosch, like the guy later claims. All Charlie talked about was the film script, and how he didn't trust Gosch. If they'd been doing a book, Charlie would have mentioned that while he was talking to me about the film script, he would have told me he was giving Gosch stuff for a book. Because by this time he's telling me all about Gosch and how much he'd been suckered by him. He would've talked about the book in that context, no longer trusting Gosch. But he didn't, which is one of the things which makes me sure there was no book in the works."

During the Christmas holidays in 1961, Luciano called New York to wish his brothers and sisters a happy holiday. Glassman says: "Charlie told his brother, Bart, that he wanted to see Gosch right away. He said, 'Gosch is double-dealing Barney. He keeps telling me I don't need Barney, that I should dump Barney and let Gosch produce the picture himself.' He told his brother that he wanted Gosch to fly back to Italy immediately. 'Tell Gosch I want to see him.' Charlie said. 'Tell him I'm going to lay it on the line to him, that I don't want to ever have anything to do with him, I never want to see him after I tell him what I think of him.' " (One of Luciano's sisters has confirmed this conversation.)

Charlie's brother called Glassman and related the conversation. Glassman, who had begun to suspect that Gosch wasn't playing straight, called him and said only that Luciano wanted to see him in Naples. Glassman didn't tell him why he'd been summoned. "Gosch said, 'Geez, I can't afford to fly over. You'll have to pay the expenses because it's your film and I'm working for you.' So I picked up the tab," Glassman says.

Gosch first had some business to take care of in Spain,

and he called Charlie to say he wouldn't arrive in Naples until the end of January. Charlie went up to his villa at Santa Marinella, where Vincent Barbi again visited him.

Barbi reports: "Charlie was very bitter about Gosch. He said, 'Gosch is a fuckin' lying son of a bitch and I'm getting him back to Naples to take care of him and then I'm shipping him back to America.' Charlie said that Gosch had welshed on everybody—that he'd been in Spain trying to peddle the rights to the film, which he didn't own, trying to raise money by cutting some other people in on it. When Charlie first heard rumors about that, he started keeping Gosch at arm's length. Charlie told me, 'Gosch is pestering my balls to work on the script and I keep telling him not now, later, because I need time to check out all the stuff I heard he's doing. Now I know it's true, I'm going to take care of Mr. Gosch.' That's exactly how Charlie put it."

Luciano returned to Naples around January 20, and Barbi went down to see him because he was concerned about Charlie's health. And when they talked again about Gosch, Charlie seemed to have grown even more bitter.

Barbi remembers: "Charlie was very sore at Gosch, because he'd really gone too far this time. Charlie said, 'The son of a bitch threatens to do the picture without my OK. He says he can do it because I'm in the public domain. If I ever catch the cocksucker, he'd gonna get it. I'll give it to him personally.' "

On January 25, 1962, Gosch called Charlie from Spain and said he'd be arriving at Capodichino Airport, outside Naples, the next afternoon. Several hours after Gosch's call, Italian customs agents raided Charlie's apartment. They found nothing, and requested that he come in for questioning the next morning. Charlie went to the customs office around 11:00 A.M. and was questioned about narcotics for a while. He was permitted to leave after a couple of hours, and he went to a cafe, the Galleria, where many American deportees hung out. He asked four of them—former American gangsters—to follow him in a car as he drove to the airport alone in his Alfa Romeo. Vincent Barbi was in the Galleria at the time.

"I talked to Charlie just before they all left for the airport. He was very pissed off at Gosch and I had a strong feeling that he was so furious he was going to do something crazy, like put a hit contract out on Gosch. That's the feeling I got about those four individuals who went to the airport with him. Just before he left Charlie shook my hand and said, 'Goodbye, Vince. Maybe we don't see each other anymore.' I didn't know if he thought he was going to die, or he was going to be thrown in jail for what he'd do to Gosch."

When Charlie arrived at the airport he learned Gosch's plane would be delayed. He went into the bar and ordered a large glass of freshly squeezed orange juice, over ice, and he sipped it slowly. After drinking down the entire glass he turned to check on Gosch's plane. He took only a few paces, and then suddenly collapsed. His four companions rushed to him and were horrified at what they saw: Charlie was vomiting up blood, his body trembling violently at the pain of his retching. An ambulance was called. Within 20 minutes Charlie was in the emergency room at the Hospitale Pace, in Naples.

Barbi recalls: "I was still in the Galleria, drinking coffee, when one of the men who went to the airport with Charlie came running in yelling that Charlie was in the hospital, and it was very bad. I ran over there; it was just a few blocks away. When I got there the doctor or an intern said to me, 'You lost a friend.' That was it. Charlie was dead. And that fucking Gosch, with all his scheming and double-dealing, he caused Charlie's death. We all felt that, everybody in Naples who knew about it felt very strongly that Charlie died because the aggravation over Gosch started his ulcers bleeding real bad."

Gosch's plane landed about ten minutes after Luciano was taken away in the ambulance. Gosch has always claimed that Luciano "died in my arms," but Barbi insists that the four men who accompanied Luciano to the airport, and others who were there, saw the ambulance drive off before Gosch arrived. Charlie never did get a chance to tell off Gosch, or to have him beaten or killed, if that's what he had been planning.

Almost immediately, a controversy began to involve Luciano's last days of life. The Federal Narcotics Bureau claimed that, at long last, it had finally gathered the evidence necessary to connect Charlie with an international drug-smuggling conspiracy, but Charlie's death had cheated them of the pleasure of arresting him. Not to be outdone, the Italian police claimed *they* had amassed sufficient evidence to send Charlie away for life and were about to arrest him when he collapsed and died.

A few days later a man described as Luciano's "former bodyguard" sold a story to a Rome newspaper claiming that Charlie had been murdered by drug traffickers who substituted poison for his heart medicine. Going that story one better, another newspaper then said Luciano had been poisoned "either by his own hand or by an underworld executioner" and that an autopsy had disclosed Charlie had "swallowed potassium cyanide—the same poison Hermann Goering used."

Actually, an autopsy disclosed that Luciano had died of a heart attack, apparently caused by a severe loss of blood from a perforated ulcer. As for reports that Luciano was about to be arrested as a narcotics merchant, the truth is that Italian police and the Federal Narcotics Bureau had put together two unrelated pieces of information and jumped to an unwarranted conclusion.

A few days before Luciano died, two New York *mafiosi* who had jumped bail after their indictment on narcotics charges the previous spring were found and arrested in Spain. Luciano received a phone call from Spain (from Gosch, of course), so his apartment was raided for evidence he'd been working with these men. When Luciano was questioned the next morning he said he had to go to the airport to meet someone flying in from Madrid. That's the capital of Spain, police reasoned, therefore Lucky is meeting someone carrying dope. U.S. narcotics agents, Italian customs officials, and probably the airport janitor, were alerted for the big arrest. Police statements that they were "closing in on Lucky Luciano when he died" were as meaningless as all such statements had always proved to be.

It didn't matter to Luciano, of course. Three days after his death a Requiem Mass was celebrated over his body in the small, ancient church of Sanctissima Trinita. During the mass about 150 photographers swarmed irreverently over the altar to get shots of Adriana sobbing as she kissed Charlie's coffin, and pictures of American friends trying to hide their faces from the cameras. Among those friends were Joe Adonis and the Fischetti brothers from Chicago. Adonis, probably remembering the gaudy wreaths sent to mobsters in the old days, ordered a floral piece with the inscription, "So long, pal." After the mass the coffin was carried to the hearse, a huge black carriage of carved wood, elaborately adorned, and drawn by eight plumed horses. Luciano's body was taken to the chapel of the English Cemetery outside Naples, to be held temporarily until his family could make arrangements for burial in New York.

A week later Luciano returned home almost precisely 16 years from the day he had sailed on the *Laura Keene*. His brothers, Bart and Anthony, met the plane with a hearse and accompanied the casket to St. John's Cemetery, Middle Village, Queens. The casket was placed inside a crypt in the mausoleum Charlie had bought for his family in 1935. His father, mother, an aunt, and an uncle were already interred there.

As the crypt was sealed, Bart Lucania sighed the only eulogy:

"Tutti finito, Salvatore," he said. "It's all over."

APPENDIX

In February, 1975, *The Last Testament of Lucky Luciano* was published by Little, Brown, in spite of a front page article in *The New York Times* the previous December which questioned the authenticity of the book. That very extensive article raised so much doubt about the book that New American Library canceled its commitment to pay $800,000 for paperback rights.

The *Times* article was written by Nicholas Gage, an investigative reporter, author of *The Mafia Is Not an Equal Opportunity Employer,* and the organized crime specialist for the *Times*. As detailed as Gage's article was, it barely scratched the surface errors of the book bylined by Martin Gosch and Richard Hammer, reportedly from notes that Gosch claimed were "dictated" by Luciano. Gage writes for a daily newspaper, and it would have taken him more months than can be spared by a newspaper to write a detailed analysis of this book. I've been studying Luciano for years and I am thus able to document the errors in this book in more detail and to go further than Gage's report that the authenticity of the book is open to serious doubt.

The problem with this book begins with Gosch himself. It seems rather strange that the blurb on the jacket of *The Last Testament* says Martin Gosch, until his death, had been a film producer, yet it does not name a single film he ever produced. Barnett Glassman, who was Gosch's employer in the few years before Luciano died, said: "That's because he never produced a film on his own. Gosch was just a hustler in the film business, conning guys all over the place."

Now that Gosch has been dead for almost two years it may seem rather unfair and callous to attack his integrity since he can no longer defend himself. But the fact is that Gosch's book is such complete fantasy that it would have come under even heavier attack were he still alive.

Gosch did not have tapes of conversations with Luciano, as his publisher once claimed. He did not even make notes of those so-called conversations with Luciano until long after the talks were supposed to have taken place. As we've learned, Luciano was about to tell off Gosch when he died.

Barnett Glassman was, apparently, the only man besides old friends and *mafiosi* with whom Luciano discussed his past. When Gosch came up with his idea for a book, long after Luciano was dead, he began to negotiate with Glassman since Glassman was his employer and holds the original film contract signed by Luciano. In the midst of those negotiations, Glassman says, Gosch took an advance from Little, Brown "and then he told me our whole deal was off."

Glassman promptly sued Gosch and the publisher. The case dragged on and the book was published—but not until Hammer's literary agent paid Glassman to drop his suit. In the settlement both Glassman and his attorney "got a substantial amount of money," Glassman says. As part of the settlement Glassman also received from the literary agent for Gosch "a large percentage" of receipts from any film which may be made of *The Last Testament*. Glassman is still suing Gosch's estate.

So much for the background. A careful analysis of the book, including research into court files and other papers dealing with Luciano, makes it evident the book cannot possibly be the posthumous autobiography "dictated by Charles 'Lucky' Luciano" that it claims to be. One thing that becomes very clear on close study of the book, is that the author did not even produce the sort of research job that the most inexperienced journalist would be capable of. From almost the opening pages of the book one can detect a steadily mounting number of major errors.

There are factual errors, about people, places, and events, which Luciano would not have made unless he were senile. There was no evidence of senility in the man; there is, in fact, much evidence to the contrary.

There are those errors which are the result of a complete fabrication by Gosch, who quotes Luciano in anecdotes that could never have happened because they are against all the evidence, including that supplied by Luciano in conversations with others.

And there are errors of omission. Gosch is such a terrible researcher that he would have us believe, for example, that Arnold Rothstein played barely any role at all in Luciano's development as a criminal superstar.

I have found, without exaggeration, at least fifty major errors in the Gosch book. I shall discuss here only a few of those errors which make it obvious that Gosch did not sit with Luciano for months while the aging mobster unburdened his every secret, as Gosch claimed.

At the very beginning of the book there is a long description of the antagonism between Charlie and his father. In it, Luciano says that he finally left home one day when his father beat him with a gold belt buckle after discovering that Charlie had stolen it from a local jeweler. Luciano has often said, however, that his father beat him frequently, not simply on this one occasion as Gosch would have it. Luciano's sister told me there were frequent beatings. Charlie told many friends, and U.S. narcotics agent Sal Vizzini, that he left home only after his father discovered his gun and threatened to shoot him. That incident is never mentioned in Gosch's book. Nor is there any mention of the wound that Charlie sustained at age fourteen, when he was accidentally shot in the leg by a friend. Certainly, in "dictating" his memoirs, Luciano would have remembered the only time he'd ever been shot.

Credibility is stretched even further, and Gosch's sloppy research for this fabrication becomes quite evident in Luciano's "reminisences" of the early years of Prohibition. The dates of events that Luciano allegedly described in such detail are absolutely incorrect. Gosch claims Luciano said he met Frank Costello in midtown, around 1913, when both here hustling on the streets. Both Luciano and Costello have often told friends and others that they did not meet until 1920, when they were brought together by bootlegging. Compounding the error, Gosch has Luciano and Genovese meeting for the first time only after Prohibition started, when all available evidence shows they had met years before.

"I remember that so clear," Luciano supposedly told Gosch in describing how Dutch Schultz came into the bootlegging partnership in the first year of Prohibition, 1920. Gosch obviously didn't check his facts when he manufactured this particular quote: Schultz was still a minor hoodlum in the Bronx as late as 1928. Further, after bringing Schultz into the game much too early, Gosch brings Joe Masseria in much too late, some time in 1923. Luciano himself has told friends and relatives that he was working for Masseria before Prohibition; investigative writers of that day noted that Charlie had his office in the curb exchange across from Masseria's office, and called them "partners." The curb exchange was put out of business in 1922, after police grew tired of all the shooting.

One of the more incredible things about this confection which Gosch baked out of the very few anecdotes he may have heard from Charlie, is that there isn't a single mention in his book of the curb exchange—which absorbed more than two years of Charlie's younger days and which made him wealthy. Luciano would certainly have remembered the curb exchange quite vividly, and would have talked about it at length.

An even more stunning omission is the minor role ascribed to Arnold Rothstein. This omission alone damages the book's purported authenticity, especially, as we shall see, when Gosch so completely misses the point about Rothstein's death and Charlie's arrest in his office. Gosch invented a pure fable to explain the arrest.

Rothstein is mentioned several times in the book. He is the model for the "certain status and power in society" that Charlie and his friends dream of attaining, around 1918. He is one of Luciano's "closest friends" around 1923, but simply lumped in with young men like Lansky, Siegel, and Lepke, to illustrate the point that Luciano associated with Jews. Rothstein was basically a gambler, Gosch says, and Luciano's main contact with him was in gambling. When Rothstein was murdered, it was as if he never existed. Gosch would have us believe that Luciano, who "confesses" so much in this book, dismissed Rothstein with this simple comment on his death: "All I knew about it was that he welshed on a bet. That was the rumor. Of course, the cops called me in and they grilled me, but I never knew who done it."

Had Gosch done his homework he would have found in very public documents—including memoirs by Rothstein's wife and the trials of men associated with Rothstein—the Luciano-Rothstein arrangement that actually existed: Luciano hired by Rothstein's aides to work in the garment center strikes before Prohibition; Luciano, Costello and others helping Rothstein set up his rum-running fleet, bribing Coast Guardsmen, arranging for overland shipment to the city, ad infinitum. Had he done his research, Gosch would have learned that Luciano suggested to Rothstein the international narcotics smuggling in which Rothstein engaged and in which Luciano was a partner. Finally, had Gosch known what he was doing, he would not have made so gross an error as he did over the circumstances surrounding Rothstein's death and the arrest of Luciano.

For Gosch, you see, did not know there was a connection between those events. To explain the arrest in November, 1928, he invents one of the most absurd stories

234

in the book. Gosch and his coauthor expect the reader to believe that Joe (the Boss) Masseria's "demands . . . for demonstrations of absolute loyalty reached a climax in November of 1928. Lucania and Masseria were together in the back seat of a car, with Adonis acting as chauffeur. 'That fat bastard pulls out a thirty-eight from his coat pocket' [Luciano is quoted as saying about Masseria] 'and hands it to me and says, "You're gonna carry this tonight on the payroll job. It ain't got no numbers." ' "

And then, says Luciano in Gosch's fantasy, Joe Masseria forced his chief lieutenant to become a common stickup man and go out on an armed robbery that Masseria had made Luciano plan. Luciano protests, "Since when do I go back on the street with a *pistola?*" But protest is useless; he must follow the Boss's orders. Charlie becomes a stickup man and joins two other members of the gang, Paul Mineo and Red Levine (which is absurd itself, because throughout the book Gosch describes how much Masseria hates Jews and won't permit his men to work with them). In any case, they hold up a payroll messenger as he comes out of a garment center bank. A bank guard shoots Mineo. Luciano heroically pulls into the getaway car the heavily bleeding man and the canvas bag containing the payroll, and they speed away. They're caught by police several blocks from the scene. "It took every bit of political muscle that Costello and me had to get the whole thing squared away," Luciano is supposed to have told Gosch. "Costello managed to get the charges squashed and the record fixed up so it was listed as an error."

Quite clearly, this anecdote told at length by Luciano is an uninformed writer's fabrication for an event he can't explain. As a writer, reporter, and researcher with more than twenty years' experience, I can see the trap into which Gosch plunged. On Luciano's police record, which has been published in the newspapers dozens of times over the years, from the day he was arrested on the vice charges in 1936 to the day of his death in 1962, is this entry: "Nov. 17, 1928—assault and robbery with a revolver; dismissed." Seeing this item, and not being able to explain it from his reading in the more obvious source works on Luciano and the Mafia, Martin Gosch invented a dramatic incident that would be perfect on the screen: Lucky Luciano participating in an armed robbery and being pursued by police in a chase scene to rival that in *The French Connection*.

What actually did occur, I found in examining the records more deeply, is that when Luciano was picked up in Rothstein's office after stealing the documents he'd been seeking, he was brought in for questioning. He refused to say why he'd been in the office, and he insisted that the police release him or charge him with a crime. In order to hold him for further questioning, police booked him for a robbery that had occurred a few days *before* Rothstein was shot, not on November 17, long after he was buried. Then the police, on orders from Jimmy Hines and other political figures trying to keep the lid on the highly dangerous Rothstein case, were forced to release Luciano. But the charge could not have been and was not erased "as an error." Luciano appeared in Magistrate's Court on November 17. The arresting officer admitted there was no evidence against him. The charges were dismissed by the judge. Had Gosch ever been a newspaper reporter he would have known that the entry on Luciano's record, "assault and robbery with a revolver; dismissed," can only refer to a *court action dismissing* the case, and not to a police "dismissal" because of "error."

The most blatant confection of all (a personal judgment, for there are many dozens of imaginative inventions here) revolves around the beating Luciano was given in October, 1929. Not only does Gosch repeat the story, which Luciano has called "bullshit," that as a result of surviving "a one-way ride" Luciano was forever after known as "Lucky," but Gosch also transforms this anecdote into a dramatic film scene that is total fiction.

Luciano, Gosch claims, told him that the beating he sustained that night came about in this fashion. The war between Masseria and Maranzano was about to break into the open. Tom Reina, boss of an East Harlem Mafia family, was scheming to throw his support to Maranzano (which is not the way Joe Valachi, Reina's son-in-law, told it). On hearing this news, Gosch claims Luciano said: "So now I knew that Maranzano was gonna call Masseria's hand and there was gonna be all-out war." Luciano set up a meeting with Maranzano, "in a place on Staten Island, a neutral territory." Charlie took the ferry, alone, and went to a pier about a half mile from the ferry landing. He met Maranzano there, and they talked for a while.

Maranzano said that Masseria must be killed. "Well, I've been thinking about that too," Luciano told him. But Maranzano insisted that Charlie personally put the bullets into Masseria. Charlie said, "You're crazy." He knew, according to Gosch, that he was being sucked into a trap because, "In the tradition-laden Sicilian underworld, one cannot kill the leader personally and then succeed to his throne; the killer cannot expect more than a secondary role in the new hierarchy and more likely he can expect to be killed himself in revenge." (There is no such tradition. I was certain of that from personal knowledge, but, not trusting even my own deep awareness of Mafia that I've had since my childhood in Brooklyn, I checked with two men who I know are Mafia. When I read them this paragraph the response of both, independently, was quite simple: "Pure bullshit." One of them added that Albert Anastasia "almost a hundred percent sure killed his boss," Mangano, and succeeded to the position.)

But the nonsense about tradition is not the vital point here. Gosch's tale continues, that when Luciano refused to kill Masseria, he was smashed over the head from behind and he "blacked out." Then Luciano is supposed to have told Gosch: "When I come to . . . I was tied up and hangin' by my wrists from a beam over me, with my toes just reachin' the floor . . . I was practically hangin' by my thumbs." Several men flashed lights on him, others beat and "tortured" him, while Maranzano tried

237

to get him to agree to his demand: "Charlie, I promise you, if you do not do it, then you are dead." But Luciano remained firm in his resolve, like a true Hollywood hero.

Now Maranzano, growing angry, personally took part in the torture. He slashed at Charlie with a knife, cutting his face and his chest. Then, when one of his men pulled out a gun and aimed it at Luciano to fulfill his boss's threat, Maranzano made a snap decision to permit Charlie to live. He again warned Charlie that he'd be killed if he didn't do as he was told, and then Charlie was thrown into a car. "Three or four minutes later they tossed me out on the road like I was a sack of potatoes," Luciano said. He lay there, regaining his strength, then crawled "to a little streetlight down the block," where police found him.

There are a number of defects in this story, besides the nonsense about Sicilian tradition. For one thing, Gosch never does explain why Maranzano, if he wanted Luciano removed from any possibility of future power, didn't simply kill him and find another traitor in Masseria's ranks? Then there is the obvious fault that Gosch's story conflicts entirely with what Luciano himself has said: That he was beaten by police seeking information about Legs Diamond. Luciano said this dozens of times, to friends, relatives, newspaper reporters, federal narcotics agents, and one of the detectives involved has admitted it.

And there is even further evidence that this anecdote is a total falsehood. Gosch's version is that Charlie said he was beaten in a building "a half-mile" from the ferry, and was then driven in a car for "three or four minutes" before being dumped on the road. In fact, Luciano was found by police in Tottenville, which is the extreme southern tip of Staten Island, about fourteen miles from the ferry and the piers along the waterfront. His captors could never have driven him there in three or four minutes; even today, with improvements to the main highway, it is a twenty-minute trip at the very least. Furthermore, evidence was found by detectives that Charlie was dumped on the beach at Tottenville, for there was sand all over his clothing, his body, and in his shoes. It is very strange that Charlie didn't mention this to Gosch, since he talked about it so many times over the years; he often said he could never forget the discomfort of sand in his mouth and eyes when he regained consciousness on the beach.

The silliest and most obscene invention of all is Luciano's "dictation" to Gosch of an anecdote involving Judge Philip McCook, who presided at the prostitution trial and sentenced Luciano to prison. It is claimed that Judge McCook came to visit Luciano in prison, begging for mercy. McCook, crying like no man Charlie had ever seen, said that ever since he had sentenced Charlie his own life had been a disaster—his house had burned down, his wife and then his child had died, and onward to a recital of every catastrophe that can befall a man. And, according to the Gosch book, Luciano said:

"When he gets all finished (telling about his troubles), he turns to me and says why did I put a Sicilian curse on him? I didn't know what the fuck to say. I just looked at him like he was loony. Then he gets down on his hands and knees, crawls over to me cryin' like a baby; he grabs hold of my hand and starts slobberin' over it . . . beggin' me to take the curse off him, pleadin' with me to help him . . . Right then and there, I knew McCook was my pigeon."

Luciano, so cunning, strikes a deal with his pigeon. He'll lift the "Sicilian curse" if the judge will help him get out of prison. Still on his knees, apparently, McCook instantly agrees. What else could the poor man do?

Later, off his knees and back on the beach, McCook waited for more than a year with the curse hanging over his head. Then, in 1942, possessed of a "more mellowed and more benevolent view of Luciano," as Gosch puts it, the judge signed the order transferring Charlie from the Siberia of Dannemora to the country club of Great Meadow. That wasn't enough to lift the curse, so McCook came through with another blow for Luciano's freedom. This time, a full two years after becoming Luciano's pigeon, McCook ruled on the motion to reduce Charlie's sentence so he'd be eligible for parole. McCook said—and Gosch stresses this to illustrate the evil forces controlling the judge—"If Luciano continues to cooperate and remains a model prisoner, it may be appropriate at some future time to apply for executive clemency."

These two acts by McCook prove, Gosch says, that Luciano owned the judge's soul. Unbelievable! Had McCook been so terrorized by Luciano's "curse" he could easily have released Charlie then and there, in 1943, on any number of grounds. He could have ruled that he had only just discovered that Luciano indeed had been convicted on perjured testimony—there was more than sufficient evidence of that in affidavits by the women who recanted their testimony, and within the trial record itself. Or McCook could have further developed the "war effort" plea and re-sentenced him to time served "so that he may continue to help the nation," or any words to that effect. McCook had any number of possibilities for lifting "the curse."

That's not all. Gosch is so intent on proving that McCook was Luciano's pigeon that he distorts the judge's ruling on the motion to reduce sentence. McCook did say that Luciano may have better luck "at some future time." But he also said the arguments that Luciano was a war hero were "far from justifying the court in granting the present application," and he once more castigated Luciano as a man who is "responsible in law and in morals for every cruel and extortionate crime" performed by him and his associates. Does this sound like a pigeon?

The second element employed by Gosch to "prove" McCook was beholden to Luciano, the assertion that the judge signed the prison transfer order, is total nonsense on the face of it. New York State judges have no authority over a prisoner once he has begun to serve his sentence, unless the prisoner approaches the judge on a matter of law. For example, requesting a new trial because of newly discovered evidence. Once a man is in prison, the decision to transfer him to another prison within the state system is made solely by the Corrections Commissioner. He signs those orders. Judge McCook was never involved in the transfer.

I could go on for another fifty pages or more, but space does not permit. To summarize, I'll briefly tick off several other errors which discolor this book. They are:

*Gosch and Hammer make the absurd claim that in the mid-1920's, "at the opening of the famed Beverly Club" outside Covington, Kentucky, Meyer Lansky suddenly announced to Luciano that he had conceived a new gambling game that would make them all rich—"the policy game," to quote the book. What an outrageous display of the authors' ignorance. Policy had been played in every American city since the Revolution; the last legal American lottery was run in the 1880's. When it was outlawed by the government, it continued to function illegally. The so-called Italian Lottery in New York was being run as early as 1905—the first mention of it that I find in newspaper clips of that day—and it had probably begun much earlier. The Harlem Lottery had been in existence since at least 1910. Furthermore, the Beverly Club did not open until 1937; Luciano was in Dannemora by then.

*In the Gosch fiction there is, most incredibly, no mention at all of the Luciano-Mafia role in the invasion of Sicily, no mention of the use of the "L-flags" which enable the *mafiosi* to attain political power as a reward for helping the American Army overrun Western Sicily. It is as if the Navy had never approached Luciano for his aid in the Sicilian invasion. In fact, the authors quote Luciano as remembering, as he entered Palermo and then drove to his birthplace in the interior along a "road full of shell holes," that both the city and the countryside had suffered "the ravages of war." Nonsense. General George Patton, and dozens of others who were there, have written that barely a shot was fired and hardly

241

any casualties suffered, because there was no opposition. An even more gross error in this book is that there is no mention of the Sicilian Separatist Party, nor of Giuliano, nor of Don Calo Vizzini. It is impossible to believe that Luciano would not have talked about this very vital phase of his exile had he talked to Gosch about anything. Rather, it can only be assumed that Gosch was not aware of that excellent book, *The Honored Society,* nor of the journalistic pieces from Italy of Michael Stern.

*Gosch claims that Luciano described meetings and conversations with his lawyers and with friends like Costello and Lansky, all of whom came to Charlie's suite in the Waldorf Towers at the end of each day of the prostitution trial. The authors even quote Luciano about one visit to his suite by Gay Orlova, which Charlie remembered so clearly because it was the first time they had sexual intercourse for weeks. None of those meetings could have occurred. Luciano was in prison from the moment of his arrest, unable or unwilling for tax reasons to raise the $350,000 bail that had been set in his case.

*Gosch, in discussing Naval Intelligence's use of Charlie's services during the war, has Luciano describing Commander Haffenden as "a typical Navy kid with pink cheeks and still wet behind the ears." Haffenden, in fact, was in his fifties at the time, with gray hair and the air of an old Navy sea dog. Luciano could not possibly have forgotten this man.

Finally, there is one more person who requires some detail. Gay Orlova, the stunning beauty whom Charlie would certainly remember quite clearly. In this fantasy that Gosch has constructed, "Luciano" remembers his woman with such fondness that he gives her roles she could never have played.

To begin with, Gosch claims Charlie met Gay in 1929, and that they were introduced by Nils T. Granlund, a radio celebrity of the day. All the evidence indicates that they did not meet until the opening of the Palm Island

Casino in 1934. Further, Granlund in his memoirs (*Blondes, Bullets and Brunettes,* published in 1957) doesn't even mention Charlie and Gay together, let alone his having introduced them. And Granlund threw in every famous racket name of the era, including Pisano, Rothstein, Nicky Arnstein (Fanny Brice's husband), Dutch Schultz, Legs Diamond, and Bugsy Siegel among them. His only mention of Luciano is to call him "Lucky of later fame" and describe him as an "assistant to Legs Diamond." Had Granlund introduced Luciano and Orlova he would certainly have used it as an anecdote in a book laden with anecdotes. Most especially since one of the two ghost writers of Granlund's book was Sid Feder, long a Mafia-watcher and coauthor of *Murder, Inc.* and *The Luciano Story.* As a journalist whose specialty was Mafia and who wrote an early biography of Luciano, Feder would certainly have pulled from Granlund every scrap of information on Charlie.

All other things considered, that is still a minor error. Other anecdotes about Gay illustrate Gosch's lack of research. Especially the anecdotes concerning her relationship with Luciano after he was sent to prison. Immigration records prove conclusively that Gay was deported in 1937 as an "undesirable alien." Reports from France during the war and after the liberation of Paris indicate she had been living in that city. When it was announced in 1946 that Luciano was to be deported, Gay called a press conference in Paris and said she was applying for emigration to Italy to visit Charlie, "because I haven't seen him since he was put in jail."

Gosch blew this one. He would have us believe Luciano told him that, some time after being transferred to Great Meadow in 1942, the warden permitted Charlie to visit bars and restaurants in Albany, accompanied by guards. "Gay Orlova met me there" one night, Charlie says according to Gosch. "Gay and me went to a nice room upstairs and we spent most of the night together. It was beautiful."

243

It was not only beautiful, but some kind of black magic, considering that Gay was not in the country.

And then, after Luciano was paroled and while he was making preparations to sail to Italy, Gosch quotes Luciano as saying: "At first, I thought Gay Orlova was gonna come with me, but she had a lotta trouble with all that red tape about passports and where she was going and that kind of crap, so she had to cancel out."

At the very time he's speaking about, Gay Orlova was in Paris giving out interviews, and then she drove down to the French-Italian border and gave out more interviews.

Enough. *The Last Testament* obviously suffers from "the Hollywood flash of a film producer chasing a buck," as one critic has called it.

the Executioner

The gutsiest, most exciting hero in years.
Imagine a guy at war with the Godfather
and all his Mafioso relatives! He's rough,
he's deadly, he's a law unto himself —
nothing and nobody stops him!

THE EXECUTIONER SERIES by DON PENDLETON

Order		Title	Book #	Price
_____	# 1	WAR AGAINST THE MAFIA	P401	$1.25
_____	# 2	DEATH SQUAD	P402	1.25
_____	# 3	BATTLE MASK	P403	1.25
_____	# 4	MIAMI MASSACRE	P404	1.25
_____	# 5	CONTINENTAL CONTRACT	P405	1.25
_____	# 6	ASSAULT ON SOHO	P406	1.25
_____	# 7	NIGHTMARE IN NEW YORK	P407	1.25
_____	# 8	CHICAGO WIPEOUT	P408	1.25
_____	# 9	VEGAS VENDETTA	P409	1.25
_____	#10	CARIBBEAN KILL	P410	1.25
_____	#11	CALIFORNIA HIT	P411	1.25
_____	#12	BOSTON BLITZ	P412	1.25
_____	#13	WASHINGTON I.O.U.	P413	1.25
_____	#14	SAN DIEGO SIEGE	P414	1.25
_____	#15	PANIC IN PHILLY	P415	1.25
_____	#16	SICILIAN SLAUGHTER	P416	1.25
_____	#17	JERSEY GUNS	P417	1.25
_____	#18	TEXAS STORM	P418	1.25
_____	#19	DETROIT DEATHWATCH	P419	1.25
_____	#20	NEW ORLEANS KNOCKOUT	P475	1.25
_____	#21	FIREBASE SEATTLE	P499	1.25
_____	#22	HAWAIIAN HELLGROUND	P625	1.25

AND MORE TO COME . . .

TO ORDER

Please check the space next to the book/s you want, send this order form
together with your check or money order, include the price of the book/s
and 25¢ for handling and mailing, to:

PINNACLE BOOKS, INC. / P.O. Box 4347
Grand Central Station/New York, N.Y. 10017

☐ CHECK HERE IF YOU WANT A FREE CATALOG.

I have enclosed $_____check_____or money order_____as payment
in full. No C.O.D.'s.

Name_____

Address_____

City_____State_____Zip_____
(Please allow time for delivery.)

Violence is a man!
His name is
Edge...

The bloodiest action-series ever published, with a hero who is the meanest, most vicious killer the West has ever seen.

It's sharp —
It's hard —
It's EDGE

GEORGE G. GILMAN

Order	Title	Book #	Price
_____	# 1 THE LONER	P596	$1.25
_____	# 2 TEN GRAND	P703	$1.25
_____	# 3 APACHE DEATH	P667	$1.25
_____	# 4 KILLER'S BREED	P597	$1.25
_____	# 5 BLOOD ON SILVER	P598	$1.25
_____	# 6 RED RIVER	P668	$1.25
_____	# 7 CALIFORNIA KILL	P599	$1.25
_____	# 8 HELL'S SEVEN	P265	.95
_____	# 9 BLOODY SUMMER	P293	.95
_____	#10 BLACK VENGEANCE	P333	.95
_____	#11 SIOUX UPRISING	P600	$1.25
_____	#12 DEATH'S BOUNTY	P669	$1.25
_____	#13 THE HATED	P560	$1.25
_____	#14 TIGER'S GOLD	P624	$1.25

AND MORE TO COME . . .

TO ORDER

Please check the space next to the book/s you want, send this order form together with your check or money order, include the price of the book/s and 25¢ for handling and mailing to:

PINNACLE BOOKS, INC. P.O. Box 4347
Grand Central Station / New York, N.Y. 10017

☐ **CHECK HERE IF YOU WANT A FREE CATALOG**
I have enclosed $_____check_____or money order_____as payment in full. No C.O.D.'s.

Name_____

Address_____

City_____State_____Zip_____
(Please allow time for delivery)

ALL NEW DYNAMITE SERIES

THE DESTROYER

by Richard Sapir & Warren Murphy

CURE, the world's most secret crime-fighting organization created the perfect weapon — Remo Williams — man programmed to become a cold, calculating death machine. The super man of the 70's!

Order		Title	Book No.	Price
_____	# 1	Created, The Destroyer	P361	$1.25
_____	# 2	Death Check	P362	$1.25
_____	# 3	Chinese Puzzle	P363	$1.25
_____	# 4	Mafia Fix	P364	$1.25
_____	# 5	Dr. Quake	P365	$1.25
_____	# 6	Death Therapy	P366	$1.25
_____	# 7	Union Bust	P367	$1.25
_____	# 8	Summit Chase	P368	$1.25
_____	# 9	Murder's Shield	P369	$1.25
_____	#10	Terror Squad	P370	$1.25
_____	#11	Kill or Cure	P371	$1.25
_____	#12	Slave Safari	P372	$1.25
_____	#13	Acid Rock	P373	$1.25
_____	#14	Judgment Day	P303	$1.25
_____	#15	Murder Ward	P331	$1.25
_____	#16	Oil Slick	P418	$1.25
_____	#17	Last War Dance	P435	$1.25
_____	#18	Funny Money	P538	$1.25
_____	#19	Holy Terror	P640	$1.25

and more to come . . .

TO ORDER

Please check the space next to the book/s you want, send this order form together with your check or money order, include the price of the book/s and 25¢ for handling and mailing, to:

PINNACLE BOOKS, INC. / P.O. Box 4347
Grand Central Station / New York, N. Y. 10017

☐ Check here if you want a free catalog.

I have enclosed $_____ check_____ or money order_____ as payment in full. No C.O.D.'s.

Name_____

Address_____

City_____ State_____ Zip_____
(Please allow time for delivery)

THE NEW SPY HERO OF THE 70'S

"Tremendous tales of high adventure and espionage." —Harold Robbins

MALKO

by gerard de villiers

MALKO is a spy, one of the CIA's most daring and effective "special" agents. He gets the impossible missions, the dirty jobs, the secret operations that demand the coolness of a million-dollar caper and the finality of a commando hit. Malko stalks the world in search of trouble.

Order	Book No.	Title	Price
_____	P235	WEST OF JERUSALEM, No. 1	$ .95
_____	P245	OPERATION NEW YORK, No. 2	.95
_____	P253	MAN FROM KABUL, No. 3	.95
_____	P316	VERSUS THE CIA, No. 4	$1.25
_____	P375	ANGEL OF VENGEANCE, No. 5	$1.25
_____	P428	KILL KISSINGER, No. 6	$1.25
_____	P500	THE COUNTESS AND THE SPY, No. 7	$1.25
_____	P541	DEATH ON THE RIVER KWAI, No. 8	$1.25
_____	P626	CHECKPOINT CHARLIE, No. 9	$1.25

AND MORE TO COME . . .

TO ORDER

Please check the space next to the book/s you want, send this order form together with your check or money order, include the price of the book/s and 25¢ for handling and mailing, to:

**PINNACLE BOOKS, INC. / P.O. Box 4347
Grand Central Station / New York, N. Y. 10017**

☐ Check here if you want a free catalog.

I have enclosed $_____ check _____ or money order _____ as payment in full. No C.O.D.'s.

Name _____

Address _____

City _____ State _____ Zip _____
(Please allow time for delivery)

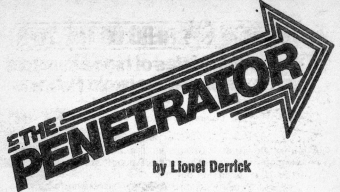

THE PENETRATOR

by Lionel Derrick

Mark Hardin. Discharged from the army, after service in Vietnam. His military career was over. But *his* war was just beginning. His reason for living and reason for dying become the same—to stamp out crime and corruption wherever he finds it. He is deadly; he is unpredictable; and he is dedicated. He is The Penetrator!

Read all of him in:

Order		Title	Book No.	Price
_____	#1	THE TARGET IS H	P236	.95
_____	#2	BLOOD ON THE STRIP	P237	.95
_____	#3	CAPITOL HELL	P318	.95
_____	#4	HIJACKING MANHATTAN	P338	.95
_____	#5	MARDI GRAS MASSACRE	P378	.95
_____	#6	TOKYO PURPLE	P434	$1.25
_____	#7	BAJA BANDIDOS	P502	$1.25
_____	#8	THE NORTHWEST CONTRACT	P540	$1.25
_____	#9	DODGE CITY BOMBERS	P627	$1.25

TO ORDER

Please check the space next to the book/s you want, send this order form together with your check or money order, include the price of the book/s and 25¢ for handling and mailing to:

PINNACLE BOOKS, INC. / P.O. Box 4347
Grand Central Station / New York, N.Y. 10017

☐ CHECK HERE IF YOU WANT A FREE CATALOG

I have enclosed $_____ check_____ or money order_____
as payment in full. No C.O.D.'s

Name_____

Address_____

City_____ State_____ Zip_____

(Please allow time for delivery)

A THRILLING
SUSPENSE TRILOGY
by CLIVE EGLETON

"... these Egleton books are among the best of their type."
—*The San Francisco Chronicle*

Russia has devastated Britain with a nuclear attack and is occupying the country. The English people unite against this oppression and form an underground resistance network to fight for their freedom against seemingly overwhelming odds.

LAST POST FOR A PARTISAN

Five years after the holocaust a split in England's resistance is jeopardizing the entire movement. David Garnett is called in to find and eliminate the traitors in a deadly game of violence and intrigue in which everyone is suspect.

P344 $1.25

A PIECE OF RESISTANCE

It is the near future and England has been conquered and occupied by the Soviets. When the assassin of a high Russian official is captured and sent to a maximum-security prison, the underground resistance plots an incredible mission to rescue the assassin.

P315 $1.25

THE JUDAS MANDATE

In the final novel of this electrifying trilogy, David Garnett must carry out his riskiest assignment yet, involving the release of political prisoners who will try to form a government in exile in the United States.

P352 $1.25

_____P344   LAST POST FOR A PARTISAN   1.25
_____P315   A PIECE OF RESISTANCE   1.25
_____P352   THE JUDAS MANDATE   1.25

TO ORDER
Please check the space next to the book/s you want, send this order form together with your check or money order. Include the price of the book/s and 25¢ for handling and mailing, to:
PINNACLE BOOKS, INC. / P.O. Box 4347
Grand Central Station / New York, N.Y. 10017
☐ CHECK HERE IF YOU WANT A FREE CATALOG.
I have enclosed $_____check_____or money order_____as payment in full. No C.O.D.'s.

Name_____
Address_____
City_____State_____Zip_____
(Please allow time for delivery.)